GENDERING SCOTTISH HISTORY

AN INTERNATIONAL APPROACH

EDITED BY TERRY BROTHERSTONE,
DEBORAH SIMONTON, AND OONAGH WALSH

THE MACKIE OCCASIONAL COLLOQUIA SERIES, NO. 1

1999

CRUITHNE PRESS

GLASGOW

Cover design: Charles Kennedy

Front cover illustrations: "Ishbel, wife of the 7th Earl of Aberdeen" (portrait by James Cant, Haddo House, reproduced by kind permission of The National Trust for Scotland); Gabrielle Keiller playing golf (photograph courtesy of The Scottish National Gallery of Modern Art).

Back cover illustration: Women at work in Tate's sugar refinery (photograph courtesy of the Imperial War Museum, London).

1999 (paper); 2000 (cased)

© individual authors

Cruithne Press
197 Great Western Road
Glasgow G4 9EB
Great Britain

British Library Cataloguing in Publication Data

A catalogue record for this book is available from the British Library

ISBN 1 873448 16 3 (paper)
ISBN 1 873448 18 X (cased)

Set in Palatino by Jazz Cornets

Printed and bound by Intype, London.

CONTENTS

To Dearbhla Hooper
born 18 September 1999
Aberdeen, Scotland
of Irish parents:
a new woman in a new world.

PREFACE AND ACKNOWLEDGEMENTS

This book derives from the fifth Mackie conference (or symposium) held at the University of Aberdeen from 30 June to 2 July 1996. These conferences are made possible by funds from the generous bequest of the late Dr J. R. M. Mackie of Glenmillan; and our thanks as ever are due to the trustees of his estate. Previous Mackie publications are detailed, and future plans are explained, in note 1 to chapter 17 below.

We are grateful to the secretarial staff in the Departments of History and Continuing Education, and to academic colleagues in these and other departments for their interest and support. Our colleagues in Residential and Catering provided the *sine qua non* of the conference most helpfully.

A special word of thanks goes to Steve Boardman, now of Edinburgh University, who was Mackie Lecturer in the Aberdeen History Department at the time of the conference. Digging deep into the reserves of his organisational skills he managed us all with an efficiency which probably surprised even him; and his indomitable cheerfulness withstood all the pressures.

Without the support of Allan Macinnes, Burnett-Fletcher Professor of History and Head of Department, the conference would not have happened. Celia Britton, Professor of French, kindly and elegantly provided the University welcome. And Grant Simpson, now emeritus Reader in Scottish History, and David Ditchburn, a former Mackie Lecturer, were generous with their advice based on past experience.

Our thanks also go to our colleagues at Cruithne Press, Ross Samson and Charles Kennedy. It is good to have publishers who take such an active interest in the books they produce.

The dedicatee's mother's maiden name is Walsh.

T. B.
Aberdeen,
Autumn 1999.

Lynn Abrams lectures in Modern European History at the University of Glasgow. She is the author of *The Orphan Country: children of Scotland's broken homes from 1845 to the present day;* and is working on a study of women in nineteenth-century Europe.

Ida Blom is Professor of History at the University of Bergen. Her main interests are political, social and medical history studied from a gender perspective. She has published several books and many scholarly articles in Norwegian and English, including "World history as gender history", in Stein Tönnesson et al. (eds), *Between National Histories and Global Histories.*

Terry Brotherstone lectures in History at the University of Aberdeen. He has edited, or co-edited, and contributed to books on protest in modern Scotland; on the history of Aberdeen; on Trotsky; and on *History, Economic History and the Future of Marxism.*

Elizabeth J. Clapp lectures in American History at the University of Leicester. Her research interests lie in the history of American women's activism in the nineteenth and early twentieth centuries. She is author of *Mothers of All Children: women reformers and the rise of the Juvenile Courts in progressive era America.*

Lesley Diack is Wellcome Research Fellow at the University of Aberdeen, working on the city's 1964 typhoid epidemic. Her Aberdeen PhD thesis is on "Women's health and charity in eighteenth-century Scotland and France", and she has published a number of articles on related topics.

Fiona Downie is a graduate of the University of Melbourne. Her PhD was awarded at Aberdeen for a thesis entitled *"Sche is but a Womman": the queen and princess in Scotland, 1414–63.* She has written on the problem of national identity in fourteenth-century Scotland and England.

Elizabeth Ewan is Associate Professor of History and Scottish Studies at the University of Guelph, Ontario. Her doctorate is from the University of Edinburgh. She is author of *Town Life in Fourteenth-century Scotland;* and co-editor of *Women in Scotland c. 1100 – c. 1700* (forthcoming).

Grethe Jacobsen is Head of the Danish Department at the Royal Library in Copenhagen. She holds doctorates from the universities of Wisconsin and Odense. She has published books and articles on women, gender and urban legislation; and on women and men in late medieval urban society.

Linda Mahood is Associate Professor of History at the University of Guelph. She is author of *Policing Gender, Class and Family 1850–1945* and *Social Control in Canada; issues in social construction of deviance;* and much else on gender, social control and punishment.

Nicholas Mayhew is Reader in Numismatics in the University of Oxford, and Acting Keeper of the Heberden Coin Room in the Ashmolean Museum. His work with Elizabeth Gemmill on Scottish medieval prices appeared as *Changing Values in Medieval Scotland*. His next book is *A History of Sterling*.

Jane McDermid lectures in Modern History at the University of Southampton New College. Her main areas of research and publication are in Russian women's history 1870–1930, and nineteenth-century Scottish women's history.

Mary Nash is Professor of Contemporary History at the University of Barcelona. Her first degree was from University College, Cork. She has been a pioneer of women's history in Spain and has published in Spanish and English on feminism; women and the labour movement; historiography; and *Defying Male Civilisation: women in the Spanish Civil War*.

Mary O'Dowd is Senior Lecturer in the School of Modern History, Queen's University, Belfast. She is author of *Power, Politics and Land: Sligo 1568–1688*; has co-edited *Women and Irish History*; and is an editor of the *Field Day Anthology of Irish Writing*, vol. IV.

Margery Palmer McCulloch teaches Scottish Literature at the University of Glasgow; and her publications include *The Novels of Neil Gunn: a critical study; Edwin Muir: poet, critic and novelist*; and the edited volume *The Man Who Came Back: essays and short stories by Neil M. Gunn.*

Siân Reynolds is Professor of French at the University of Stirling. She has published on French and Scottish history, as well as translating into English several works by distinguished French historians. She is author of *France Between the Wars: gender and history.*

Deborah Simonton lectures in Cultural History and Women's Studies at the University of Aberdeen, where she is a Continuing Education Organiser. She is author of *A History of European Women's Work, 1700 to the Present,* and other work on the social and cultural history of women in Europe since 1700.

Oonagh Walsh is Lecturer in History at the University of Aberdeen. Her PhD is from Trinity College, Dublin. She has published articles on Irish women's history, and on nineteenth-century psychiatry; and is working on a study of Ireland's war of independence.

Introduction

Terry Brotherstone, Deborah Simonton, and Oonagh Walsh

The *naming of books*, to adapt a feline allusion from T. S. Eliot, "... is a difficult matter. / It isn't just one of your holiday games."[1] And the emphatic and comprehensive title of this volume was not lightly chosen. Perhaps, however, it deserves some explanation. When the fifth Mackie Conference was in the planning stages, it was envisaged as an opportunity to draw together an international group of scholars who would consider two interrelated themes: the current state of the writing of women's history in Scotland and elsewhere; and the relationship between the history of Scottish women and that of women in other countries. We were interested too in exploring the impact that a developing historiography of women has had upon the writing of Scottish history as a whole and, conversely, the manner in which Scottish women's history has contributed to the international picture. When the conference was first proposed, we operated under the working title "Women's history at the margins" – a dual reference to the position of women's history in the canon and to the fairly common idea that areas of Western culture geographically distant from centres such as London, Paris, Berlin, or New York are, or were in the past, "marginal". This Janus-faced approach was intentional: we sought to position ourselves above the doorway to a new phase in Scottish women's history and to encourage a discussion looking simultaneously in different directions, both backwards and forwards, and also at each of the types of marginalisation which must be overcome. We think that the individual responses to our broad agenda – which, much revised, now constitute the chapters of this book – not only make major contributions to a diversity of subjects in their own right, but also belong together by virtue of being informed by this more general approach.

As is by now well established, women's history has earned a central place in the broader discipline. Joan Hoff has written of the three stages through which the writing of women's history passes in most countries[2] – the compensatory, the pre-feminist, and the feminist. The first two phases are necessary in establishing visibility for female historical figures, but each is necessarily limited – by the focus upon individuals in the first instance and by an overly critical examination of the limitations of female participation in the second. It is within the third, or modern feminist phase, which draws upon a wider range of primary and secondary tools, that we would want this volume to be perceived. Drawing upon literary as well as standard historical sources, and employing a comparative methodology, its chapters "trac[e] lines of connection not only among the histories offered here but also between them and other histories of women."[3]

We also suggest that *Gendering Scottish History* should be seen in the context of the direction in which both women's history and gender history are moving. When the journal *Gender and History* was launched in 1989, its editors raised the question: "why gender and history?" A decade later the answer has been provided not only in theory but by a corpus of practical historical work. It was knowledge of much of that work which has enabled us to bring this book together. And gender – not a simplistic view of a compensatory "women's history" – is the fundamental unifying concept underlying it. The chapters which follow address the issue of gender relations from a feminist (rather than from a women's) perspective throughout. As the original *Gender and History* editors put it:

The integration of the experiences, languages and perspectives of women into our understanding of the past ... requires a fundamental transformation of received categories and modes of thinking, as well as a new conceptualization of the very definition of historical study and of the nature of those who have the power to define it.[4]

Gendering Scottish History, then, is situated in a discourse which addresses gender relations at all levels and in every sphere. If gender creation is seen as a process, then these chapters in part chronicle that process, while suggesting how historians may read and understand the past more pro-foundly by viewing it with the assistance of new and critically applied ideas about gender relations. The interdiscipinary nature of the research reported or reflected on here also indicates how feminist historians have been questioning the categories and processes of historical writing, and are, in many different countries, in the vanguard of those reinterpreting the past.

Parallel to all this, in the methodological underpinnings of this volume, lies the thought that Scotland should not – any more than Ireland, Denmark, Norway, or Spain – be seen as peripheral to European culture in any but a narrow geographical sense. It can be argued, indeed, that the focus on the European Union, and on the position of a country like Scotland within a North Atlantic research community which includes Ireland and the Scandinavian countries, can point to new perspectives, distinct from those which centre on the old imperial nation states. The study of Scottish women's history in an international context can help to make this case, perhaps in a qualitatively new way. As Grey Osterud commented following her participation in the Mackie conference:

> The field of history has been transformed [in recent years] by the integration of women as historical subjects, and the history of Europe looks different when viewed from its outer edges than [it does] when viewed from such metropolitan centres as London or Paris.... Recognising women as social actors and reframing the historical narrative in terms appropriate to places like Scotland alters our sense of the past and the process of social change in related ways.[5]

The chapters which follow constitute, we think, an important contribution to this corrective perspective. They help to weigh up the "gendering" of Scottish history, utilising a range of international viewpoints, and they put down a marker for the position of women's history at the end of the twentieth century. The book comments, as Osterud remarked of the conference papers, on

Scotland's international links and suggests some possible lines of comparison between Scottish women's history and the histories of women elsewhere on the "margins" of Europe. The Mackie symposium offered rich resources, both conceptual and empirical, for such analyses. Readers may draw their own conclusions from these collected papers, tracing lines of connection not only among the histories offered here but also between them and other histories of women. [6]

The chapters have been arranged into two broad groups. The first is broadly historiographical, dealing with issues of women's history from a variety of international and theoretical perspectives. Siân Reynolds' opening chapter raises key issues in Scottish women's history by fore-grounding a specific event: the creation of the League of Nations. The Covenant of the League accorded women equal status with men as repre-sentatives, delegates, and officials, an equality successfully fought for by Ishbel Gordon, Lady Aberdeen. Reynolds argues that this symbolic his-torical moment represents a "breach in the male monopoly of official international relations", and may be thought of as symbolic of the possib-ilities confronting women's history more generally. In the context of this volume, the symbolism is twofold, as Lady Aberdeen's story calls both for a "women's history" approach to what has mainly been a male his-torical record, and for the assertion of the importance of Scottish history within a thereby newly defined approach to British diplomatic history.

Chapters two and three provide historiographical overviews of Scot-tish women's history. Elizabeth Ewan examines the medieval and early modern period. As she points out, historians working on Scottish women in the medieval period are relatively few, and those considering gender as a critical tool even fewer. Ewan demonstrates how Scottish women's history has moved from a narrow consideration of "women worthies" to a more challenging examination of the roles women have played in shap-ing Scottish history, in contrast to the assumption that they were simply acted upon by forces largely outside their control. It is cheering to note that "more historical work has been done on women in Scotland than is commonly realised", but her conclusion points up the many areas which remain untouched. She argues, for example, that historians need to address themselves to areas such as the participation of Scottish women in the empire, but that they should do so in order to evaluate their con-tribution within a gendered context, not merely to add footnotes to a broader imperial narrative. Jane McDermid's chapter engages with research into Scottish women's history of the nineteenth and twentieth centuries, and places that history firmly at the centre of the broader debate over the development of Scottish history as a whole. She challenges the assumption that the construction of Scottish national identity, and the historical origins of that identity, are necessarily masculine. McDermid demonstrates how feminist historians have interrogated the constructs of labour, politics, and education, while sounding the cautionary note that much remains to be done. As she indicates, practitioners of Scottish women's history not only have the difficulties of asserting the validity of women's history *per se* but have to avoid their work being assimilated unproblematically into the new accounts of Scottish history on the one hand or of British feminism on the other.

In contrast to these historiographies of Scotland, Grete Jacobsen's chapter throws the development of Scandinavian women's history into relief, and offers a framework within which comparative studies of other countries could be made. Jacobsen offers the intriguing proposal that the model of Scandinavian women's history – that of Denmark, Norway, and Sweden, as well as Iceland and the Scandinavian parts of Finland – may serve as a means of creating a theoretical basis for women's history generally.[7] The histories of these countries are often uncritically presumed to be common: what does this say about similar presumptions in the field of women's history? Jacobsen's emphasis on the arguments amongst feminist historians, as much as on their points of agreements, further illustrates the advances made in women's history. Dissent marks an arrival at a state of confidence in the subject.

The following three chapters focus on specific themes to illuminate general issues of historical approach. Deborah Simonton examines the ways that work was defined, and consequently gendered, so that women were frequently not perceived as "workers". Concentrating on Europe between 1750 and 1820, her starting points are the significance of the ways that skill and status were coded as male, and the patriarchal operation of the workplace. Exploring the link between females and the home in the period before "domesticity", she demonstrates how ideas about home and workplace combined with concepts of skill and perceptions of technology to conceptualise women as casual, temporary, unskilled workers, and men as the skilled artisans. She argues that "division of labour along sexual lines ... was about power, status, position, and masculinity,"[8] while women's skills and place were described in terms of the physical and ideological space of the home. Defence of the male workplace and status provided the underlying theme for redefinitions of work and skill which devalued women's skills and economic role.

[xv]

The division between public and private spheres has been extensively explored by feminist historians, with the pioneering work of Nancy Cott and Barbara Welter providing a theoretical model for later historical analysis.[9] Taking the Norwegian welfare state as a starting point, Ida Blom's article tackles this public/private dichotomy, and teases out the implications for a truly gendered history in presuming that the former is always masculine and the latter feminine. On the contrary, Blom suggests that not merely could the public, masculine, political arena "demonstrat[e] instrumentally feminine qualities"[10] through the provision of welfare, but the development of the welfare state was a complex mix of public and private initiatives, in which strict distinctions between masculine and feminine spheres of control were blurred. Furthermore, Blom presents the possibility that welfare-dependent women, formerly read as powerless dependants of the state, may in some cases have been empowered by the assistance which liberated them from husbands and fathers.

Margery Palmer McCulloch's chapter raises a key element in women's history – the variety of sources used to document women's historical experiences – through an exploration of the city in Scottish women's fiction. She also engages with the issue of image and reality. Linking the literary representations with actual experiences of city-dwelling women in the early twentieth century, Palmer McCulloch demonstrates how urban living could be a liberating experience for women. The relationships of women to the city, and the Scottish city to European capitals, are ones in which gender distinctions are blurred and often breached, offering another perspective from which to view the question of women's history. She argues that

> Scottish authors and their characters [were] rewriting female scenarios and in so doing [were] pointing with understanding to the changes occurring in women's lives.... Women authors were not only writing themselves; they were also writing the city as a place where they could find a truer way to themselves.[11]

By engaging with the literary text, Palmer McCulloch gives us an insight to the ways other sources can be used by the historian who is traditionally wary of literature as evidence.

The final chapter in this section both draws together many of the issues raised in the preceding chapters and points the way forward to the second, more empirical section. Opening with a discussion of comparative issues in a European context, Mary Nash challenges the concept of

"European" itself when applied to women's history. The Spanish case, for example, is markedly different from that of Britain or France, which are commonly taken to represent a standard "European" experience. Thus historians of women need to be mindful of the particular cultural environment within which any given group operated. Nash further explores the construction of motherhood in early twentieth-century Spain, and argues that contrary to the traditional assumptions about the Catholic idealisation of mothers, motherhood can be redefined "as a prime mobilising force in the fight of women against fascism." [12]

The book's second section, while employing many of the theoretical strategies outlined in the first, comprises largely empirical studies of women's experiences in Scotland and abroad from the fifteenth to the twentieth centuries – studies which illuminate specific aspects of gendered research. In the opening chapter Fiona Downie explores the institution of marriage for the medieval nobility, and shows that although queens were rarely born, they could be made, or could make themselves, through marriage. The intimate association between marital and political alliances allowed certain women to play crucial roles as power brokers and peacemakers in the fifteenth century. Downie draws particular attention to the permeable barrier between the public and private spheres by pointing out that young titled women were often informally "apprenticed" to powerful female patrons, who instructed them in court etiquette and, more importantly, prepared them for the complex diplomatic roles they were expected to assume after marriage. Far from wielding power through a son, the traditional interpretation of female influence in this period, medieval noblewomen operated as political agents in their own right.

Nicholas Mayhew's examination of the records of the Aberdeen Burgh Court provides a sharp contrast in terms of class to the preceding chapter. Focusing mainly upon women "candle-makers, cake-bakers, petty retailers, servants and ... brewsters", [13] this chapter indicates the strength of women in Aberdeen as manufacturers and retailers. Their importance as regulators of the local economy – the October burgh court of 1522 agreed that women should, in consultation with the local growers, determine the market price for malt and meal – is emphasised, although they were largely confined to products and areas which were regarded as low-status. Women were dominant in the brewing business, and remained so well into the sixteenth century. Part of the reason, Mayhew suggests, was because it was domestic in origin, and even when placed on a commercial footing, it remained "women's work". Public and private spheres were thus blurred, although in this case for the economic benefit of women.

Mary O'Dowd's chapter on women and the colonial experience in Ireland raises some key issues for women's history generally. Pointing out that the roles of women as agents and objects of colonialism have been ignored by most historians, O'Dowd also indicates that the sources for women in Ireland in the early modern period are scanty. However, while women's personal or collective testimony may be difficult to recover, the accounts of male administrators survive, many of which comment forcefully on what was regarded as the dangerously destabilising influence of Irishwomen on the English garrisons. Women were viewed as lawless sexual beings who transgressed acceptable gender boundaries and militated against the rule of English law. The presentation of women as guileful, untrustworthy creatures in need of firm control raises echoes in other women's histories, and emphasises the need for more comparative work.

Lesley Diack's essay on motherhood and poverty in eighteenth-century Aberdeen also focuses on a central female experience as recorded by men. Although, as Diack points out, the sources for a study of maternity in poverty are good, there is little testimony from the women themselves, and the historian is dependent upon middle-class, male-generated material. Thus the records of the kirk sessions of the Church of Scotland for the eighteenth century reveal an avid concern, bordering on the voyeuristic, to interrogate, judge and reprimand unmarried mothers. Establishing paternity was crucial for the session, in order that possible financial obligations might be removed from the church poor relief funds and placed on the putative father, but the persistent and often callous manner in which women were questioned – one appeared seventeen times before the session – led to infanticide and suicide.

Lynn Abrams' chapter questions the meaning of national identity for women in the nineteenth century. Arguing that Scottish women's history has thus far offered "few insights into the relationship between Scottish women's experience and their political and national identity",[14] Abrams turns to Germany as an example of how women used the period between 1871 and 1914 to fashion a sense of national identity which allowed a full expression of women's lives. Interestingly, German feminists of the 1890s defined women as both mothers and citizens, and even advocated their exclusive occupation of the domestic sphere. Far from viewing "home" in opposition to "work" or "politics", these feminists argued that women's roles as guardians of morality automatically entitled them to the full rights of citizenship.

The relative experiences of men and women as both staff and patients in the asylum system are considered by Oonagh Walsh. Concentrating mainly on the Irish case, Walsh demonstrates how nursing represented an employment opportunity for women throughout the nineteenth century, and how these positions offered a degree of power and authority not normally available to unskilled women. Much of the power was however exercised at the expense of the inmates. In analysing patterns of admission, Walsh indicates that young single patients, and especially males, were committed with the greatest frequency, and were most likely to be detained in the asylum long-term. Marriage, it would appear, offered a degree of protection to both men and women, but whether this was against insanity, or merely committal, remains open to question.

Elizabeth Clapp, in her examination of the Chicago Juvenile Court in the 1890s, demonstrates how perceptions of women and their roles were modified to suit particular historical moments. Philanthropic endeavour has always blurred the distinctions between public and private spheres, and Clapp demonstrates how women consciously used the notion of maternal duty to expand the parameters of their activities. Arguing that the contribution of women to the reform of the juvenile court movement has been sidelined in the emphasis upon individual male reformers, Clapp shows not only that women were central to the reform process, but that they were conscious of the gendered implications of their participation. By clothing their demands for change in the innocuous garb of maternalism, women achieved legislative reform without alienating the men to whom they appealed.

The final substantive chapter in the book – prior to some personal concluding observations by Terry Brotherstone – continues the themes of women's relationships to institutions, and that of delinquency. Commenting on how interpretations of the female delinquent have altered over the years, Linda Mahood presents a gendered reading of delinquency theory and of the institutions established in the late nineteenth and early twentieth centuries to deal with "problem girls". Despite the changing discourse of female delinquency over the years, Mahood points out that some things remained constant – girls were believed to be more difficult to rehabilitate than boys, and the reclamation of girls who were deemed sexually corrupt required an especially strict regime. While boys were encouraged to make contacts outside of reform institutions as part of their rehabilitation, girls were isolated from unapproved contact which might retard their progress.

During the 1996 Mackie conference it became clear that two obvious questions were not being explicitly addressed. The contributors did not ask what is distinctly "Scottish" in the historical experiences of women, nor did they confront directly the question of how the integration of women and gender transforms the writing of Scottish history. Grey Osterud saw this as

a well-considered effort to avoid the pitfalls of narrowly nation-alist histories. Indeed, the nationalist problematic that has dominated much modern Scottish historical writing has excluded and subordinated women, along with other social groups which were not represented in "high" politics, and has neglected Scotland's links with places other than the British metropole. Initial research in Scottish women's history, too, often took its conceptual frameworks from better-researched regions such as England, even though these were not necessarily applicable to Scotland and ought not to set the standard of comparison. [15]

Gendering Scottish History, however, does not ignore the question of what is distinctive about women's history in Scotland. It tries to allow what is particularly "Scottish" and what is shared with other histories of women to emerge from empirical work, rather than to have such points dictated by the presuppositions of writers whose main emphasis is understandably on particular national histories. It also aims to let Scotland figure, "not solely in a vexed relation to 'England', but rather in relation to diverse societies on the European 'periphery' – in Ireland, British North America, Scandinavia, the Mediterranean and Central Europe." [16]

By exploring parallel, divergent, and connected developments in a wide range of societies, this book intends to contribute to the process of shifting the focus of historical narrative from the nation-state to broader processes of social change. It is one of our hopes that overarching themes are at least adumbrated in this collection – themes which perhaps suggest future directions for women's history, Scottish history and the relation between gender and nation in the writing of women's history. We are not so ambitious as to suggest that this book in itself will serve to "gender Scottish history". But we think it takes an important step forward along the road to this end; and that, in doing so, it helps to demonstrate two important truths. The first is that the new Scottish history must become more outward-looking and self-critical, with its practitioners asking themselves more seriously how they could – during the past generation or two – have achieved so much while paying comparatively so little attention to women and to gender. And the second is that, if this happens, there are communities of historical scholarship "furth of Scotland" (to use a native term) ready to take a serious interest in this small northern European country's place in history; and to enter into a mutually productive, and publicly needed, international dialogue about both the methodology and the intellectual content of historical work.

NOTES

1. T. S. Eliot, "The naming of cats", in *Old Possum's Book of Practical Cats* (London, 1939), p. 11. ("The Naming of Cats is a difficult matter,/ It isn't just one of your holiday games;/ You may think at first I'm as mad as a hatter/ When I tell you a cat must have THREE DIFFERENT NAMES.")
2. "The impact and implications of women's history" in M. O'Dowd and M. Valiulis (eds.), *Women and Irish History* (Dublin, 1997), p. 25.
3. We are grateful to Grey Osterud, who, despite her participation in the Mackie conference, was unfortunately not able to contribute directly to this book, but whose draft comments on the conference and the texts which came out of it have been invaluable to the editors in providing an outside insight into the importance of the project, and in helping to shape this introduction. See Grey Osterud, "Women's history at the margins: Scottish and international perspectives", unpublished draft ms., 1996.
4. *Gender and History*, vol. 1, no. 1 (Spring, 1989), p. 4.
5. Osterud, "Women's history at the margins ...".
6. *Ibid.*
7. Jacobsen provides a salutary reminder that concepts of "margins" and "centres" largely depend upon one's own geographical or theoretical position – Iceland considers itself part of the north, and not primarily part of Scandinavia, despite what mainland Europeans may think. See below, p. 47.
8. See below p. 63.
9. Barbara Welter, "The cult of true womanhood, 1820–1860", *American Quarterly*, vol. 18 (1966); Nancy F. Cott, *The Bonds of Womanhood: women's sphere in New England, 1780–1835* (Yale, 1977).
10. See below, p. 86.
11. See below, p. 110.
12. See below, p. 116.
13. See below, p. 145.
14. See below, p. 187.
15. Osterud, "Women's history at the margins ...".
16. *Ibid.*

PART ONE

Historiography and gender: Scottish and international dimensions

Siân Reynolds

This chapter starts and finishes with a famous international event – the Treaty of Versailles, signed on 28 June 1919. It may not seem an obvious choice to illustrate an essay about historiography and gender, let alone one with Scottish dimensions. Signatories to the treaty were all male, and Scotland was of course not represented separately from the rest of Britain. What is the link?

The conference on which this book is based was held in Aberdeen, the regional capital of north-eastern Scotland. Twenty miles from the city is Haddo House, the home of a Scotswoman who was present in Paris during the peace conference of spring 1919, Ishbel Gordon, Lady Aberdeen. She went to Paris in her capacity as president of the International Council of Women (ICW).[1] With her committee, she successfully helped lobby the world leaders and diplomats who were simultaneously drafting the rules for the League of Nations, so that a clause of its covenant, signed in April 1919, enabled women to be delegates, representatives, and officials within the League of Nations on the same terms as men. This was not the case in most national civil services at the time, let alone diplomatic corps.

The clause marked a small, often unnoticed breach in the male monopoly of official international relations at the beginning of the twentieth century; and it makes a symbolic starting-point for some more general reflections. This chapter concentrates on the role of gender as a structuring concept in the debates over the way we write history. It will seek to reconcile a Scottish vantage point with some of the international dimensions of those debates.

I

Most readers, whether they find the concept of gender congenial or not, will be familiar with the ideas of women's history. And women's history itself has a history. Indeed it has an under-valued pre-history, but for practical reasons the following remarks refer only to what has been written since the early 1970s. We have come a long way since then, but the shock waves of that period are still being felt. If all history is to some extent a conversation with other historians, then the arrival of a critical mass of women's history was – or should have been – one of the biggest and noisiest conversations of recent times. It remains potentially disruptive to accepted frameworks of historiography. But if women's history has forced its way on to the historical agenda in some countries, the process has by no means been universal. There are quite significant national differences in the way women's history has, or has not, been accepted. To illustrate such mixed fortunes, I have chosen the four countries I know best from the "northern" geographical areas represented in this volume: the United States of America, England, Scotland, and France.

In the USA, where it already had a weighty pre-history, the expansion of women's history accompanied the women's movement and was associated with radical politics: the civil rights protests of the 1960s and the anti-Vietnam War campaigns of the 1970s. Women's history shared in the massive growth of women's studies in American universities, and has developed in a particularly dynamic relationship with separate histories, such as that of women of colour, and with the various strands of radical feminism. Its diversity remains extraordinary. A history graduate from as late as the mid-1960s would rub her eyes in astonishment to see the number of papers given at the Berkshire Conferences of recent years[2] – the great majority by American historians and on American topics, but with many international sessions too. Women's history in America certainly has critical mass.

[2]

In England (and "England" sometimes stood for "Britain" at first: it was taken to include Wales and Scotland, if not Ireland) women's history was from the start closer to an older radical tradition, that of labour history. Many of the women's historians of the 1970s were influenced by, for instance, E. P. Thompson's *The Making of the English Working Class*, first published in 1968; and they wrote for journals like *New Left Review*, and, later, the very important *History Workshop Journal*, which was launched in 1972.[3] The approach of writers like Sheila Rowbotham, Anna Davin, and Sally Alexander was shaped by socialist politics. This was not necessarily true of the women's movement in Britain as a whole, but it was certainly true of women's *history*, which was initially greatly concerned with the debates about the compatibility, or incompatibility, of Marxism and feminism. For anyone of my generation, working in the south of England throughout the 1970s and 1980s, this could be taken for granted. Whether despite or because of this emphasis, women's history in "Britain" (though perhaps I mean "England" here) has a solid presence in the academic world, and is taken seriously – although the historical establishment remains largely masculine.

In both these countries, women's history, however controversial, was unarguably successful in "becoming visible". In the other two examples – Scotland and France – the picture is more clouded. This might seem a paradoxical remark to make about France. There is after all a huge and conspicuous volume of work published on the history of women in France. There too, it resulted from the wave of feminist politics starting in the early 1970s, after the upheaval of 1968. But the practitioners of women's history in France remain even today surprisingly isolated within the academy and certainly in university history departments. The five-volume *History of Women in the West*, written almost entirely in France and containing much French material, was an extraordinarily successful publishing venture.[4] But the environment is not woman-friendly. Very few senior historians supervise PhDs in this area; and women's history is viewed as an unwise career choice – something that was briefly fashionable, but which has never been seriously welcomed by the historical establishment, despite some sympathy from individuals.

This is partly because of the theoretical dimension of French republicanism which, in the name of universalism, has been very male-centred; and partly because of the practical dimension represented by male-dominated power structures in strongholds of social history, such as the *Maison des Sciences de l'Homme* (MSH). In a book published under the MSH imprint in 1995 on "the profession of historian" and the writing of history in France over the last fifty years, only three of thirty-eight contributors were women. Women's history was conspicuous by its absence; and Arlette Farge, having been invited to write instead on "social history", commented on the "relative isolation of this field of research [i.e. women's history]". She wrote that it

> has not really "caught on" in the discipline. It seems to be in some obscure way devalued, even if historians claim it is there to stay. The comparative silence [sic] surrounding this history is itself part of history.[5]

I turn, finally, to Scotland, where women's history got off to a late start. *History Workshop*, in its early years, published some Scottish material, and it has carried more recently. But by the mid-1980s there had still been comparatively little work on Scottish women's history. In 1990 Eleanor Gordon and Esther Breitenbach in their introduction to *The World is Ill-divided* – a collection of essays on women and work in Scotland – said that "sadly" there was still little material published on Scotland, and they pointed to the "enormous disjuncture between research and interest on the one hand and published material on the other". They ascribed this to "ethnocentrism on one side of the border and male prejudice on the other". In other words, the writers on women's history did not trouble themselves with Scotland, while the writers of Scottish history did not trouble themselves with women.

There had been one or two pioneer studies in the 1970s and early 1980s, and today there is a greater volume of research reaching print,[6] such as the work of the contributors to the Gordon and Breitenbach book, of Leah Leneman, of Elspeth King, of Linda Mahood – soon to be joined, it is to be hoped, by the publications of a younger generation of postgraduate researchers. Many recent studies concentrate on the nineteenth and twentieth centuries, and perhaps this is no accident. Not only was there a set of well-established Scottish historical traditions to contend with – warrior history; legal and ecclesiastical history; and, later, labour history (none with much space for women) – but it has also been suggested that modern Scottish historians were chiefly concerned with building a Scottish national history and identity, with roots in the centuries before the Act of Union of 1707. As this book itself illustrates, this is not necessarily incompatible with women's history, yet, in practice, the two seem to have been kept separate.

In other countries represented by chapters in this volume – Ireland, Spain, Norway, Denmark, Germany – there are other tales to tell, which might reflect one of these models or be specific in other ways. The field of research is still contentious, still a fight, and the notion of injustice is not far below the surface. The motivating force behind the original dynamics of women's history remains the need to let unheard voices speak, anonymous people find a name, unknown faces be seen, unrecorded experience be taken into account. This role has not by any means become redundant – since, even where women's history has tenure, so to speak, that is of very recent origin.

As the titles of some of the chapters of this book indicate, however, women's history has led to something that would never have emerged from previous (i.e. male-centred) history – the development of gender as an analytical concept, and as something with a force in history comparable to class. Gender is the theorised version of sexual difference: maleness/femaleness or masculinity/femininity. When the concept first began to be used, it was distinguished from sex. Sex referred to biological features, regarded (in those days more than they would perhaps be now) as given. Gender referred to the sexual differences constructed by society. The early debates will by now be familiar to many readers, and are reflected in the rise of journals such as *Gender and History*, which first appeared in 1989. There is still some tension between those who see women's history as unavoidably a crusade against patriarchy in all its forms, and those who see gender as a concept, applicable to both men and women. Those who feel most strongly on either side see their positions as incompatible. In my own view, reconciliation is not impossible: as a feminist, I am myself happiest working with gender as a way of exploring the past, though I recognise that this may often mean working on women's history more than on men's. If we dwell too much on this quasi-internal debate, we may underestimate the ways in which both women's history and gender history relate to another general debate, since they both pose a challenge to traditional forms of writing history.

That debate hinges on the "linguistic turn" – sometimes referred to as post-structuralism or post-modernism, sometimes as relativism. Any attempt to see where we are now cannot ignore this issue. It is one of the biggest, but most oblique debates in history today, and in many ways it is closely associated with the gender issue. Wherever one looks, it continues to be discussed: in the pages of *Social History* and *Past & Present*, to name only two mainstream journals.[7] While it has long been a feature of American historical debates, quite recently, Keith Thomas could suggest that it had yet to hit Britain. Reviewing sympathetically a book entirely devoted to the question, he wrote in 1994:

The intellectual uncertainties which are chronicled in this book have gone much further in the US than in this country ... for the most part British historians are a stolidly untheoretical lot, neither has the challenge of multiculturalism and ethnic minorities so far provoked much of a response from the writers of the nation's history.[8]

But, in the latter 1990s, these uncertainties and challenges have become part of the British historiographical landscape too.

The linguistic turn has been much caricatured by those who dislike it. Some of its opponents characterise relativism as the extreme proposition that there is no such thing as historical truth, and no point in seeking it. A more moderate characterisation would be to say that the relativist considers absolute truth about the past impossible to grasp, and assumes that there are many ways of trying to approach it. The spin put on this by the post-modernist is that written history should be viewed as a series of texts, or narratives, with their own formal shape, their own detailed rhetoric, their own context. Narrative here does not always mean chronology so much as a story, *something with a shape*. An extreme relativist might take the view that no particular narrative has more claim to tell the "truth" about the past than any other; that history is always written by someone; and that someone in turn can hardly do other than select from the past the things that either may be fashionable at the time or may fit her view of the world or may have been drawn to her attention by other historians, and so on.

At one level this is merely common sense. Most historians are trying to make sense of something very complex, to unscramble the past. E. H. Carr in *What is History?* famously said something superficially not so different: first identify your historian – let us call him Jones of St Jude's – and then find out what "bee he has in his bonnet". Today it might be phrased as "what is his or her agenda?".[9] It is an entirely reasonable question to ask. But that is not quite the same thing as taking a post-modernist view. Carr assumes Jones to be a completely free agent, consciously choosing his bee. A post-modernist would argue that Jones was at least in part *being spoken*, without his being fully aware of it, by the discourses available to him. He did not choose the bee, if you like, the bee chose him. The kind of history he wrote would take shape according to the discursive practices – more plainly put, the patterns of thought and expression – which he found all round him. To anyone from a literary background, used to reading texts as texts, or to anyone who has trans-

[6]

lated works of history out of another language, the idea that history has its own textual specificity and rhetoric is not particularly difficult to accept. And to this extent, unlike some fellow-historians, I regard the linguistic turn as, in some respects, little more than a statement of the obvious.

But there is some understandable resistance to extreme relativism – do *no* narratives have any claims to take precedence? Are we not defending truths when we write the kind of history that, for example, brings to light hidden aspects of women's lives? Is there no hierarchy of more or less serious texts? Points like this have been made in some quite noisy conversations from their different perspectives (by Lawrence Stone or Joan Hoff, for instance).[10] It is a debate that has not only divided those who have had nothing at all to do with women's history, but if possible, even more violently those who *do* write women's history. Paradoxically, while in some quarters women's history and gender history are seen as among the chief forces propelling relativism along, there have been some extremely negative reactions from within women's history itself.

I think we ought to be able to absorb this debate without allowing ourselves to be fazed by it. Of course it is important to be scrupulous in the way we do things, the way we use our evidence. Of course there are such things as facts, and sometimes we can even agree which ones are more important than others. But the important point to bear in mind is that first women's history then gender history gave a jolt to historiography and are rightly seen as having "relativised" much that went before – although the full implications of that jolt are by no means universally realised, even today. Take Jones of St Jude's. Part of the rhetoric a history don at Oxford in the 1950s or 1960s would take for granted would be a male form of discourse, using male pronouns automatically and omitting any mention of women except in certain preconceived ways. When we read such work now, we may react rather strongly, but the historian did not consciously imagine he was writing an *anti-feminist* kind of history. A *tour de force* of St Jude's speak is the first page of A. J. P. Taylor's *English History 1914–1945* published in the mid-1960s. Here are some extracts:

> Until August 1914, a sensible, law-abiding Englishman could pass through life and hardly notice the existence of the state, beyond the post office and the policeman. He could live where he liked and as he liked. He had no official number or identity card. He could travel abroad or leave his country for ever without a passport or any sort of official permission.... An Englishman could

enlist, if he chose, in the regular army.... He could also ignore if he chose, the demands of national defence. Substantial householders were occasionally called on for jury service.... [The state] imposed safety rules in factories, and prevented women, and adult males in some industries, from working excessive hours.... Broadly speaking, the state acted only to help those who could not help themselves. It left the adult citizen alone. [11]

If we now find this kind of formulation rather lopsided, it is because the gender debate has given a boost to relativism – not so much invalidating old narratives as destabilising them, and showing that the same period could be viewed in an entirely different light. How could all that great mass of history have been written with hardly a mention of women? The further point about gender history was that it drew attention to the specificity of men as well. One was not so much making the picture more complete, correcting it, by "adding" women, so to speak: it simply was no longer the same picture. Once gender has been recognised as a force in history, one cannot go on playing by the old rules. Something has to give and that something may be the innocent faith in objectivity.

What was more, not only did a gendered kind of history cast disturbing new light on secondary works, which were often narratives produced by men about men, it also unsettled one's faith in the archives. In case this sends a shiver down the spine, let me declare that I am in no doubt that archives may provide genuine and authentic documents, traces of the past. A letter from Lloyd George written during the peace conference, for instance, may tell you something about his state of mind that the official record leaves out. But women's history has helped de-fetishise the archives too. Which documents survive? What is thought worthy of preservation? In large measure, the records contain male-compiled collections of male-authored texts, concerning the doings of men: trade union minutes, military records, police reports. And these all have not only male authors, they also have a certain form and rhetoric, which alters over time. Once linguistic doubt has crept in, it points to other textual doubts, which may or may not concern gender. Minutes of meetings for example are conventionally written in the passive mood – "it was decided to", "a resolution was passed". The participation or silence of those in the room may go unrecorded. A letter may seem a better guide to "what really happened" than someone's unreliable memoirs, but even a letter is conceived according to certain textual imperatives: the writer knows who will, or might, read it, so it has a rhetoric of its own.

[8]

Two letters written by the same person on the same day may carry different accounts of the same events. You do not have to be a feminist or a women's historian to see this, but we have become somewhat expert at finding the gaps and inconsistencies in the sources. Archives are not innocent, transparent windows to the past: at best they are fragments of glass, some clear, some clouded, with frightening gaps all round them.

Key names in the broad debate about relativism (or post-modernism or post-structuralism) include Michel Foucault, Richard Rorty, and Hayden White – who were/are not particularly, or necessarily, interested in gender (it just happens that they are men ...). But their work has been used by those who are concerned with gender. In Britain, Keith Jenkins has popularised these ideas, while in the field of gender history itself the unavoidable name at the centre of the debate has been that of Joan Scott.[12] (I am tempted at this point to give a different meaning to the Aberdeen symposium's original title, *Women's History: Scottish and international perspectives*, and say that the debate in women's history has shown signs of becoming one between a Scott-ish history and its adversaries.) What Scott and Jenkins have in common is their sceptical distrust of the grand narrative. In their book *Telling the Truth about History*, Joyce Appleby et al., who engage fully with this debate – is it an accident that they are all women? – show remorselessly how certain grand narratives have shaped our view of the past. This has been especially true of national history – whether in the myth of the frontier, the advance of science, or the Whig view of progress – because it suited someone's agenda at the time. Again, although the writers of *Telling the Truth ...* choose not to over-stress the gender aspect, these grand narratives could be attacked by writers of women's history for their constant marginalising of gender, their reductionism. Yet these are the narratives that govern the textbooks, those pillars of mainstream history, with their constant stress on political history – that is, on such events as the Treaty of Versailles. To quote Breitenbach and Gordon:

> the lack of visibility of women in Scottish life up till now is not a result of their absence from political social or public life. It is a result of the blindness of historians to the significance of women's experience, not to say on occasion to the fact of women's existence.[13]

If we seek to take stock, then, we need to propose new agendas all the time, to keep thinking of new ways to see history. To try to illustrate what I mean, I shall try to "en-gender" the Treaty of Versailles, to discuss it in the light of the various approaches opened up by the debates I have discussed, and, incidentally, to link Scotland to the international stage, if only via Lady Aberdeen, who can be a useful guide. I have chosen the Treaty of Versailles deliberately because international history, diplomacy, and foreign policy have traditionally been somewhat resistant to approaches via gender.

II

Back, then, to Paris. How can gender be brought to bear on the events of 1919? One approach is to look for named women – in this case, Lady Aberdeen – who were recognised by many of the leading actors of the time, or by the press, as persons of note, but who are not now household names in the way that even fairly minor government ministers may be. Of course, it did no harm to be an aristocrat's wife, and a luminary of the British Liberal Party. Lady Aberdeen's guest list reads like a roll-call of all contemporary politicians of note. She was a woman whose biography cries out to be written: a genuine philanthropist and liberal, an activist in many causes. But her importance at this particular time was as a well-connected lobbyist – to whom Lloyd George would not be able to refuse an audience – acting on behalf of other women in her capacity as president of the ICW. Lady Aberdeen has left plenty of traces in the record – she is not at all anonymous and obscure. Yet she is rather hidden from history and can be part of a straightforward recovery programme – along the line of thought that is sometimes known as the "women worthies" tradition.

Alongside her, one could cite other women closely connected to centres of power in Paris, some professionally, such as the emerging number of women journalists, newspaper owners, or editors, who were taken very seriously in their time. They would include Séverine, Louise Weiss, Genevieve Tabouis, or Lady Rhondda.[14] Certainly by the time of the treaty, such women's actions are quite recoverable: it would be possible to find out a good deal about them and to write their biographies. Others are more like Lady Aberdeen: Mme de Jouvenel, society hostess, was known as "queen of the peace conference". Political or diplomatic wives are an underestimated élite group. Pat Jalland's account of British political families is a good example of historicising the informal kinship and gender patterns of élites.[15] Informal is the key word, but analysis of decision-making has for some time now recognised that informal factors, though resistant to historical investigation, may have been more important than was once thought. Partly this is because women's history has shifted attention somewhat – even though it is still seen as dangerous territory – on to an informal, separate world, linked to family and blood. One of the interesting things to be found in Sir Maurice Hankey's memoirs, a source for much information about the day-to-day handling of the peace talks, is the number of references he makes to his wife. [16]

A second line of approach, perhaps more comfortable to most women's historians, would be to concentrate on the ICW – the association, founded in 1888, that Lady Aberdeen was representing at Versailles. This approach represents the structural preference, inherited perhaps from labour history in England, for studying movements rather than individuals. By far the most studied of women's movements are the suffrage organisations. By 1919, however, women's international organisations were no longer a novelty: they had built up a corps of women who had the experience to deal with foreign travel, organisational machines, lobbying, and so on. It was of course the suffrage issue that provided the original motivation. So this new phenomenon can be historicised as never before, since it was probably in the inter-war years that most critical mass was acquired: indeed it seems to have been the heyday of such groups. [17] Inevitably, since they had no support system, and no expense accounts such as were provided for career diplomats, the women who were most active in such organisations often had enough private means to travel: they were well-off and well educated; they could speak foreign languages; they were often professionally qualified, and so on. They were, on balance, from élite backgrounds – Lady Aberdeen more than most. But, then, so were most of their male counterparts.

For diplomatic historians, women's organisations – such as the ICW, the IWSA, the Women's International League for Peace and Freedom, etc. – have not seemed very important: after all they did not inflect national policy. Most such historians have never given them a first, never mind a second, thought. More recently, a new wave of scholarship associated with the study of the League of Nations and in particular with peace movements has resuscitated these movements, and is looking at them for what they can tell us about women as political pressure groups. [18] The peace talks in Paris were accompanied by an informal meeting of the ICW and allied suffrage groups, whose main concern, as noted earlier, was to lobby for women to have full access to membership of the delegations to the League of Nations, as well as to its bureaucracy, and for due consideration to be given for what were thought of as "women's issues". These included equal pay, the abolition of white slavery, child welfare,

[11]

etc. We may today regard this as accepting only stereotyped roles (Vellacott's view),[19] but at the time many women in mainstream feminist movements saw the purpose of the right to vote as having a voice on these issues; they regarded the existence of discriminatory practices as being a matter on which international pressure was worth applying.

Not all women campaigners wished to be so confined. At the same time as Lady Aberdeen and her friends were lobbying Clemenceau, Wilson, and Lloyd George, another – and more radical – conference was meeting in Zurich. It was deliberately held away from Paris, so that women from the defeated powers, Germany and Austria, could attend. This was the second conference of the group which was to become known as the Women's International League for Peace and Freedom. It had held a conference in the Hague in 1915 in the teeth of massive international and national disapproval, which divided the suffrage movements that were invited. A Scotswoman, Chrystal McMillan, was one of only three British women who beat a channel blockade to get there. And the Hague conference's resolutions have a good claim to have helped inspire Woodrow Wilson's Fourteen Points. The same women meeting in Zurich in 1919 were among the first people to read the terms of the Treaty of Versailles (which appalled them by their punitive character). They did not dissent from the ICW lobbying in Paris, but wanted women to have a say in the fundamental negotiations designed to create peace – not just on women's issues.

Nevertheless, the point about all these associations is that they were *women's* movements; they were united by this, if often internally divided. Official diplomacy was a gendered group too (male), although of course it did not see itself in that way. Most diplomatic services explicitly prevented women joining at this time. Lady Aberdeen's lobby drew attention to the practices of exclusion operating in the Foreign Office, the Quai d'Orsay, and all the chancelleries of Europe, to which the League of Nations brought just a little change. They drew attention to the fact that the treaties were all signed on behalf of the world's citizens by men. The changes achieved were small and not far reaching. Few women were ever delegates or sent on missions. Yet permanent officials of the League were sometimes formidable women of that generation before women's careers really got going. And the politics of women's organisations at international level often cut across national policy. This is an alternative politics with its own history, waiting to be discovered, and with no lack of sources.[20]

The third approach goes further than the previous two towards both gender history and post-modern analysis. It may be very worthwhile to demonstrate that some women played a role in international relations – contrary to what every book on diplomatic history would lead you to think – but this does not answer that famous nagging question: "that is all very well, but my understanding of the French Revolution (or the Treaty of Versailles) is not changed by knowing that women participated in it". While this statement in fact seems to me open to question, to answer the objection another way a more radical approach is necessary.

This approach consists of a thorough reappraisal of the whole field of international history from the point of view of gender. In other words the *presence* or *absence* of one or the other sex, and the power relations on which that may depend, need to be analysed at every level. I have argued elsewhere that the French Republic was not simply constructed without women, as some kind of oversight, but that at various historical moments it was constructed against them.[21] Investigating this proposal can tell us quite a lot about the republic as well as about women. If we are serious about analysing power, we need to ask some of these questions. To quote Joan Scott again: "political history has been enacted on a field of gender".[22] To fail to see that we are on a field at all will lead to failure to appreciate the rules and structures of the game, and to misinterpret the result.

To take an example from Paris again, during the talks, Lloyd George took his advisers off to Fontainebleau and had them engage in role-playing: each player had to pretend to be a different country. At one point, the British chief of staff, General Henry Wilson,

> spoke as a French woman, for, as he insisted, *the unenfranchised French women were the real source of French public opinion*. The losses of so many of their husbands, sons and men folk, the unbearable anxiety and long separations, the financial losses and the desperate struggle and overwork to keep their homes going, the wanton destruction and frequent prolonged occupation by German, British or French troops were his themes. These all contributed to an overwhelming insistence on retribution and full reparation by the enemy above everything else, the punishment of the guilty and absolute guarantees that Germany should pay the bill and make up all losses, and that the terms of peace should ensure *the complete disarmament of Germany* and that a war of this kind should never happen again. In his delivery, pathos and humour were skilfully blended [emphasis added].[23]

In this extract we can see at work both a human recognition, at some level, that women were in the world and part of the nation, and an assumption that all women would inevitably think alike – not to mention the unwarranted conclusion that all French women would *automatically* favour a stern line on reparations. Some women, admittedly a minority, whose views we do have from the time, happened to think the opposite. This kind of thing is what constitutes the "field of gender".

To take one very accessible attempt to map that field, the political scientist Cynthia Enloe has analysed the fabric of contemporary international relations from the point of view of gender in her book *Bananas, Beaches and Bases*.[24] Taking the commercial, military, and diplomatic aspects of international relations, she looks at the gendered structures of, for example, military bases (with their support systems made up of cleaners, clerical staff, etc. and the intermarriage between soldiers and local civilians); embassies (with similar support systems, and with the particular reliance placed on diplomats' wives); and international trade (the construction of markets, the gendered division of labour, depending on cultural factors). She argues that these structures are not random, natural, or neutral, but rather represent the construction of power. They take for granted a certain number of things about the appropriate roles of men and women, which thus have an impact on the whole.

These assumptions can take many forms. There is indeed a symbolic order at work in international relations. Take three examples of its often unperceived effect on our thinking. First, a dissertation could be written about the use of metaphors of marriage and sexuality in international exchange – terms such as courtship, alliance, divorce, etc. Second, war throughout much of history has been presented as the mobilisation of young male forces (whether that is literally so or not) to defend a civilian population assumed to consist of adult women, plus children and the elderly of both sexes: we now know that that is not a timeless reality. And, third, married women's nationality has been constructed as that of their husbands in international law: for many years they had no right to separate passports. (The Joint Council of Women's Organisations protested at this in 1932 without success.) In general, higher value in international relations has been placed on manhood than on womanhood. These are all elements of international exchange that form part of the "taken for granted" in history. But they are not by any means stable and fixed in some sort of monolithic patriarchal order. They have been changed or modified over time, and indeed women have sometimes negotiated positions of authority for themselves within the available structures, whether as the powerful wives of ambassadors or as wealthy tourists creating a certain kind of international market, airline customers, and so on. Even the linguistic and symbolic agenda changes over time: the political correctness furore, whatever else it is, is a sign that symbolic and linguistic structures are a site of conflict and change, and can be historicised like anything else.

III

The kinds of questions raised by this approach cannot be answered just by a trip to the archives. They require a rethinking of the narratives of history and of the symbolic systems by which we represent gender, and a salutary re-examination of our own assumptions. When I went to a conference of international historians at the London School of Economics in 1993, I was struck by the shared culture of many of the historians who spoke, or were quoted there.[25] It is not that this is a "naturally masculine" culture – to say that would be essentialism. But it is a culture shaped by and around men who have often followed a certain *cursus* through a sequence of often all-male institutions, historically and until recently entirely inhospitable to women – public schools; Oxbridge colleges; even, for long enough, university history departments. On the whole, one suspected, there had always been someone else around to do the washing-up. The ideas about men and women held by such historians will have reflected their culture to a certain degree, whatever their private relationships. This proudly shared culture, which produced impressive results, also brought considerable rewards in the shape of regius professorships, outside recognition, and so on. The entry of a few women historians to the culture could not, and cannot, in itself make much difference: on the whole individuals are changed more by the milieu they enter, especially if it carries high status, than the other way around. The point is that the questions asked from inside this cultural context do not exhaust the possible range of questions to ask. The generation of historians – not all of them necessarily women – who cut their teeth during the women's history revolution of the 1970s and after will surely ask different questions of the archives and state papers, just because they come from a different historical, and, to some extent, social culture. Such questions will be asked by a generation of historians who cannot avoid being influenced by the debates of their youth, and who cannot fail to be self-aware, rather than assume a dangerous objectivity.

The chapters in this book, whether on Scotland or on other national

[15]

approaches to women's history, all ask questions that have received relatively little attention hitherto. This could, and I hope will, be a starting point for some fruitful new departures. To speak personally, I found that the 1996 Mackie conference on which this book is based pushed me towards a project in comparative history. And one way to help bring Scottish women's history to broader visibility is to work on genuinely comparative topics which involve looking at Scottish data together with material from elsewhere. All the contributions in this book are, in some sense, re-thinking history. Not necessarily for all time, but certainly for now.

NOTES

1. Lady Aberdeen (1857–1939) was born Ishbel Marjoribanks and married John Gordon, 7th Earl of Aberdeen in 1877. She followed her husband to his high-level postings in Dublin and Canada, and was a hostess in Liberal circles. A keen suffragist, she was for several terms of office president of the International Council of Women. The family home was Haddo House near Aberdeen. There is a biography by a family member, Marjorie Pentland, *A Bonnie Fechter: the life of the Marchioness of Aberdeen* (London, 1952).
2. The Berkshire Conference on the history of women was founded in 1929. It was revived in recent years. It meets at intervals of two – or now three – years at different venues in the USA. The eleventh meeting is at Rochester, NY, in 1999.
3. *History Workshop Journal*, in 1982, changed its subtitle from "a journal of socialist historians" to "a journal of socialist and feminist historians". In 1995, however, it dropped the subtitle altogether.
4. George Duby and Michelle Perrot (eds), *Histoire des Femmes en Occident* (Paris, 5 vols, 1988–92), translated by A. Goldhammer as *A History of Women in the West* (Cambridge, Mass., 1992–95).
5. Arlette Farge, "L'histoire sociale" in François Bédarida (ed.), *L'histoire et le métier d'historien en France 1945–95* (Paris, 1995). The quotation is from pp. 294–295. A conference held in Rouen in 1997 under the title "Une histoire sans les femmes est-elle possible?" ("Is a history without women possible?") sought however to attract mainstream attention, and included papers from some leading historians of both sexes. The proceedings, edited by Anne-Marie Sohn, were published in 1999 (Paris) under the same title.
6. Some examples since 1980 which contain suggestions for further reading are: Rosalind Marshall, *Virgins and Viragos* (London, 1983); The Glasgow Women's Studies Group, *Uncharted Lives: extracts from Scottish women's experience, 1850–1982* (Glasgow, 1983); Esther Breitenbach and Eleanor Gordon's two key collections, *The World is Ill-divided: women's work in Scot-*

land in the 19th and early 20th centuries (Edinburgh, 1990) and *Out of Bounds: women in Scottish society 1800–1945* (Edinburgh, 1992); Eleanor Gordon, *Women and the Labour Movement in Scotland 1850–1914* (Oxford, 1991) and Leah Leneman, *A Guid Cause: the women's suffrage movement in Scotland* (Aberdeen, 1991). Since this chapter was completed, more titles are appearing, notably Elizabeth Ewan and Maureen Meikle, *Women in Scotland c. 1100–c. 1700* (East Linton, forthcoming 1999?).

7. See for example James Vernon, "Who's afraid of the 'linguistic turn'? The politics of social history and its discontents", *Social History*, vol. 19, no. 2 (January 1994), pp. 81–97, which discusses the debate, and refers to the articles by Lawrence Stone, Patrick Joyce and Catriona Kelly in *Past and Present*, nos 131, 133 and 135. Cf. note 10 below.

8. Keith Thomas, review of Joyce Appleby, Lynn Hunt and Margaret Jacob, *Telling the Truth about History* (New York, 1994), in *The Guardian*, 9 September 1994.

9. E. H. Carr's *What is History?* was first published in 1961 and has been reissued in several editions since. For a critique of it by one of Britain's leading relativists, Keith Jenkins, see his *On "What is History?"* (London, 1995). Jenkins's *Rethinking History* (London, 1991) is a useful introduction to the current debates, cf. also his *The Postmodern History Reader* (London, 1997), one of a number of books in this area to be published in recent years by Routledge.

10. There has of course been much criticism from historians of what is variously described as "relativism", "post-modernism", and even "post-structuralism" (the label may cover a number of perspectives). See for example Lawrence Stone, "History and postmodernism", *Past and Present*, no. 131 (May 1991), pp. 217ff.; for a certain perspective from within women's history, see Joan Hoff, "Gender as a post-modern category of paralysis", *Women's History Review*, vol. 3, no. 2 (June 1994), pp. 149–168. This last article – which I am not alone in finding somewhat intemperate – is largely directed at Joan Scott, cf. note 12 below.

11. A. J. P. Taylor, *English History 1914–1945* (Oxford, 1965), p. 1.

12. On Jenkins see note 9 above. Joan Scott is the leading advocate of what might perhaps be called post-modern scepticism in the field of gender studies. Her position has been set out in a number of articles too numerous to cite here, and in her book *Gender and the Politics of History* (New York, 1988) which has fuelled a long-running debate.

13. Gordon and Breitenbach, *Out of Bounds*, p. 2.

14. On "the well-connected woman" in the French context, see chapter 7 ("The permeability of public life: mainstream and alternative politics") in S. Reynolds, *France between the Wars, gender and politics* (London, 1996).

15. Pat Jalland, *Women, Marriage and Politics 1860–1914* (Oxford, 1988).

16. For details of the conduct of the Paris conference leading to the Treaty of

Versailles, see the first hand accounts by Lord Hankey (formerly Sir Maurice Hankey), *The Supreme Control at the Paris Peace Conference of 1919* (London, 1964); and Harold Nicolson, *Peacemaking* (London, 1934).

17. The literature on women's suffrage associations, in Britain and elsewhere is of course enormous. For Britain, see for example Leneman, *A Guid Cause*, bibliography. The literature on the international women's organisations is very scattered, but see for example Leila Rupp, "Constructing internationalism: the case of trans-national women's organisations 1888–1945", *American Historical Review*, vol. 99, no. 5 (Sept. 1994) pp. 1571–1600, which contains many references.

18. See Rupp, article cited above note 15; Jo Vellacott, "A place for pacifism and trans-nationalism in feminist theory: the early work of the Women's International League for Peace and Freedom", *Women's History Review*, vol. 2, no. 1 (March 1993), pp. 23–56; Carol Miller, "'Geneva – the key to equality': inter-war feminists and the League of Nations", *Women's History Review*, vol. 3, no. 2 (June 1994), pp. 219–246.

19. Vellacott, "A place for pacifism", p. 31.

20. On WILPF and its meetings of 1915 and 1919, see Anne Wiltsher, *Most Dangerous Women: feminist peace campaigners of the Great War* (London, 1985); Jill Liddington, *The Long Road to Greenham, feminism and antimilitarism in Britain since 1820* (London, 1985); Norman Ingram, *The Politics of Dissent: pacifism in France 1919–1935* (Oxford, 1991); cf. James Smyth, "Rent, peace votes: working-class women and political activity in the First World War", in Breitenbach and Gordon, *Out of Bounds*, pp. 174–196.

21. "Marianne's citizens? Women, universal suffrage and the republic in France", in S. Reynolds (ed.), *Women, State and Revolution: gender and politics in Europe since 1789* (Brighton, 1986).

22. Scott, *Gender and the Politics of History*, p. 49.

23. Hankey, *The Supreme Control*, p. 101.

24. Cynthia Enloe, *Bananas, Beaches and Bases: making feminist sense of international politics* (London, 1989).

25. "Historians and Officials: the development of international history in Britain and the world", conference held in honour of Donald Cameron Watt, London School of Economics and Political Science, 28–30 June 1993.

2

A realm of one's own? The place of medieval and early modern women in Scottish history

Elizabeth Ewan

When in 1990 the Scottish Medievalists' Conference canvassed for historians to address their chosen theme, "Medieval Women", it became clear that there were not too many candidates. The four who did agree to speak were an archivist from the Scottish Record Office, a medieval literature specialist from Liverpool, an Aberdeen graduate student, and an historian from Canada. In Scotland there were no academics in post as historians who were working in the field.

Three years later, a conference at the University of Strathclyde addressing the question "Whither Scottish History" surveyed the state of historical research on every period from the Middle Ages to the present. Each historian referred to women's history, mostly to comment on the lack of work available.[2] But for the period before 1800, the *implications* of considering women and gender were not addressed. This chapter argues that this cannot have been because there was no work on medieval and early modern women's history in Scotland – more than is commonly realised has been done – but that this work has yet to make an impact on mainstream Scottish historical writing. It will look at a selection of what is available,[3] consider the present state of the field, and suggest what contributions attention to women's history can make to the practice of Scottish history more generally.

Women's history in Scotland began, as elsewhere,[4] with nineteenth-century studies of "women worthies", usually noblewomen or queens. In Scotland, St Margaret and Mary Queen of Scots, who both affected the political or religious life of their day, were prominent examples. There were those commemorated for other reasons, such as Lady Sarah Bruce distinguished by living "to be one of the oldest women of quality in the three kingdoms".[5]

Most early works were collective biographies. J. Anderson's *Ladies of the Covenant* (1850) showed "the active part taken by our countrywomen in succouring and encouraging God's people."[6] Biographies of Border women and women songwriters appeared.[7] The most popular subjects were heroines. R. S. Fittis' *Heroines of Scotland* (1889) was followed eight years later by J. M. Dryerre's *Heroes and Heroines of the Scottish Covenanters*. Fittis' preface rang with pride:

> The annals of every nation record the deeds of heroic women....
> Our authentic records bear the names of many Scotswomen who distinguished themselves by a fearless and self-sacrificing sense of duty.

One wonders what type of heroism he hoped to inspire in choosing a selection of heroines "memorable for their patriotism, their romantic destinies, their misfortunes, or their sufferings".[8]

Contemporary discussions about women raised questions about traditional Scottish society.[9] Henry Grey Graham, in *The Social Life of Scotland in the Eighteenth Century*, published in London in 1899, wrote that "it is in the inner life of a community that its real history is to be found – in the homes, and habits, and labours of the peasantry; in the modes, and manners, and thoughts of society; what the people believed and what they practised...."[10] He included many references to women. Unfortunately, few followed his lead.[11]

The "women worthies" tradition continued, inspired by the women's suffrage campaign,[12] which sought examples of women who had held power and used it wisely. Not everyone felt Mary Queen of Scots was a good role model, nor were Robert Ford's *The Heroines of Burns* (1906) exactly what many women had in mind. More suitable models included

St Margaret and Flora MacDonald.[13]

The preface to Harry Graham's *A Group of Scottish Women* (1908) commented on contemporary attitudes. Never

> has the position of women claimed so large a share of the public thought ... Whether the hand that rocks the cradle is competent to rule the world is one of the controversial questions of the moment.[14]

Perhaps mindful of sales, he avoided providing an answer, but showed how women had inspired genius and noble actions. He reported he had written his book to correct a serious omission in the historical education of the public. A group of Edinburgh ladies had raised money for a statue of a famous and typical Scotswoman for one of the niches of the Scottish Portrait Gallery, but found they could not decide on any woman worthy of the honour. Graham's book apparently fulfilled its educational aim. The following year, a great pageant was held in Edinburgh showing famous women from Scotland's past, both historical and legendary. [15]

The 1910s and 1920s saw biographies of contemporaries, active in the cause of women's rights.[16] Royal and aristocratic women continued to be popular subjects.[17] That women were capable of "men's work" was shown by John Fairley's *Agnes Campbell, Lady Roseburn, Relict of Andrew Anderson: a contribution to the history of printing in Scotland*, published in Aberdeen in 1925; but it is significant that in the title of the book Campbell was identified with her husband, not as historically important in her own right.

In the 1930s historians began to examine the lives of ordinary people,[18] and some looked at women. Eunice Murray – whose historical work grew out of her experiences as an active member of the suffrage movement and from her family background[19] – dedicated *Scottish Women in Bygone Days* (1930) "To the women of all ages who defied convention and held aloft the banner of progress."[20] Breaking with the traditional approach, she discussed social and domestic life, funeral practices, witchcraft, education, and sports and pastimes. Later she turned to the older model, producing biographies in *A Gallery of Scottish Women* (1935). Another collective biography, *Great Scotswomen* (1933), was written by Margaret Keary.

In many countries the 1940s saw the development of social history, challenging more traditional political and constitutional history. In Scotland, Ireland, and Wales, where the emphasis was on political history and national identity, this development was delayed[21] and the few works on women were mostly about heroines.[22] But again Murray was an exception. Her *Scottish Homespun*, published in 1947, was dedicated to "my fellow members of the Scottish Women's Rural Institutes who are the Guardians of the Future and the Custodians of the Past". Murray stressed the role women play in safeguarding the nation's history:

> Women have a two-fold calling, for not only are we as wives and mothers the guardians of the future, but we are also the custodians of the past.[23]

She urged the establishment of folk museums to preserve the past of everyday people. A few writers followed Murray's lead. Marion Lochhead's *The Scots Household in the Eighteenth Century* came in 1948, focused mainly on aristocratic life, but on domestic, not political, affairs. And women occasionally appeared in labour histories, such as Robin Page Arnot's *A History of the Scottish Miners* (1955).

The publication, in 1969, of T. C. Smout's *A History of the Scottish People 1560–1830* brought new life to Scottish social history. A groundwork was laid for the history of women by Michael Flinn's *Scottish Population History from the 17th century to the 1930s* (1977), which provided data on population growth, fertility, marriage, and other demographic factors affecting women's lives. Yet few historians in the 1970s focused specifically on women. One who did was Rosalind Marshall, whose *Days of Duchess Anne* (1973) was the first of her several publications on women. Working at the Scottish Portrait Gallery, she produced two exhibition catalogues, one on childhood and one on women.[24] Although the nature of portraits meant that their focus was on upper-class families, these books reinforced the point that women, in Scotland as elsewhere, did have a history worth studying.

Elspeth King's *The Scottish Women's Suffrage Movement*, published in Glasgow in 1978, pointed the way to a history that would include women's experience by placing the suffrage struggle in the long-term context of women's history in Scotland. Hampered by the lack of research into women's lives before 1800, she came to some controversial conclusions about the impact of the Reformation, but her attempt to provide a background for women's militancy showed the need for medieval and early modern historians to start looking at women's lives in order to understand the present.

With the publication, in 1981, of Christina Larner's *Enemies of God: the witch-hunt in Scotland* – posing complex questions about women's position in the past – and, two years later, of Rosalind Marshall's survey *Vir-*

gins and Viragos: a history of Scottish women from 1080 to 1980, women's history began to be recognised as a field of serious historical study. Since the early 1990s and the publication of the essay collections The World is Ill-Divided and Out of Bounds,[25] a critical mass of people interested in women's history has developed. The Scottish Network for Women's History has drawn scholars together. Articles have appeared in journals such as the Scottish Historical Review and the Innes Review; and, in larger numbers, in newer publications such as Scottish Affairs, Scotlands, and Études Écossaises. Several articles have pointed out how slow the development of women's history in Scotland has been and have themselves acted as an incentive to quicken the pace.[26] A major exhibition of the work of Scottish women artists during Glasgow's year as "European City of Culture", in 1990, also broadened public awareness of women's role in Scottish cultural history.[27]

Most recent historiographical articles have focused on the modern period, surveyed in this volume by Jane McDermid. But what has been done on medieval and early modern women in the past two decades? The study of individual women has continued,[28] with greater efforts to understand them within the context of their own times. Knox may have sounded his trumpet against the monstrous regiment of female rulers but this has not discouraged recent historians: recent work indeed has suggested intriguing new approaches for the study of queens.[29] Indeed the female allies of Knox are being examined, with some historians even undertaking the challenging task of revising Knox's reputation as a misogynist.[30] The active role of Covenanting and post-Reformation Catholic women has attracted new attention.[31] Women's medieval religious life is still poorly studied, although archaeologists have examined some nunneries. The discovery of separate women's cemeteries raises issues about religious beliefs.[32]

One contentious question is the impact of the Reformation on ordinary people. Recent work has questioned the view that the Reformation was beneficial for women.[33] Historians of Scottish women have seen its impact as largely negative, despite a lack of knowledge of women's conditions before 1560. This is one area where much more research is needed. The Reformation has been a dividing wall for too long. Judith Bennett has questioned whether there was much change at all in European women's position between medieval and early modern times.[34]

An important issue for early modern women was the witch-hunt. Larner suggested that before the Reformation women were rarely prosecuted in the courts, but that after 1560, especially with the introduction of laws on witchcraft and infanticide, women became "criminalised", legally responsible for their own criminal actions.[35] This argument has been accepted by several historians, although Deborah Symonds' recent study of infanticide suggest that perceptions of women's criminal nature changed over time.[36] More generally, we do not yet know enough to argue conclusively that such a "criminalisation" occurred. Although women's formal legal status was inferior to that of men,[37] in practice women both before and after 1560 were able to overcome many of their legal disabilities; some indeed were positively litigious.[38] More work is needed on crime and women's criminality.[39]

There are recent studies which shed light on early modern women's socio-economic status, but less has been done on the medieval period. Several essays in *Scottish Society 1500–1800* (1989) discuss women and one gives an overview of the state of knowledge.[40] The Whytes' study of women's geographical mobility dispelled illusions of an immobile female population.[41] Much recent knowledge, indeed, has come from demographic studies.[42] In Edinburgh, Helen Dingwall has shown the high proportion of female-headed households and the wide variety of women's occupations, while Elizabeth Sanderson has studied women's work in the eighteenth century.[43]

Comparative studies have suggested that Lowland women's lives were similar to those of other women in north-western Europe. Many spent a period as domestic servants. Wages were about half those of men, their work had less status and was fitted around domestic duties, and they were unlikely to be formally trained.[44] However:

> notions of what constituted women's work were not fixed, but varied over time and place. The factors which determined women's employment pattern were a complex mix of economic, social and ideological factors.[45]

Economic evidence has been provided by Alex Gibson and Christopher Smout in *Prices, Food and Wages in Scotland 1550–1780*, and by Elizabeth Gemmill and Nicholas Mayhew in their *Changing Values in Medieval Scotland* (1995)[46] – both books published by Cambridge University Press. Gibson and Smout suggest we cannot truly understand the history of changes in standards of living unless we examine the total family economy – looking at men's wages alone will not explain the patterns. They argue that the rise in living standards in many areas in the late eighteenth century was entirely due to household income provided by the labour of women and children. As they point out, there "is much more work to be done on the interface of women's history and economic history".[47] An excellent example is provided by Christopher Whatley's article on the role of women in Scottish industrialisation.[48]

Demographers have begun to provide a picture of household structures, marriage age, and other basics of family life.[49] Types of marriage have been a major focus.[50] Recent work on Lowland families suggests marriages occurred relatively late. Scots may have adjusted to changed economic circumstances by accepting a reduced standard of living rather than adjusting marriage age as seemed to be English practice.[51] The implications for women's lives need to be explored. Scotland is both familiar and unique.

Gibson and Smout have suggested a typical pattern for early modern working-class people of relative ease in adolescence and young adulthood, poverty when establishing a new household, hardship when children were born, some easing as children found work, and then an old age, or widowhood, of deep poverty if they survived. Was this true for other periods as well? They also discuss the nature of child labour. In the seventeenth century young girls earned roughly the same money as did young boys.[52] What did this mean for the formation of gender identity and self-worth?

One aspect which has engaged attention outside Scotland is the attempt to control sexual behaviour. Peter Laslett called Scotland "the classic country for illegitimacy";[53] but an important finding of recent work is the amount of regional variation.[54] Attempts by the authorities to impose social discipline have been examined.[55] Michael Graham has suggested that the apparent obsession with sexual crimes may reflect as much the courts' lack of ability to enforce conformity in other matters as the excessively prurient interest in sexual matters with which they are often charged.[56]

Gender is a social construct: how masculine and feminine roles and behaviours are defined changes over time. And this is beginning to be explored. Most work is by literary scholars, examining attitudes towards women in the mainly male writings of the period.[57] A few sources provide contact with the female voice. The works of Gaelic poets and the waulking songs of Highland women give insight into female views of life.[58] In Lowland Scotland, claims have been made for ballads as a woman's tradition.[59] Such sources offer insights into popular culture, a culture which may have become more particular to women as men's literacy grew.[60]

The gendered nature of language in which church, state, and morality

[25]

were discussed is being studied. Enlightenment thinkers debated "the feminine character" and argued that "women were able to soften the harsh emotions of men". However, while great moral influence was ascribed to them, "their very susceptibility to feeling defined women as perpetual adolescents".[61] By the nineteenth century a powerful ideology of separate spheres, the private world for women, the public world for men, was common. However, reality did not match ideology.[62] "Separate spheres" applied even less to pre-industrial women; public and private life were not sharply demarcated, and historians need to remember this.

It is important to study how gender divisions are constructed. Education could play a role in preserving male dominance, with different schooling for boys and girls.[63] Labour divisions are also important. In early modern Europe, guilds increasingly excluded women from membership; professionalisation of certain occupations had a similar effect.[64]

Perceptions of gender can have far-reaching consequences. Larner argued that witch hunting "is the hunting of women who do not fulfil the male view of how women ought to conduct themselves".[65] What was that view? Early modern ordinances suggest that the authorities believed women should be in a household, under the rule of the male head. It appears the only things authorities feared more than masterless men were masterless women.[66]

There are many gaps still to be filled. One extremely important area, the experiences of women in the Highlands before 1750, is very under-researched. A recent discussion of early modern Scottish clans had almost nothing to say about women except as objects as exchange (and not the most valuable ones).[67] Because much recent work has been concerned with the basic task of finding historical women, questions of gender relations and the impact that gender can have on politics, society, etc. are only just beginning to be discussed.[68]

Despite these many gaps, this chapter has already shown that much more historical work has been done on women in Scotland than is commonly realised. Why, then, has women's history taken so long to develop? And why has it not yet had much impact on mainstream Scottish history?

Several factors have contributed. One is the particular development of Scottish history. In the late nineteenth century, as Scots became increasingly involved in the empire, their own history seemed less important, and English/empire history became dominant.[69] With imperial decline, English history faced new challenges. Increasingly, the emphasis on political and constitutional history was questioned, and social and economic history and other fields began to develop. Elsewhere, in the 1970s, social history, combined with the women's movement, led to the development of women's history. Within Britain, however, there was another challenge. Increasingly, Scotland, Ireland, and Wales perceived a need to research their own histories, and the 1960s and 1970s saw the rise of these histories as academic subjects.[70] But national history emphasised political history,[71] questions of nationality, and Scottish identity, and women's experience was not seen as central to these.[72] Moreover, in Scottish historiography, there has also been an unusually strong preoccupation with religious conflict and schism, areas in which the woman's role has traditionally – though perhaps erroneously – been seen as secondary.[73]

Popular ideas about Scottish history tend to be masculine in character. Military prowess is glorified in such popular heroes as William Wallace, Robert Bruce, and Rob Roy. Scotland's pride in its traditional heavy industry emphasises male muscular strength, while the radicalism of Red Clydeside is identified mainly with the skilled male workforce.[74] Popular Scottish history has few strong female figures, resulting in a stereotyped view of women as either victims or nurturers, as passive and not active historical actors, and therefore unworthy of attention.[75] Recent work suggests that women were by no means passive.[76] Moreover, the form of subordination is worth investigation.[77] However, the stereotype has created constraints which need to be overcome. "If you don't expect women to do anything much, then you are likely to miss the impact of what they do accomplish."[78] And you are unlikely to look for them.

The Scottish historical profession is small. With many specialised fields, there is a lack of personnel in any one. Outside Scotland, Scottish historians are usually marginalised within history departments. This makes it difficult to achieve the active interchange of ideas with others in the same field that has so helped the development of women's history elsewhere. The development of technology such as the internet can help break down some of these barriers.

Related to this is a lack of women's historians within the academy. Much recent work has been done by those outside the historical establishment. This is partly the result of economic factors – as interest in women's history began to develop, job opportunities declined. Without teachers interested in the topic, it is hard to encourage students to pursue it, and so the pattern can continue.

Finally, there are problems associated with publicising work. Scottish publishers are now publishing books on women's history. However, getting the results of recent work to an audience outside Scotland has proved more difficult. Scottish historians know the problem; publishers outside Scotland usually regard books on Scottish topics as of local interest only. As one historian has put it, Scottish women's historians often face a double closure – first as Scottish and second as women. [79]

One positive result is the comparative approach adopted by researchers to show the significance of their work to the field. Scottish historians often find themselves in conference sessions with women's historians from elsewhere because they are the only Scottish historian there: this facilitates fruitful interchange of ideas. The field can also take advantage of its relatively late development. Although still largely at the "excavation" stage, recovering women's stories, it can use conceptual advances from countries where women's history is more developed. This can help it make its own contribution to debates within women's history. [80]

How does women's history fit into Scottish history? A continuing debate is whether Scottish historians should focus on Scotland's uniqueness or on similarities to other societies. Should we be writing Scottish history or British/European history? How much should Scottish history be influenced by questions from elsewhere?[81] Scottish women's history can contribute to this debate. It is not "in a realm of its own". There are several ways in which it interacts with other fields.

Scholars researching Scottish women come from historical geography, archaeology, demography, literature. The value of the inter-disciplinary approach has been well demonstrated. There is much co-operation between those within and outside academia. Co-operation between researchers within and outwith Scotland is strong. Exposure to other histories helps broaden the conceptualisations within which historians work. Essay collections comparing Scotland with elsewhere, and the Mackie conferences themselves, show the value of this.

Scottish women's history shows how historians of different periods can collaborate. One difficulty many historians face is mastering the volume of literature for their own period, not to mention others. This is not yet such a problem in Scotland. One division is between medieval and early modern, but historians of women before and after 1800 can also learn from each other. The questions posed by modern historians can inform the work of historians of the earlier period and vice-versa. History is about both continuity and change; the opportunity to develop a picture of the *longue durée* should be taken. The field of Scottish women's history is small enough at present for researchers to keep up with work in most periods.

Women's history contributes to "British history". Whatley's discussion of industrialisation places women firmly within a British context, comparing them with those elsewhere in the British Isles. The lives of pre-industrial Lowland women appear similar to those of women in northern England. Some have suggested British history should be seen in regional rather than national terms.[82] Women's lives can help bridge the national gap. Many Scotswomen married into English families.[83] Did this strengthen "British" identity?

Women's history is an essential part of Scottish history. Its findings need to be integrated into the historical picture: one challenge is how consideration of the role of gender might change perceptions, even the framework, of the Scottish past. Historians need to

> establish the presence of women in history and in society, produce new narratives and reconstruct our history, and generate identities of historical women that will reflect the complexity and variety of women's experience.[84]

By incorporating women and gender into Scottish history, researchers will create a new history, one including the whole population, women and men, so that no-one will exist in "a realm of one's own". The fact that the advent of Scotland's first parliament for almost three hundred years has been accompanied by a discussion about how gender equality might be achieved amongst the MSPs (members of the Scottish parliament) indicates the advances women have made in becoming part of Scottish political consciousness. If contemporary politics continues to influence historical writing in Scotland, perhaps this advance will be reflected in Scottish historical consciousness as well.

NOTES

(1). I would like to thank the Social Sciences and Humanities Research Council of Canada for help with the funding of the research for this chapter. My thanks also for the valuable comments on the ideas presented here made both by the participants in the Mackie conference at the University of Aberdeen, from which this book derives, and by the members of the Scottish History seminar at Edinburgh University.

2. *Scottish Historical Review*, vol. 73 (spring 1994).

3. The following discussion is by no means comprehensive. A bibliography may be consulted at website http://www.uoguelph.ca/~ewan. Joan Thirsk has recently examined the question of whether male and female English historians have tended to address different historical topics: see her "The

history women", in M. O'Dowd and S. Wichert (eds), *Chattel, Servant or Citizen: women's status in church, state and society* (Belfast, 1995), pp. 1–11. This is an approach which might also be worth exploring in a Scottish context.

4. Gerda Lerner, "Placing women in history: definitions and challenges", in *The Majority Finds its Past* (New York, 1979).

5. John Ramsay, *Scotland and Scotsmen in the Eighteenth Century* (ed. Alexander Allardyce), (Edinburgh, 1888) vol. 2, pp. 146–151; James Rennie, *Mary Queen of Scots* (Glasgow, 1826); Elizabeth O. Benger, *Memoirs of Elizabeth Stuart, Queen of Bohemia* (London, 1825); Turgot's twelfth-century life of St Margaret was published in 1884.

6. James Anderson, *Ladies of the Covenant* (1850), in *The Scots Worthies their Lives and Testimonies ... Also a Supplement Containing Memoirs and Historical Sketches of Ladies of the Covenant* (London, 1879).

7. Walter Ridell Carré, *Border Memories, or, Sketches of prominent men and women of the border* (Edinburgh, 1876); Sarah Tytler and S. L. Watson, *The Songstresses of Scotland* (London, 1871).

8. Fittis, *Heroines*, pp. 1, 3, 5.

9. Robert Chambers, *Domestic Annals of Scotland* (Edinburgh, 1858–74); Charles Rogers, *Scotland Social and Domestic* (London, 1869).

10. Graham, *Social Life*, p. vi.

11. James Murray, *Life in Scotland a Hundred Years Ago* (Paisley, 1900); R. Menzies Fergusson, *Scottish Social Sketches of the Seventeenth Century* (Stirling, 1907).

12. Elspeth King, *The Scottish Women's Suffrage Movement* (Glasgow, 1978); Leah Leneman, *"A Guid Cause": the woman's suffrage movement in Scotland* (Aberdeen, 1991).

13. Samuel Cowan, *Life of the Princess Margaret, Queen of Scotland 1070–1093* (Newcastle, 1911); John Maclean, *Flora Macdonald in America, With a brief Sketch of her Life and Adventures* (Lumberton, NC, 1909).

14. Graham, *Scottish Women*, p. vii.

15. King, *Scottish Women's Suffrage*, p. 3.

16. Lady Frances Balfour, *Dr Elsie Inglis* (London, 1918); David Murray, *Janet Ann Galloway and the Higher Education of Women* (Glasgow, 1914).

17. Louis Barbé, *Margaret of Scotland and the Dauphin Louis: a historical study based mainly on original documents* (London, 1917); Katherine Parker, *My Ladie Dundie: being a very true accompt of her life, death & burial & of the finding of her body so perfect one hundred years later* (Paisley, 1926). For other prominent women, see also Louis Barbé, *Sidelights on the History, Industries and Social Life of Scotland* (London, 1919) which devotes three chapters to this subject.

18. I. Donnachie and C. Whatley (eds), *The Manufacture of Scottish History* (Edinburgh, 1992), pp. 4–5.

19. Her father, David Murray, was an historian (see note 16 above) and an

advocate of women's education, while her mother was a writer. See King, *Scottish Women's Suffrage*, pp. 20, 27; and Eunice Murray, *Frances Murray: a memoir by her daughter* (Glasgow, 1920).

20. Murray, *Scottish Women*, dedication.
21. See discussion below, pp. 26–27
22. A. M. D. Henderson-Howat, *Royal Pearl: the life and times of Margaret Queen of Scotland* (London, 1948); David McRoberts, *St Margaret Queen of Scotland* (Glasgow, 1957).
23. Murray, *Scottish Homespun*, preface, p. 105.
24. R. Marshall, *Childhood in Seventeenth-century Scotland* (Edinburgh, 1976); R. Marshall, *Women in Scotland 1660–1780* (Edinburgh, 1979).
25. Eleanor Gordon and Esther Breitenbach (eds), *The World is Ill-divided* (Edinburgh, 1990); Breitenbach and Gordon (eds), *Out of Bounds* (Edinburgh, 1992).
26. Joy Hendry, "Snug in the asylum of taciturnity: women's history in Scotland", in Donnachie and Whatley, *Manufacture of Scottish History*; Jane McDermid, "Placing women in Scottish history", *Journal of Women's History*, vol. 4/2 (fall 1992); A. Brown, "Gender and national identity: introduction", *Scottish Affairs*, no. 18 (winter 1997); Siân Reynolds' chapter above.
27. Jude Burkhauser (ed.), *The Glasgow Girls* (Edinburgh, 1990).
28. Rosalind Marshall, *Mary of Guise* (London, 1977); Victoria Chandler, "Ada de Warenne, Queen Mother of Scotland (c. 1123–1178)" *Scottish Historical Review*, vol. 60 (1981); Fiona Downie's chapter in this volume; Maggie Craig, *Damn Rebel Bitches: women of the '45* (Edinburgh, 1997); Rosalind Marshall, *The Winter Queen: Elizabeth of Bohemia* (Edinburgh, 1998); and see several essays in E. Ewan and M. Meikle (eds), *Women in Scotland c. 1100–c. 1750* (East Linton, 1999).
29. See Fiona Downie's chapter below; Louise O. Fradenburg, "Troubled times: Margaret Tudor and the historians" in S. Mapstone and J. Wood (eds), *The Rose and the Thistle* (East Linton, 1998), and Fradenburg's *City, Marriage, Tournament: arts of rule in late medieval Scotland* (Madison, 1991); Alan Wilson, *St Margaret Queen of Scotland* (Edinburgh, 1993); P. Buchanan, *Margaret Tudor Queen of Scots* (Edinburgh, 1985); and Jenny Wormald, *Mary Queen of Scots: a study in failure* (London, 1988).
30. R. M. Healey, "Waiting for Deborah: John Knox and four ruling queens", *The Sixteenth-century Journal*, vol. 25 (1994); Susan Felch, "The rhetoric of biblical authority: John Knox and the question of women" *The Sixteenth-century Journal*, vol. 26 (1995).
31. Alasdair Roberts, "The role of women in Scottish Catholic survival", *Scottish Historical Review*, vol. 70 (1991); David Mullan, "Mistress Rutherford's narrative: a Scottish puritan autobiography", *Bunyan Studies*, 7 (1997).
32. J. O'Sullivan, "Excavation of an early church and a woman's cemetery at St Ronan's medieval parish church, Iona", *Proceedings of the Society of Anti-*

quaries of Scotland, vol. 124 (1994); Alison Reid and Dorothy Lye, "Elcho Nunnery", in *Pitmiddle Village and Elcho Nunnery* (Perth, 1988). And see Roberta Gilchrist, *Gender and Material Culture: the archaeology of medieval women* (London, 1994).

33.   Lyndal Roper, *The Holy Household: women and morals in Reformation Augsburg* (Oxford, 1989); Merry Wiesner, *Women and Gender in Early Modern Europe* (Cambridge, 1993), pp. 179–213.

34.   Judith Bennett, "Medieval women, modern women: across the great divide" in David Aers (ed.), *Culture and History 1350–1600* (Detroit, 1992). For an example of the negative view of Scotland in this respect, see Elspeth King, *The Thenew Factor: the hidden history of Glasgow's women* (Edinburgh, 1993).

35.   Larner, *Enemies*, p. 51.

36.   Deborah Symonds, *Weep Not For Me: women, ballads and infanticide in early modern Scotland* (University Park, Penn., 1997). For Larner's view, see Rosalind Mitchison and Leah Leneman, *Sexuality and Social Control: Scotland 1660–1780* (Oxford, 1989); and R. A. Houston, "Women in the economy and society of Scotland 1500–1800", in R. A. Houston and I. D. Whyte (eds), *Scottish Society 1500–1800* (Cambridge, 1989).

37.   A. D. M. Forte, "Some aspects of the law of marriage in Scotland: 1500–1700", in E. Craik (ed.), *Marriage and Property* (Aberdeen, 1984); Houston, "Women in the economy and society of Scotland".

38.   Janet Kennedy, James IV's mistress, frequently appeared in court to safeguard her lands. Ishbel Barnes, "Janet Kennedy", paper delivered to Conference of Scottish Medievalists, Pitlochry, January 1991. See also Elizabeth Ewan, "Scottish Portias: women in the courts in mediaeval towns", *Journal of the Canadian Historical Association*, n.s., vol. 3 (1992); John Finlay, "Women and legal representation in early sixteenth-century Scotland", in Ewan and Meikle, *Women in Scotland*.

39.   Keith Brown, "The laird, his daughter, her husband and the minister: unravelling a popular ballad", in Roger Mason and Norman MacDougall (eds), *People and Power in Scotland* (Edinburgh, 1992). And see the essays in J. Kermode and G. Walker (eds), *Women, Crime and the Courts in Early Modern England* (Chapel Hill, 1994). Anne-Marie Kilday has completed a PhD thesis on "Violent Women in South-west Scotland, 1750–1815" (Strathclyde University, 1998).

40.   Houston, "Women in the economy". And see the discussion by Joy Hendry, "Snug in the asylum", pp. 138–139.

41.   Ian and Kathleen Whyte, "The geographical mobility of women in early modern Scotland", in Leah Leneman (ed.), *Perspectives in Scottish Social History* (Aberdeen, 1988).

42.   R. A. Houston, *The Population History of Britain and Ireland 1550–1750* (Cambridge, 1992); Robert Tyson, "Household size and structure in a Scottish burgh: Old Aberdeen", *Local Population Studies*, vol. 40 (1988); Lesley

Diack's chapter in this volume.

43. Helen Dingwall, *Late Seventeenth-century Edinburgh: a demographic study* (Aldershot, 1994); Elizabeth Sanderson, *Women and Work in Eighteenth-Century Edinburgh* (London, 1996).

44. Tyson, "Social structure", pp. 42–43; Elizabeth Ewan, "Mons Meg and merchant Meg: women in late-medieval Edinburgh" in Terry Brotherstone and David Ditchburn (eds) *Freedom and Authority; essays on Scottish history c. 1050–c. 1650 presented to Dr Grant G. Simpson* (East Linton, 1999).

45. Eleanor Gordon, "Women's spheres" in W. Hamish Fraser and R. J. Morris (eds), *People and Society in Scotland*, vol. 2, *1830–1914* (Edinburgh, 1990) p. 209.

46. Both books present large amounts of economic data.

47. Gibson, *Prices*, p. 356.

48. Christopher Whatley, "Women and the economic transformation of Scotland c. 1740–1830" *Scottish Economic and Social History*, vol. 14 (1994).

49. Tyson, "Household size"; Dingwall, *Edinburgh*, chapter 2; R. A. Houston, "Age at marriage of Scottish women, c. 1660–1770", *Local Population Studies*, vol. 43 (1990).

50. T. C. Smout, "Scottish marriage, regular and irregular, 1500–1940", in R. B. Outhwaite (ed.), *Marriage and Society: Studies in the Social History of Marriage* (New York, 1981); Mitchison and Leneman, *Sexuality and Social Control*. Mitchison and Leneman's book is to be republished in a revised and expanded form as *Girls in Trouble: sexuality and social control in rural Scotland 1660–1780*, and *Sin in the City: sexuality and social control in urban Scotland 1660–1780* by Scottish Cultural Press. For divorce, see Leah Leneman, *Alienated Affections: the Scottish experience of divorce and separation, 1684–1830* (Edinburgh, 1998).

51. Houston, *Population History*, pp. 75–76.

52. Gibson, *Prices*, pp. 347–349, 290.

53. Peter Laslett et al. (eds), *Bastardy and Its Comparative History* (London, 1980), p. 41.

54. Leah Leneman and Rosalind Mitchison, "Girls in trouble: the social and geographical setting of illegitimacy in early modern Scotland", *Journal of Social History*, vol. 21 (1988).

55. G. Parker, "The 'kirk by law established' and the origins of 'the taming of Scotland': St Andrews 1559–1600", in Leneman, *Perspectives in Scottish Social History*; Leah Leneman and Rosalind Mitchison, "Acquiescence in and defiance of church discipline in early modern Scotland", *Scottish Church History Society Records*, vol. 25 (1993); G. DesBrisay, "'Menacing their persons and exacting on their purses': the Aberdeen Justice Court, 1657–1700" in David Stevenson (ed.), *From Lairds to Louns: country and burgh life in Aberdeen 1600–1800* (Aberdeen, 1986).

56. Michael Graham, *The Uses of Reform: "Godly discipline" and popular behaviour in Scotland and beyond, 1560–1610* (Leiden, 1996).

57. Evelyn Newlyn, "Of 'vertew nobillest' and 'serpent wrinkis': taxonomy of the female in the Bannatyne Manuscript", *Scotia*, vol. 14 (1990); Priscilla Bawcutt, "Images of women in the poetry of Dunbar", *Études Écossaises*, vol. 1 (1992); Anne McKim, "'Makand hir mone': masculine constructions of the feminine voice in Middle Scots complaints", *Scotlands*, vol. 2 (1994).

58. Catharine Kerrigan (ed.), *An Anthology of Scottish Women Poets* (Edinburgh, 1991); *The Gaelic Songs of Mary Macleod* (Scottish Text Society, 1935); A. Frater, "Scottish Gaelic Women's Poetry up to 1750" (PhD thesis, University of Glasgow, 1994).

59. Catherine Kerrigan, "Reclaiming history: the ballad as a women's tradition" *Études Écossaises*, vol. 1 (1992). Symonds, *Weep Not For Me* makes major use of ballad evidence. See too D. Gifford and D. MacMillan (eds), *A History of Scottish Women's Writing* (Edinburgh, 1997).

60. R. A. Houston, *Scottish Literacy and the Scottish Identity* (Cambridge, 1985), pp. 57–70. David Mullan is editing a spiritual autobiography of a seventeenth-century woman.

61. John Dwyer, *Virtuous Discourse* (Edinburgh, 1987), pp. 118, 137; and, for an earlier period, David Mullan, "Women in Scottish divinity c. 1590–c. 1640", in Ewan and Meikle, *Women in Scotland*.

62. See essays in the Breitenbach and Gordon collections, *Out of Bounds* and *The World is Ill-divided*.

63. Houston, *Scottish Literacy*, p. 239.

64. Dingwall, *Edinburgh*, p. 204. However, see Sanderson, *Working Women*, pp. 74–76.

65. Larner, *Enemies*, p. 100.

66. Michael Lynch, "The social and economic structure of the larger towns, 1450–1600", in Lynch et al. (eds), *The Scottish Medieval Town* (Edinburgh, 1988), pp. 277–278.

67. R. A. Dodgshon, "'In pretense of blood' and 'place of thair duelling': the nature of Scottish clans 1500–1745", in Houston and Whyte, *Scottish Society*, p. 190. For new research, see Anne Frater, "Women of the *Gaidhealtachd* and their songs to 1750", and Domhnall Uilleam Sti/bhart, "Women and gender in the early modern *Gaidhealtachd*", both in Ewan and Meikle, *Women in Scotland*.

68. See Elizabeth Ewan, "Women's history in Scotland: towards an agenda", *Innes Review*, vol. 46 (1995), for suggestions on areas of inquiry.

69. David Cannadine, "British history as a 'new subject': politics, perspectives and prospects", in Alexander Grant and Keith Stringer (eds), *Uniting the Kingdom?* (London, 1995), pp. 13–16. For the decline in Scottish history, see Marinell Ash, *The Strange Death of Scottish History* (Edinburgh, 1980).

70. Cannadine, "British history", pp. 20–21.

71. For the lack of social history until the 1980s, see R. A. Houston and I. D. Whyte, "Introduction: Scottish society in perspective", in their *Scottish Society*, pp. 1–2.
72. Jayne Stephenson, "Scottish women's studies", a review article in *Women's History Review*, vol. 2 (1993), p. 149; Esther Breitenbach, "'Curiously rare'? Scottish women of interest or the suppression of the female in the construction of national identity", *Scottish Affairs*, no. 18 (winter 1997), pp. 82–89. For reflections on the complex relationship between nationalism and feminism in Scotland, see Christopher Whyte's, "Introduction" to the volume he edited, *Gendering the Nation: studies in modern Scottish literature* (Edinburgh, 1995).
73. I would like to thank Michael Lynch for his insights on this point.
74. Breitenbach, "Curiously rare", discusses some images.
75. Breitenbach, "Curiously rare", pp. 84–87; Breitenbach and Gordon, *Out of Bounds*, pp. 2–3. One way to counteract this is to promote popular knowledge of historic women: see Ellen Kelly, *Edinburgh Women's Achievement Trail: a guide to the location of the plaques of 24 of Edinburgh's most outstanding women* (Edinburgh, 1995), and Jane Leggett, *Local Heroines: a women's history gazetteer to England, Scotland and Wales* (London, 1988). Popular histories are now beginning to include women: see, for example, Maurice Fleming, *The Real MacBeth and Other Stories From Scottish History* (Edinburgh, 1997). In August 1998 Anne Lorne Gillies and Maggie Craig discussed the actions and poetry of historical women at the Edinburgh Book Festival.
76. Cynthia Neville, "Widows of war: Edward I and the women of Scotland during the War of Independence", in S. Sheridan Walker (ed.), *Wife and Widow in Medieval England* (Ann Arbor, 1993); C. Whatley, "An uninflammable people?", in Donnachie and Whatley, *The Manufacture of Scottish History*; James D. Young, *Women and Popular Struggles* (Edinburgh, 1985).
77. Siân Reynolds, *Britannica's Typesetters* (Edinburgh, 1989), pp. 141–143.
78. Hendry, "Snug in the asylum", pp. 130–131.
79. Sue Innes as quoted in R. J. Morris and Graeme Morton, "Where was nineteenth-century Scotland?", *Scottish Historical Review*, vol. 73 (1994), p. 98. Also Breitenbach, "Curiously rare", pp. 89–90.
80. Wiesner, *Women and Gender in Early Modern Europe*, and Olwen Hufton, *The Prospect Before Her* (London and New York, 1996) include some Scottish examples.
81. Keith Wrightson, "Kindred adjoining kingdoms: an English perspective on the social and economic history of early modern Scotland", in Houston and Whyte, *Scottish Society*, p. 250.
82. Houston, *Scottish Literacy*, pp. 256–266; Alexander Grant, "Scottish foundations: late medieval contributions" in Grant and Stringer, *Uniting the Kingdom?*, pp. 106–107.

83. Patricia Otto, "Daughters of the British Aristocracy: their marriages in the eighteenth and nineteenth centuries with particular reference to the Scottish peerage" (PhD thesis, Stanford University, 1974), p. vii.

84. Breitenbach, "Curiously rare", pp. 92–93.

3

Missing persons? Women in modern Scottish history

Jane McDermid

As late as 1991 Rosalind Mitchison's edited collection *Why Scottish History Matters* failed to consider why it mattered to Scottish *women*, or indeed why women should matter to Scottish history. The proceedings of the Strathclyde University "Whither Scottish History?" conference of 1993 show the speakers lamenting briefly the paucity of women's history in Scotland, yet implying that it was still not central to the debate on the condition of Scottish historical studies.[1] Ironically, at the same time, work published on Scottish women revealed that they have largely been excluded from history precisely by the nature of the discussion about Scottish national identity which has been conceived as a masculine construct.[2]

What survived the Union of 1707 was pride in Scotland's intellectual achievement and martial tradition. Hence Scotland's essentially masculine national character had to be preserved if Scotland was to play a significant, distinctive, and respected part in the union. By the early nineteenth century the main concern was over anglicisation and loss of national identity, reflected in twentieth-century works such as George

Elder Davie's *The Democratic Intellect* (1961) and *The Eclipse of Scottish Culture* (1989) by Craig Beveridge and Ronald Turnbull. In neither was there any consideration of the absence of women from the "democratic" intellectual tradition. Bearing this context in mind – and following on from the previous chapter – I shall focus here on the historiography of women in modern Scotland, concentrating on the nineteenth and twentieth centuries.

Most works on nineteenth-century Scotland recognise the tensions which militated against a unifying national mythology: tensions between being Scottish and British; Highland and Lowland; urban and rural; from the east or from the west; Protestant and Catholic; and, after the 1843 Disruption in the Church of Scotland, Free Church, and Established Church.[3] The focus of Scottish history on key aspects of national identity, such as labour history and educational history, has been one reason for the neglect of women's history; but, since the late 1980s, there has been significant revision which has not simply reinstated women as active participants but has also challenged certain assumptions and concepts.

Siân Reynolds, in her *Britannica's Typesetters: women compositors in Edwardian Edinburgh* (1989), Eleanor Gordon, in her *Women and the Labour Movement in Scotland, 1850–1914* (1991), and the collection *The World is Illdivided* (1990), edited by Gordon and Esther Breitenbach, all question the concept of "skill" as above all a masculine construct, with women at best as semi-skilled – and then only at the expense of the "dilution" of male skills. Reynolds argues convincingly that skilled female compositors were not considered as equal to the men because the former learned on the job while the latter served long apprenticeships which were not open to women.

Nineteenth-century Edinburgh provided few jobs for women apart from domestic service – so the female compositors represented some degree of progress for women workers. Christopher Whatley has argued that women's and children's labour was significant, if not crucial, for Scotland's early economic transformation.[4] Gordon's *Women and the Labour Movement* challenged earlier labour historians who equated lack of formal trade union organisation among women with passivity and highlighted the importance of female labour in a particular region, upsetting broad generalisations by demonstrating the need to consider locality and industry and not just the labour market as a whole. Dundee and its textile industry were dominated by female labour as early as the middle of the nineteenth century, and skilled men tended to leave to find work elsewhere, notably in Glasgow's heavy industry and shipbuilding.

By the last quarter of the nineteenth century, Glasgow witnessed a decline in job opportunities for working-class women, not only in textiles but also in domestic service. *The World is Ill-divided* revealed a gender-segregated work-force, though the contributors also questioned the assumptions that paid employment was necessarily a negative experience for women: certainly, women's work was inferior to men's in terms of status, skills, and pay, but those essays in the book based on oral history show that women took pride and found pleasure in their work.[5] Women also remained important in the farm labour force.[6] Often, working on farms was a family affair, with daughters being taken on through the father, and with female wages always treated as a proportion of the man's. The practice of employing seasonal workers ensured that women's wages especially remained low. Improved education and job opportunities outside farming led to the migration of female farm labourers to the towns in the late nineteenth century.

Scottish political history has been male dominated, but again that has been challenged recently. In *Politics and Society in Scotland* (1996), Alice Brown, David McCrone, and Lindsay Paterson question the relative absence of women from Scottish politics.[7] They conclude that a Scottish parliament should provide more opportunities for female representation, and that hope may be substantiated with the Scottish Office's appointment in 1998 of its first official adviser on women's issues, Esther Breitenbach. Yet we need perhaps to widen our definition of "political" to give a fuller and fairer assessment of the role of women. To concentrate on parliamentary politics alone is to remain within too narrow an orbit.[8] Ironically, even in terms of the movement for female suffrage, Scottish women were largely absent from a mainly English and especially Pankhurst-dominated story until the pioneering work of Elspeth King on the west of Scotland suffrage movement.[9] Leah Leneman's longer study argues that the women's suffrage movement differed in significant respects from the English movement, in the independence of the Scottish Women's Social and Political Union (WSPU) from London, in the left-wing politics of many of the leading Scottish suffragists, and in the successful co-operation of all the suffrage organisations in Scotland.[10] Leneman also convincingly disputes the facile distinction often made which explains the suffrage issue in Scotland in terms of social class but in England in terms of women as a whole.[11]

One of the prominent Scottish suffragists, Dr Elsie Inglis, served at the front during World War I, with little encouragement from the male establishment.[12] Medicine was one of the most difficult of the professions for women to penetrate.[13] Not only were those who managed to do so a minority but female students in higher education were a minority among Scottish women. In the first half of the twentieth century the majority of women would have had a primary (or elementary) education at best.[14] Education was – and is – seen as integral to Scottish distinctiveness but until recently the educational tradition was gender blind. The collection of essays *Girls in Their Prime: Scottish education revisited* (1990) include a mixture of historical and contemporary studies which challenge comfortable stereotypes of the *lad o' pairts* and the dominie. The contributors see the Victorian ideal of domesticity as gendering education in Scotland, just as in England and in Wales, and argue that the tradition of co-education (more accurately, mixed-sex schooling) discriminated against women.[15] Lindy Moore reveals a more complex picture in which parents, and some teachers, resisted the teaching of sewing and domestic economy because of a belief that intellectual discipline was the best means of developing an intelligent, moral, and cultured individual.[16] Ironically it was upper- and middle-class women, including feminists, who criticised the male educational establishment for its opposition to domestic training.[17]

The gender-specific curriculum was class based, directed at working-class girls. Indeed, *Out of Bounds* reveals that the progress made by middle-class women in the late-nineteenth century in terms of educational and professional opportunities was, to a considerable degree, gained at the expense of working-class girls who were exhorted by their social superiors to accept their domestic destiny. Working-class women did not always passively accept institutional ideologies of domesticity and femininity.[18] Nevertheless, such ideas were relentlessly directed at them wherever they were schooled – notably in industrial schools and ragged schools established as reformatories or to provide against the potential of vagrancy. In such punitive institutions, girls were specifically prepared for domestic service. Linda Mahood argues that female delinquents were treated more harshly than boys, because girls were seen as especially vulnerable to the temptations of the street, which could lead them into prostitution. Hence girls were sent to reformatory and industrial schools not only as punishment but also as protection against committing future offences.[19] There were similar interventionist responses to the sexual morality of the working classes in the twentieth century, and some women's organisations were prepared to support local initiatives – for example on controls to prevent the spread of venereal disease. Others, however, were opposed to such measures on the grounds that prostitutes and other female patients of public clinics were targeted, when it was men who constituted the majority of those failing to complete their course of treatment.[20] Why were lower-class girls deemed to be "in moral danger"? Mahood's work focuses on the city, and Glasgow in particular, but in fact illegitimacy in the nineteenth century was higher in rural areas, particularly in south-western and north-eastern Scotland.[21]

The education of working-class girls opened up increasing opportunities for middle-class women, whether as lady child-savers or as domestic-science teachers.[22] By the end of the nineteenth century women were numerically dominant in the schooling of infants and girls. The profession itself, however, remained dominated by men, which kept Scottish women teachers at a disadvantage. Indeed Helen Corr's contrast between what she sees as a feminist presence among English teachers, and the acceptance by their Scottish counterparts of a subordinate place in a male-dominated profession, suggests that the latter were accomplices in the maintenance of the patriarchal tradition.[23] That argument, however, overlooks the relative lack of professional careers open to women in Scotland compared to England and underestimates the ways in which women manoeuvred within a patriarchal system, and did not passively submit.[24]

These last two points are highlighted in *A History of Scottish Women's Writing* (1997), which challenges the "male generated and male fixated" Scottish tradition in literature in general, and Hugh MacDiarmid's dismissal of Scottish women's writing in particular.[25] Many writers in this collection link the inferior status of women in Scottish society to the Reformation and to Calvinism, but Calum Brown and Jayne Stephenson have shown that Presbyterian women also manoeuvred within the patriarchal church to establish an influential, if still subordinate, place for themselves.[26] Lesley Orr Macdonald further argues that there was a feminisation of Presbyterianism in the late nineteenth and early twentieth centuries, which saw women increasingly engaged with social and public issues such as temperance, education, and suffrage.[27] And Graham Walker points out that the male officials of the Orange Order in Scotland recognised that there was a role for women when they agreed to the establishment of the first women's lodges in 1909. By 1934 there were a hundred and ninety-one female lodges with the women soon proving themselves "expert organisers, indefatigable workers for charity, in particular local hospitals", and confirmed conservatives in their politics.[28] The Roman Catholic church in Scotland, another deeply patriarchal institution, also saw women as playing a key role in preserving their minority community and culture within a hostile environment.[29] That

[41]

role was primarily domestic, though crucially it involved teaching, in which the trainees were told that they stood "between the priest and the parent and like them derive authority from Almighty God".[30] This was another case of manipulating patriarchy – while still also being manipulated by it – which forces us to confront our rather patronising assumption of female passivity in Scottish history and to widen our concept of the "political".

The place of women in Scottish history is gradually being asserted and slowly being integrated into mainstream studies, but much research still needs to be done. The hope is that theses on women's history will find publishers.[31] There are also books which appeal to a wider audience than academics, though they are still useful to the latter.[32] For those who want to research the present-day position of women, there are the *Gender Audits*, compiled by the Engender organisation since 1993. As Esther Breitenbach has pointed out, however, the struggle to escape marginalisation is on three fronts: not only within Scottish history and within the debates on nationalism but also within British feminist history.[33] That is a considerable task, but one which, as this chapter and the previous one have tried to show, is being undertaken with energy and determination.[34]

NOTES

1. *Scottish Historical Review*, vol. LXXIII (1), no. 195 (April 1994).
2. See, for example, F. M. S. Paterson and J. Fewell (eds), *Girls in Their Prime: Scottish education revisited* (Edinburgh, 1990); E. Gordon and E. Breitenbach (eds), *The World is Ill-divided: women's work in Scotland in the nineteenth and early twentieth centuries* (Edinburgh, 1990); E. Breitenbach and E. Gordon (eds), *Out of Bounds: women in Scottish society 1800–1945* (Edinburgh, 1992).
3. See, for example, M. Ash, "William Wallace and Robert Bruce: the life and death of a national myth", in R. Samuel and P. Thompson (eds), *The Myths We Live By* (London, 1990); T. C. Smout, "Perspectives on Scottish identity", *Scottish Affairs*, no. 6 (winter 1994), pp. 101–113; J. Foster, "Nationality, social change and class: transformation of national identity in Scotland", in D. McCrone, S. Kendrick, and P. Straw (eds), *The Making of Scotland: nation, culture and social change* (Edinburgh, 1989); Richard S. Finlay, "Heroes, myths and anniversaries in modern Scotland", *Scottish Affairs*, no. 18 (winter 1997), pp. 108–125.
4. Christopher A. Whatley, *The Industrial Revolution in Scotland* (Cambridge, 1997), pp. 72–75; and his "Women and the economic transformation of Scotland, c. 1740–1830", *Scottish Economic and Social History*, vol. 14 (1994), pp.

19–40. See too James H. Treble, "The characteristics of the female unskilled labour market and the formation of the female casual labour market in Glasgow, 1891–1914", *Scottish Economic and Social History*, vol. 6 (1986), pp. 33–46.

5. See, for example, Jayne D. Stephenson and Calum Brown, "The view from the workplace: women's memories of work in Stirling c. 1910–c. 1950", and James. J. Smyth, "'Ye never got a spell to think aboot it': young women and employment in the inter-war period – a case study of a textile village", both in Gordon and Breitenbach, *The World is Ill-divided*.

6. See Barbara W. Robertson, "In bondage: the female farm worker in south-east Scotland", in Gordon and Breitenbach, *The World is Ill-divided*; T. M. Devine (ed.), *Farm Servants and Labour in Lowland Scotland 1770–1914* (Edinburgh, 1984), especially Devine's own chapter on "Women workers 1850–1914"; I. MacDougall (ed.), *"Hard Work Ye Ken": Midlothian women farmworkers* (Edinburgh, 1993); Lynn Jamieson and Claire Toynbee, *Country Bairns: growing up 1900–1930* (Edinburgh, 1992).

7. Alice Brown, David McCrone and Lindsay Paterson, *Politics and Society in Scotland* (Basingstoke and London, 1996). See also Esther Breitenbach, "Out of sight, out of mind?: the history of women in Scottish politics 1900–1914", in Lynn Jamieson and Helen Corr (eds), *State, Private Life and Political Change* (London, 1990).

8. See Esther Breitenbach, "Sisters are doing it for themselves: the women's movement in Scotland", in A. Brown and R. Parry (eds), *The Scottish Government Yearbook* (Edinburgh, 1990).

9. Elspeth King, *The Scottish Women's Suffrage Movement* (Glasgow, 1978).

10. Leah Leneman, *A Guid Cause: the women's suffrage movement in Scotland* (Aberdeen, 1991).

11. This is argued by James D. Young, *Women and Popular Struggles: a history of Scottish and English working-class women 1500–1984* (Edinburgh, 1985).

12. See Leah Leneman, *In the Service of Life: the story of Elsie Inglis and the Scottish women's hospitals* (Edinburgh, 1994); Eileen Croft, *The Women of Royaument: a Scottish women's hospital on the Western Front* (East Linton, 1997).

13. See Wendy Alexander, *First Ladies of Medicine: the origins, education and destination of early women medical graduates of Glasgow University* (Glasgow, 1987); J. Geyerkordesch and R. Ferguson, *Blue Stockings, Black Gowns, White Coats: a brief history of women entering higher education and the medical profession in Scotland in celebration of 100 years of women graduates at the University of Glasgow* (Glasgow, 1995); Sheila Hamilton, "The first generations of university women 1869–1930", in G. Donaldson (ed.), *Four Centuries: Edinburgh University life, 1583–1983* (Edinburgh, 1983); Lindy Moore, "The Scottish universities and women students, 1862–1892", in Jennifer J. Carter and Donald J. Withrington (eds), *Scottish Universities: distinctiveness and diversity* (Edinburgh, 1992); Lindy Moore, *Banjellas and Semolinas: Aberdeen University*

and the education of women, 1860–1920 (Aberdeen, 1991).

14. See Paterson and Fewell, *Girls in Their Prime*; J. McDermid, "Women and Education", in June Purvis (ed.), *Women's History in Britain, 1850–1945* (London, 1995), and her "Working-class girls' education in Glasgow", in *History Teaching review Yearbook of the Scottish Association of Teachers of History*, vol. 8 (1994); Lindy Moore, "Invisible scholars: girls learning Latin and mathematics in the elementary public schools of Scotland before 1872", *History of Education*, vol. 13, no. 2 (June 1984), pp. 121–137.

15. See too Helen Corr, "An exploration into Scottish education", in W. H. Fraser and R. J. Morris (eds), *People and Society in Scotland: vol. 2, 1830–1914* (Edinburgh, 1989).

16. Lindy Moore "Educating for the 'woman's sphere': domestic training versus intellectual discipline", in Breitenbach and Gordon, *Out of Bounds.*

17. See Helen Corr, "'Home Rule' in Scotland: the teaching of housework in Scottish schools 1872–1914", in Paterson and Fewell, *Girls in Their Prime*; Tom Begg, *The Excellent Woman: the origins and history of Queen Margaret College* (Edinburgh, 1994); E. Millar, *Century of Change 1875–1975: one hundred years of training home economics students in Glasgow* (Glasgow, 1975).

18. For the class connotations of the ideology of domesticity, see Eleanor Gordon, "Women's spheres", in Fraser and Morris, *People and Society.*

19. Linda Mahood, *The Magdalenes: prostitution in nineteenth-century Scotland* (London, 1990).

20. Roger Davidson, "'A scourge to be firmly gripped': the campaign for V. D. controls in inter-war Scotland", *Social History of Medicine*, vol. 6, no. 2 (August 1993), pp. 213–235.

21. See Andrew Blaikie, *Illegitimacy, Sex and Society: north-east Scotland, 1750–1900* (Oxford, 1994); T. C. Smout, "Aspects of sexual behaviour in nineteenth-century Scotland", in P. Laslett, K. Oosterveen, and R. M. Smith (eds), *Bastardy and Its Comparative History* (London, 1980).

22. Barbara Littlejohn and Linda Mahood, "Prostitutes, Magdalenes and wayward girls: dangerous sexualities of working-class women in Victorian Scotland", *Gender and History*, vol. 3, no. 2 (summer 1991), pp. 160–175.

23. Helen Corr, "Dominies and domination: schoolteachers, masculinity and women in nineteenth-century Scotland", *History Workshop*, no. 40 (autumn 1995), pp. 151–164, and her "Teachers and gender: debating the myths of equal opportunities in Scottish education 1800–1914", *Cambridge Journal of Education*, vol. 27, no. 3 (November 1997), pp. 355–364.

24. Jane McDermid, "'Intellectual instruction is best left to a man': the feminisation of the Scottish teaching profession in the second half of the nineteenth century", *Women's History Review*, vol. 6, no. 1, pp. 95–114.

25. Douglas Gifford and Dorothy McMillan (eds), *A History of Scottish Women's Writing* (Edinburgh, 1997), p. xix; and see Jenni Calder, "Heroes and hero-makers: women in nineteenth-century Scottish fiction", in Douglas Gifford

(ed.), *The History of Scottish Literature: volume 3 – the nineteenth century* (Aberdeen, 1988).

26. Calum Brown and Jayne Stephenson, "'Sprouting wings'?: women and religion in Scotland, c. 1890–1950", in Breitenbach and Gordon, *Out of Bounds*; and see too references in Calum Brown, *The Social History of religion in Scotland, 1780–1914* (London, 1987).

27. Lesley Orr MacDonald, "Women and presbyterianism in Scotland, c. 1830–1930", PhD thesis, University of Edinburgh, 1995.

28. Graham Walker, "The Orange Order in Scotland between the Wars", *International review of Social History*, vol. xxxvii, part 2 (1992), pp. 177–206, 203–204.

29. Alasdair Roberts, "The role of women in Scottish Catholic survival", *Scottish Historical Review*, vol. 70, no. 190 (1991), pp. 129–150.

30. Bernard Aspinwall, "Catholic teachers for Scotland: the Liverpool connection", *Innes Review*, vol. xiv, no. 1 (spring 1994), pp. 85–108; Jane McDermid, "Scottish Catholic girls' education", *Innes Review*, vol. 47, no. 1 (spring 1996), pp. 69–80.

31. For example, in addition to Lesley Orr Macdonald's thesis (see footnote 27 above), there is David James Lamond's "The Female Experience of Schooling in Scotland, 1872–1945: lassies o' pairts or lassies apart?", PhD thesis, University of Glasgow, 1996.

32. Elspeth King, *The Thenew Factor: the hidden history of Glasgow's women* (Edinburgh, 1992); Sheila Livingstone, *Bonnie Fechters: women in Scotland, 1900–1950* (Motherwell, 1994).

33. Esther Breitenbach, "'Curiously rare'?: Scottish women of interest *or* the suppression of the female in the construction of national identity", *Scottish Affairs*, no. 18 (winter 1997), pp. 82–84; and see also Breitenbach, Alice Brown and Fiona Myers, "Understanding women in Scotland", *Feminist Review*, vol. 58 (spring 1998), pp. 44–66.

34. See *Gender and Scottish Society: politics, policies and participation. Report of a conference held on 31 October 1997 at the Unit for the Study of Government in Scotland, University of Edinburgh* (June 1998) – especially the section "Gendering History", pp. 116–135, with papers by Esther Breitenbach, Helen Corr and Lesley Orr Macdonald.

4

Telling the story of women in medieval Scandinavia

Grethe Jacobsen

In 1524 *Margaret Archbald*, wife of David Gudlawde of St Andrews, and her mother Christine Petbladow, wife of Andro Archbald, left their husbands and travelled – fled, perhaps, since they were both suspected of adultery – to Denmark, where Margaret found another man and apparently lived happily ever after.[1] She was not the only Scotswoman – or Scotsman – who travelled to, and settled in, Denmark at that time. Ties between Denmark and Scotland were many and strong during the fifteenth and sixteenth centuries.[2]

An advantage of discussions such as those at the fifth Mackie conference is that they can increase awareness of the importance not just of connections but also of comparisons between the study of women in both countries. What this chapter offers is a presentation of Scandinavian sources relevant to problems and issues in medieval women's history, which could form the foundation for comparisons to be made by future scholars. The exciting part of doing research in women's history is the revelation of hitherto hidden facets of well-known events and of the fact that events such as the Reformation, or the revolutions of 1848, do not necessarily explain the changes that women of the past experienced, whether for better or worse. Women's history and gender history have been treated on a more theoretical level in the chapter by Siân Reynolds but I must begin by outlining briefly the relationship between women's history and gender history as I see it.

Gender history is distinguished by its recognition of the fact that every known human society has been populated by two sexes, the female and the male. Accompanying this is the awareness that the sexes had different roles. Gender history is the story of how that difference and that awareness shaped the structures of the society in question. How was it, for instance, that some men were able to talk passionately about liberty and equality and brotherhood for all mankind and then turn around and behead the woman who dared to ask that liberty and equality be extended in equal measures to womankind, as happened during the French Revolution.[3] Similarly, the difference between the genders has shaped the manner in which the history of past societies has been told. One example is the Danish medievalist, known to be a very cautious scholar hesitant to say anything definite about any medieval topic unless it was thoroughly documented in the sources, yet he could blithely state, just seventeen years ago, that "assumptions that ... women were always less socially active than men need no historical evidence to be generally accepted".[4]

Gender history is an approach that permeates – or ought to permeate – all other kinds of history, be it that of men, of women, of groups of men, of groups of women, of formal institutions, or of informal institutions. Women's history is the history of women in past societies in which there was a gender hierarchy, an asymmetrical relationship between the sexes that generally favoured the male sex in the distribution of control over resources. These considerations form the background for the following contemplations about sources, issues, and problems in women's history as it unfolded in the Scandinavian countries during the Middle Ages, and as it has been retold by historians past and present.[5]

First, some geographical considerations may be appropriate. By "Scandinavian" I mean the three Scandinavian countries, Denmark, Norway, and Sweden, together with Iceland even though it considers itself not part of Scandinavia but of the north. Being aware, however, that the terms "north" and "northern" may have other meanings in a European, a Scottish, or an English context, I shall stick to the term "Scandinavia" – asking that you keep in mind that it includes Iceland and, indeed, the Swedish parts of Finland as well.

Periodisation is also a bit tricky when one is referring to the Middle Ages as the use of that term in Scandinavia differs a bit from the period it refers to in Europe in general. While Europeans are held to have been living through the early Middle Ages (from AD 500 to 1000) the peoples of Scandinavia were in the Germanic Iron Age (to AD 800) and the Viking Age (AD 800 to 1050). As everyone knows, the important event of 1066 was that the last Viking fell at Stamford Bridge that year. Then Scandinavia joined the the rest of Europe for the high Middle Ages (AD 1050 to 1300) and the late Middle Ages for the period AD 1300 to 1450. Then the waters separate again as Scandinavians extend the Middle Ages to the early sixteenth century. In dealing with periodisation, it is important to note which periods are favoured and which are not, and to be aware of the traditional time-span that may hide significant breaks in women's history – or, conversely, hide continuities. In Scandinavian historiography, the focus has, in general, been on the Viking Age, and on the thirteenth and fourteenth centuries. The break with the early modern period has been made either in 1536 (the Lutheran Reformation) or more generally around 1500. It is also the case that the sixteenth century has, with a few notable exceptions, been left to the theologians or church historians. Only within the past few years has the period 1300–1550 gained the attentions of medieval historians.

In Icelandic historiography, the fall of the Free State in the late thirteenth century signalled the coming of a long series of calamities, which accelerated in 1385 when, along with Norway, Iceland became part of the Danish kingdom, and which ceased only when Danish rule ended in 1944. Focus has been, therefore, on the tenth to the thirteenth centuries, the truly glorious period in Icelandic history, which witnessed the creation of the sagas, Iceland's unique contribution to world literature. Similarly, but not quite as bitterly, Norwegians for years referred to the period of the joint kingdom of Denmark-Norway (1385–1814) as the "four hundred dark years". However neutral, scientific, and rational modern historians have claimed to be, such assumptions and attitudes do influence historical writings, including those dealing with women. If women were written into history at all, it was assumed that dark periods in men's history naturally had to be dark periods in women's history too.

One of the early battle cries of the new feminist wave in women's history, which began about the mid-1960s, was that the dark ages for men were the bright ages for women. The early Middle Ages were seen as great for women, and then it went downhill, reaching a low point at the Reformation.[6] Taking a longer view, the Middle Ages were seen overall as very positive for women – and then things got worse, reaching the nadir at the time of the French Revolution and Napoleon. I myself adhered to this line for a long time, and have still not completely let go of it. Working on women in medieval Danish towns between 1400 and 1600, I was, however, unable to find a straight decline in women's opportunities; I had – reluctantly – to concur with the view voiced by one of the most important and inspiring American medievalists, Judith Bennett. She concluded her analysis of thirteenth-century English village women with the statement that

> neither capitalism nor state formation was a necessary cause of women's second-rank status in English society. The subordination of women in Brigstock was rooted in neither government nor economy, but rather in the household. [7]

Bennett represents a branch of feminist history which argues that no basic changes occur in the relationship between the sexes. European women's history for the past two thousand years is seen not as the history of revolutions but as that of changes in the visible upper parts of the social structures – the purpose of which is to adapt to the underlying and hidden structures of society in order to uphold a gender hierarchy, placing males in a more favourable position than females. Or, as it has been formulated recently by one of Judith Bennet's students: "upholding the patriarchal equilibrium".[8] This was reflected already in 1981 in the theme of the Fifth Berkshire Conference, which focused on women and the structure of society. The five following Berkshire conferences have gone on to find new routes through women's history by focusing on different strategies – trying to look beyond the private-public dichotomy, and looking at women, gender, power, and transformations. The conference held in June 1996 had the title "Complicating categories: women, gender and difference". Complicated and complicating is exactly what women's history has become. In that respect, it is no different from men's history.

I

Returning to the writing of medieval Scandinavian women's history, I must note at the outset that this process has not moved swiftly forward along grand theoretical lines. On the contrary, until recently, theory has been absent. When medieval women's history began seriously in Scandinavia in the early 1980s, we all dug into our sources in order to unearth evidence about the past of women. We found a great deal – not necessarily what we expected, nor as much as we had hoped for – but nevertheless so many histories which had been forgotten or ignored. This so angered, pleased, and frustrated us that we just kept digging and digging. Then we began getting together to compare notes. Since 1981 a small group of scholars from all five Nordic countries have met regularly, but it was not until 1990 (in Norway) and 1993 (in Denmark) that we consciously attempted to reflect on our progress, and to take stock of where we are going, and how. In 1990 the topic of the meeting was the source material for medieval Scandinavian history, and, in 1993, the contributors were asked – under the general heading of "Women and the church" to present papers which included theoretical and methodological reflections. The papers from this symposium have been published, as have the papers from previous meetings.[9] And, although the resultant volumes are slim, they are important witnesses to the research which has been done on Scandinavian women's medieval history and thus form a good foundation for a discussion of the problems and issues writing this history.

The topics covered show a certain fluidity. During the symposia of the 1980s – where a general topic was chosen to guide the content of the subjects discussed – there was always room for a paper that went in a different direction. That was due less to our open minds than to the lack of scholars interested in the chosen topic, but we made a virtue out of necessity, and this has provided us with some unexpected insights. The first symposium, in Göteborg in 1979, had as a programme title, "Women's economic position". The papers covered a wide range of topics as well as sources, predominantly laws and account books – the latter from the fifteenth and sixteenth centuries.[10] This in turn inspired the topic of the programme for the third symposium in 1983, which was "Women's work"[11] – although, when you compare the published volumes, it can be seen that some articles in the one might as well have been published in the other.

One obvious area of study was traditional women's work. Some articles, including one which was published separately,[12] pointed to evidence that textile work, primarily the weaving of coarse cloth in Iceland and Norway, was specifically female work. Missing from the sources, however, is evidence of the many types of female work found in central and southern Europe – such as embroidery, lace-making, gold-spinning, and other fancy textilework. The National Museums of Iceland and Denmark contain examples of Icelandic embroidery, particularly altarcloths with images of saints and holy men and women, but not on a large scale: most of them were produced by bishops' wives and daughters.[13] The crafts found in the Scandinavian countries relate to leatherwork (shoemakers, cordwainers, saddlers, furriers, skinners, etc.); smithing (blacksmith, pewterers, sword makers); and wood (coopers, turners, carpenters). All are crafts that women could engage in, but which had become traditionally male occupations.[14] But this only means that we have to take a gendered look at work in general.

Further topics covered have been women's health – including childbirth and the practice of the exposure of infants – to which the fourth and fifth symposia in 1985 and 1987 were devoted (this choice had not a little to do with what we could get funding for);[15] and "Changes in the conditions of women during the Middle Ages" – the subject of the second symposium.[16] It was significant that the changes dealt with were those associated with the transition from pagan to Christian society, rather than with the Reformation. So there remain important changes and transitions to be dealt with, and we have still much to discuss concerning the question of evolution versus revolution. On the other hand there are themes which recur at almost every symposium, whatever the topic of discussion, notably that of literature. We have had papers on literature *about* women, including the lives of saints; on literature, especially scaldic poety, that may have been written *by* women; and on the transition from an oral to a written culture.

II

One of the major problems we have continually dealt with is that of the source material. As is the case for Scotland, sources for the Scandinavian Middle Ages are very unevenly distributed, geographically and chronologically. They favour the late Middle Ages and certain categories of documents, such as those relating to the law, and especially to property. One must also be aware of what is accessible and in what way. It has been possible, because of their relative scarcity, to produce printed scholarly editions of practically all the sources dealing with Scandinavian society before 1500. However, the organisation of such materials, and the availability of tools such as indices, are heavily influenced by political history. This reflects the inclination and training of the editors. Indices of personal names, place names, and dates are easily found, but subject indexes are rare. Nor are there attempts to identify any but the most prominent women, such as queens.

A second problem we have considered is the use of the sources, the prime example being the presentation of the Viking woman in the Sagas. The *Laxdoela Saga* recounts an episode in the life of Egil Skallagrimson, a mighty warrior and feared chieftain of the tenth century. Egil wanted to marry his daughter to a promising young man, Olaf Pá, son of another great chieftain, and of an Irish princess who had been captured and held as slave. Because of Olaf's mother's status as a slave woman in Icelandic society, Egil's daughter Thorgerd, initially refused the marriage proposal. Egil could, according to the law, force his daughter to marry whomever he chose but he did not do this. Instead, he asked his daughter to talk to the young man and not to reject him out of hand. Thorgerd agreed, met with Olaf, and the couple talked all day. Then Thorgerd told her father that it was his decision whom she was to to marry. Egil then accepted Olaf's proposal and the marriage turned out to be a happy and prosperous one.[17]

The *Saga of Njál*[18] tells the story of another happy marriage, that of Njál and Bergthora. Njál and his family were drawn into one of the many feuds of Icelandic society, and the farm where Njál, his wife, their sons, and their families lived was attacked. Before setting fire to the farm the attackers offered safe conduct to the women and children inside the house. But Bergthora refused to leave saying, "I was young given to Njál and I have solemnly promised him that we would share the same fate." They went into their chamber, lay down in their marriage bed and perished together.

The picture presented is most appealing: in the heathen past men and women respected each other, and marriages, if agreed to by both partners, would be happy. There are also contrary examples in the sagas – of women forced to marry against their will – and such marriages invariably ended in disaster. This rosy picture of women, and marriage, is an important ingredient in the notion, which first appeared in the late-eighteenth century, that the pagan Viking period was a golden age for women and that the advent of Christianity brought an end to this happy state, not least because it was the "wrong" Christianity which came to Scandinavia in the tenth and eleventh centuries – namely that of the Roman Church. To Protestant and atheist historians of the following two hundred years, it may be surmised, the Catholic church could not possibly have heralded anything positive; although, of course, these historians – claiming to be objective and rational, and therefore scientific historians – never expressed such views openly.

In the mid-1970s, I began looking more carefully at the sources for this picture, and concluded that while it might be true for Iceland, and partly true for Norway, it certainly was not true for southern Scandinavia, Denmark in particular. My own research on the Viking women centred on the question of whether the changes Christianity brought were for the better or for the worse, and I concluded that the former had been the case. The advent of Christianity was a benefit to women.[19] I did, however, see Iceland as the remaining shining light in an an otherwise dim pagan past, owing to the fact that Iceland was a pioneer society. Alas, this hypothesis was shot to pieces by the Danish-American scholar, Jenny Jochens, who began publishing her work on women in Old Norse society at the same time. She argued that the image we find in the sagas reflected, not an earlier golden period but rather propaganda by the clergy of the twelfth and thirteenth centuries. The leading clergymen were eager to impose Christian norms of marriage upon a society in which having multiple sexual partners and engaging in temporary relationship, was the norm; in which marriage was determined by political and economic considerations, not personal feelings; and in which celibacy was regarded an abnormal condition. The authors of the sagas promulgated marriage as a bond, tied after mutual consent by a man and a woman, which had sacramental rather than political and economic meanings, and which was to last until death and even beyond.[20] Analysing the sagas, lives of the saints, laws, letters, wills, and charters, Jochens searched for, but found no trace of, the traditional Icelandic heroine. Instead she found a society in which some women had great power and others had little. It was also a society with a gender hierarchy very similar to that found elsewhere, in that it favoured the male sex.[21]

The free Viking woman, then, is as much a myth as the horn-helmeted Viking blowing on his lure. This image of the male belongs to the Bronze Age, and that of the free Viking woman to the realm of fiction. But this fact by no means diminishes the importance of the age of the Vikings, and of the advent of Christianity, to women. Rather, it makes clear that transitions from pagan to Christian society, and from chiefdoms to kingdom, meant different things to different men and women, and that the impact upon women's lives and history depended upon the individual woman's social, economic, and civil status. What we are discussing now is not whether the advent of Christianity, or the advent of the larger kingdoms, were good or bad for women, but rather in what ways the changes affected women's lives and history.

One offspring of this discussion has been research, by a Swedish historian, Birgit Sawyer, on tenth-century runic inscriptions. This evidence should, according to her major thesis, mirror a clash between a rising

[53]

monarchy, supported by the church, and local chieftains. Consequently, one of the dominant motives for the erection of rune stones was to establish the legal claims of those erecting them to the inheritance of the deceased commemorated in the inscription. The property and authority of a deceased chieftain would normally go to his sons or brothers, but, if they were not alive, women could assume ownership and power – alone or with other male relatives. This explains the appearance of women on only one quarter or less of the runic stones. It is not an indication that women were unable to inherit, nor that they could not act independently, only that women were not the first in line to assume political power after a chieftain's death.[22] What Sawyer's work also demonstrates is that by looking for women in a familiar source – but with a gendered view – the historian has been forced to reconsider the role of the runic stones in their contemporary social context, and therefore to return to political history from which women had previously been been excluded, and which had been avoided by feminist historians dealing with the Middle Ages in Scandinavia.

III

The discussion of women in the high Middle Ages has centered on the great work of the Danish historian, Saxo Grammaticus who wrote his *Gesta Danorum* ("Deeds of the Danes") during the second half of the twelfth century. It has of necessity been a discussion on the "image of woma/en" and on "images and reality". Again it began as a one-sided question: was Saxo positive or negative toward women? But this discussion has developped into an analysis of how gender roles, and a gender hierarchy, are reflected in Saxo's writings and in those of his contemporaries. In 1990, one of the prominent participants in this debate, the Danish historian Nanna Damsholt, asked us to step inside the head of the medieval male historian. Arguing that most medieval authors we know are male, she presented a picture of their world, and of the ways it shaped their perceptions and hence their writings about women as well as about men.[23]

One of her students, Niels Henrik Holmqvist-Larsen, had earlier illustrated this albeit not so directly in his book dealing with the treatment of women in selected chapters of Saxo's history. Saxo recounts the story of Frode, a legendary king who supposedly ruled in Denmark at the time of Christ, making him a contemporary of Emperor Augustus. Frode created a peaceful society in which he could hang golden bracelets on trees along common roads and they would not be stolen. Frode also gave women the right to freely choose their spouse. As Holmqvist-Larsen, one of the few male historians engaged in women's history, points out, this reveals the two faces of Saxo: one is that of the educated cleric, knowing that the Church favoured mutual consent in marriage, the other is that of a male member of the ruling élite of contemporary Danish society, who knew what would be best for that society. The moral of Saxo's story was really this: that in an ideal state, such as Frode lived in, we could hang gold bracelets on trees, and give women the right to freely choose their spouse but in our sinful, contemporary society neither can be recommended.[24] Thus the discussion of Saxo and of twelfth-century Danish Latin literature has demonstrated both that the Church cannot be seen simply as good or bad news for women, and, more important, that it was not a fixed entity in medieval society, but had many local expressions which affected women's lives differently.

Another source for women's history of the high Middle Ages has been the law, primarily the provincial law codes compiled during the twelfth and thirteenth centuries. The earliest laws are those of Norway and Iceland from the twelth century – the Danish and Swedish laws date from the thirteenth. Court records are very few for the period before 1500; and wills, deeds, and charters date mostly from the late Middle Ages.[25] With a few exceptions, the legal sources have been used as a supplement to other sources, a supplement from which evidence of real life can be extracted. Legal sources, in my view, could be better utilised. I have recently focused on borough customs in Denmark to analyse not only what the laws say, but also what they do not say. Whom do they regulate? Who is not regulated – and hence not defined?[26] Knowing that women were active outside the home in Danish urban society, I expected to find women defined as something other than as daughters, wives, and widows, but I did not. Women were represented not as economically active agents, only as family members. I had hoped to uncover laws allowing women to engage in trade or preventing them from doing so. Instead, I found silence. But there was also the outline of a space that existed between the private and the public sphere. This space was governed not by written law but by informal norms shaped by written law. Women were not outside the law when they ventured out of the home. They moved in a space that was encircled by the law, and in which women were able to engage in economic activities – outside the family, yet not formally inside the public sphere. This enabled women to be active, to earn a living, and to support their families. But, because their sphere was a judicial void – that is, governed by the absence of written rules – women did not gain legal status and authority by acting on their own. They were not conceptualised as anything other than as daughters, wives, and widows.

IV

My research has also focused on the late Middle Ages and the Reformation period, that is 1400 to 1600 – with the specific aim of understanding a period that has so often seemed disconnected from what went before and came afterwards. My purpose has not been to find the supposed abrupt break with the Reformation but rather to examine changes which had the effect of adjusting to a new political and religious situation in ways which upheld the patriarchal equilibrium. Many of these changes were for the worse for many women, but some benefited.[27] In working on the late Middle Ages, I have been rather alone. Research on women in Denmark is almost totally lacking for the whole period 1400–1850. Women historians have worked either on the medieval period or on the modern period. With regard to the latter, the tendency has been to begin with the labour movement and then to venture into women's history. In contrast the women's history of seventeenth- and eighteenth-century Norway and Sweden is currently being extricated from the archives, and some papers at one of our early symposia did deal with aspects of the fifteenth and sixteenth centuries.

One field that has expanded considerably in recent decades has been medieval archaeology. This discipline has immensely increased our knowledge of the material conditions of women's and men's lives. Unfortunately, a gendered analysis is absent from the many reports and stories written on the basis of the excavations – with one exception. This is the study of humans remains, in which one regular participant in our symposia, Berit Sellevold, has worked and has shared her discoveries of what the skeletal remains told her. First, they told her that restrictions in access to resources, including food, can produce very tangible evidence. Looking at skeletons from the Iron Age through to the Middle Ages, she compared the height of men with that of women, and charted the differences over time. Having found that this difference varied – though with a constant pattern of men being taller than women – she argues that the variations are caused by the amount of food allocated to each sex. In short, in some periods women were allowed to eat as well as men, in other periods the men keep the major part to themselves. This pattern fits in with the evidence of the grave goods left in the pagan period. Taller women also commanded better grave goods.[28]

Second, Sellevold has looked at the general health picture of women during the Iron Age and the Middle Ages, as well as evidence of health problems specifically connected to pregnancy and childbirth.[29] Most recently she has looked at burial customs in and around the churches in Scandinavia, concluding that while law codes and regulations demanded that women be buried in the north side of the church and men on the south side, in fact social and economic status also played an important role in determining where a person was buried.[30]

What has been left out from our work so far? One thing immediately comes to the mind: biographies of the two great women of the later Middle Ages, Queen Margrete, who died in 1412, and St Bridgid of Sweden, who died in 1375. Margrete succeeded where many men have failed before and since, namely in uniting the three Northern kingdoms into one, and ruling them. She ruled Denmark and Norway for several years as a guardian for her young son who died when he was only seventeen. Then she ruled the three kingdoms for her grandnephew for fifteen years. This was a traditional role for women, but Margrete was also a ruler in her own right during a ten-year period between the death of her son in 1387 and the proclamation of her grandnephew as king in 1397 – when she reigned as "husband, mighty mistress, and guardian of the entire kingdom of Denmark", combining the male and the female role for a decade.

A paper given at our first symposium in 1979 did in fact deal with Margrete.[31] One of the learned professors took on her "role as woman" – with the purpose of extricating the queen from the fangs of women's history by asserting some unquestioned assumptions about female traits, and then postulating that Margrete had none of these, but was indeed "one of the guys". It would give too much credence to this article to suggest that it has kept us from writing about Margrete. Much more relevant is that, when we began in earnest to analyse women's history, the time had passed for the "women worthies" approach, and "compensatory history" ("women certainly also contributed to history") had proved itself a dead end. What mattered was women in general, in all spheres of society, in their own separate space and in the joint spheres. Now, however, the time has come for us to take a good – gendered – look at the women worthies of our medieval past. A solid account of Margrete and her times did, in fact, appear some years ago,[32] and in 1997, on the occasion of the six-hundredth anniversary of the Calmar Union, a major exhibition, travelling to four of the Nordic countries with an accompanying catalogue, had Margrete as the central character. [33]

That other famous woman – not just in medieval Scandinavia but in Europe more generally – St Bridgid of Sweden, founder of the Brigettine Order, belonged to the considerable number of female mystics and reformers prominent in late-medieval society. In her case, however, we do have a feminist analysis of her significance, by another regular member of our circle, the Swedish historian, Beata Losman. [34]

In closing, I want briefly to consider the impact of this new knowledge on recent writing about medieval Scandinavian societies and to say a word about the future course of our work. Has our work been utilised by those who claim to write general history? As far as Denmark is concerned, there has been little sign of this amongst established historians, that is those at the universities. A recent major popular multi-volume history of Denmark, which devoted no less than four volumes to the Middle Ages, used the standard cookbook approach: follow your usual recipe, add women, and stir! In this case the addition was limited to a sprinkle. It is symptomatic that one of the leading periodicals, the (Dansk) *Historisk tidsskrift* ("Danish Historical Review") has yet to publish one article dealing with women's history. Sweden and Norway both have a chair in women's history, and in these countries our research has been more visible. This is particularly true in Norway, where the official organ, the (Norsk) *Historisk tidsskrift* ("Norwegian Historical Review"), has devoted several issues specifically to women and frequently carries articles on women. This has meant that recent surveys have indeed included women – though again rather as a separate dish without which the meal is incomplete. It was also on a Norwegian initiative that a three-volume global history of women was published some years ago as a joint Danish-Norwegian venture[35] – to much acclaim and attention in Norway and to almost total silence in Denmark.

Finally: where do we go from here? First, we have to get into the universities and into publication. This is very difficult at the moment in Denmark; the openings are few and far between. It is to be hoped that a generational change during the coming decade – when the great majority of the academic staff currently in post will retire – will open the way for women's history at the universities. Things look better in Norway and Sweden, where there are female professors; and many students writing dissertations on topics in women's history. Second, we have to continue to develop even more sophisticated tools of analysis and methods to aid young scholars in writing both women's history and gender history. And third, we must never forget that there are very many good stories yet to be told to our sisters, our daughters, and our grand-daughters – as well as to their brothers. And that we have the duty to tell them.

NOTES

1. In 1560 David was granted a divorce from Margaret. Their story is found in David Hay Fleming (ed.), *Register of the Minister Elders and Deacons of the Christian congregation of St Andrews*, part first: 1559–1582, publications of the Scottish History Society, vol. IV, no. 1 (Edinburgh, 1889), pp. 44–50.
2. See Thomas Riis, *Should Auld Acquaintance Be Forgot ...: Scottish-Danish relations c. 1450–1707*, vols I-II (Odense, 1988).
3. Darline Gay Levy and Harriet Branson Applewhite, "Women and political revolution in Paris", in Renate Bridenthal, Claudia Koonz and Susan Stuard (eds), *Becoming Visible: women in European history*, vol. 2 (Boston, 1987), pp. 279–306; and their "A political revolution for women?: the case of Paris", in the third edition of the same work, edited by Bridenthal, Stuard and Merry E. Weisner (Boston, 1998), pp. 264–292.
4. Kai Hørby, "The social history of medieval Denmark", in Niels Skyum-Nielsen and Niels Lund (eds), *Danish Medieval History: new currents* (Copenhagen, 1981), p. 50.
5. In the following, references will be made primarily to literature relevant for women's history. For an English-language reference work, see Phillip Pulsiano (ed.) and Kirsten Wolf (co-ed.), *Medieval Scandinavia: an encyclopedia* (New York and London, 1993).
6. Jane Schulenburg, "Clio's European daughters: myopic modes of perception", in Julia A. Sherman and Evelyn Torton Beck (eds), *The Prism of Sex: essays in the sociology of knowledge* (Madison, Wisconsin, 1979), pp. 33–53.
7. Judith M. Bennett, *Women in the Medieval English Countryside: Gender and Household in Brigstock before the Plague*, (New York: Oxford University Press 1987), p. 198.
8. Cited by Judith Bennett at the 1996 Berkshire Conference.
9. See Appendix. All volumes have English-language résumés of the articles.
10. *Kvinnans ekonomiska ställning* (see Appendix).
11. *Kvinnearbeid i Norden* (see Appendix).
12. Nanna Damsholt, "The role of Icelandic women in the sagas and in the production of homespun cloth", *Scandinavian Journal of History*, vol. 9, no. 2 (1984), pp. 75–90.
13. Elsa E. Gudjónsson, "Islandske broderier og broderersker i middelalderen", in *Förändringar i kvinnors villkor* (see Appendix), pp. 127–158; English version in her *Traditional Icelandic Embroidery* (Reykjavík, 1985), pp. 55–57.
14. Grethe Jacobsen, entries under "crafts" and "guilds" in Pulsiano, *Medieval Scandinavia*, pp. 113–115, 248–249.

15. The papers are collected in one volume under the title *Kvinnors rosengård* (see Appendix).
16. *Förändringar i kvinnors villkor under medeltiden* (see Appendix).
17. For editions and translations of the saga see Sverrir Tómasson, "Laxdoela saga", in Pulsiano, *Medieval Scandinavia*, pp. 387–388.
18. For editions and translations of the saga, see Vésteinn Ólason, "Njál's saga", in Pulsiano, *Medieval Scandinavia*, pp. 432–434.
19. Grethe Jacobsen, "Ændrede kvinders stilling sig ved overgangen til kristendom i Norden? En komparativ analyse", in *Förändringar i kvinnors villkor under medeltiden* (see Appendix), pp. 26–40.
20. Jenny M. Jochens, "The Church and sexuality in medieval Iceland", *Journal of Medieval History*, vol. 6 (1980), pp. 377–392; and see her *Women in Old Norse Society* (Ithaca, 1995).
21. Jenny M. Jochens, "Consent in marriage: Old Norse law, life, and literature", *Scandinavian Studies*, vol. 58 (1986), pp. 142–176; and her "The medieval Icelandic heroine: fact or fiction?", *Viator: Medieval and Renaissance Studies*, vol. 17 (1986), pp. 35–50.
22. Birgit Sawyer, *Kvinnor och familj i det forn – och medeltida Skandinavien* (Skara, 1992); and her "Det vikingatida runstensresandet i Skandinavien" *Scandia*, vol. 55, no. 2 (1989), pp. 185–202.
23. Nanna Damsholt, "Hvorfor skrev den middelalderlige historieskriver som han gjorde?", in *Fokus på kvinner i middelalderkilder* (see Appendix), pp. 32–42.
24. N. H. Holmqvist-Larsen, *Møer, skjoldmøer og krigere: en studie i og omkring 7. bog af Saxo's "Gesta Danorum"*, Studier fra Sprog – og Oldtidsforskning, no. 304 (Copenhagen, 1983).
25. Thelma Jexlev, "Wills, deeds, and charters as sources for the history of medieval women", in Birte Carlé, Nanna Damsholt, Karen Glente and Eva Trein Nielsen (eds), *Aspects of Female Existence: proceedings from the St Gertrud symposium "Women in the Middle Ages"*, Copenhagen, September 1978 (Copenhagen, 1980), pp. 28–40.
26. Grethe Jacobsen, *Kvinder, køn og købstadslovgivning 1400–1600: lovfaste Mænd og ærlige Kvinder, mit deutscher Zusammenfassung*, Danish Humanist Texts and Studies, vol. 11 (Copenhagen: Det kongelige Bibliotek, 1995).
27. Grethe Jacobsen, "Nordic women and the Reformation", in Sherrin Marshall (ed.), *Women in Reformation and Counter-Reformation Europe: public and private worlds*, (Bloomington, Indiana, 1989), pp. 47–67; and her "The Reformation of the women II: a response from a Northern perspective", in Hans R. Guggisberg and Gottfried G. Krodel (eds), *Archiv für Reformationsgeschichte. Sonderband: Die Reformation in Deutschland und Europa: Interpretationen und Debatten* (Gütersloh, 1993), pp. 209–220.
28. Berit Sellevold, "Knokler, oldsaker og kvinner", in *Kvinnearbeid i Norden* (see Appendix), pp. 63–77.

29. Berit Sellevoid, "Fokus på kvinner: Kvinnders helse i middelalderen belyst gjennem skjelettstudier" and "Fødsel og død", in *Kvinnors Rosengård* (see Appendix), pp. 59–96.

30. Bergit Sellevold, "Kvinnen, kirken og døden", in *Kirkehistorier* (see Appendix), pp. 151–169.

31. Erik Lönnroth, "Drottning Margaretas kvinnoroll", in *Kvinnans ekonomiska ställning* (see Appendix), pp. 105–109.

32. Vivian Etting, *Margrete den første* (Copenhagen, 1986).

33. The title of the exhibition was "Margrete I, Nordens frue og husbond, Kalmarunionen 600 år" – in English, "Margrete I, Regent of the North". The exhibition travelled from Denmark to Sweden, Finland and Norway during 1997: see *Margrete I, regent of the North – the Kalmar Union 600 Years: essays and catalogue* (Copenhagen, 1997).

34. Beata Losman, "Birgitta, en kvinnlig väckelsepredikant", in *Förändringar i kvinnors villkor* (see Appendix), pp. 82–104.

35. Ida Blom (ed.), *Cappelens kvinnehistorie* (Oslo, 1992) and *Kvinder – Fra urtid til nutid* (Copenhagen, 1992).

APPENDIX

Reports from the Nordic symposia:

Kvinnans ekonomiska ställning under nordisk medeltid. Uppsatser framlagda vid ett kvinnohistoriskt symposium i Kungälv 8–12 oktober 1979, ed. by Hedda Gunneng and Birgit Strand (Lindome, 1981).

Förändringar i kvinnors villkor under medeltiden. Uppsatser framlagda vid ett kvinnohistoriskt symposium i Skálholt, Island, 22.-25. juni 1981, ed. by Silja Adalsteinsdóttir and Helgi Torláksson. Ritsafn Sagnfræðistofnunar, 9 (Reykjavík: Sagnfræðistofnum Háskola Islands, 1983).

Kvinnearbeid i Norden fra vikingtiden til reformasjonen. Foredrag fra et nordisk kvinnehistorisk seminar i Bergen 3–7 august 1983 (Bergen, 1985).

Kvinnors Rosengård. Medeltidskvinnors liv och hälsa, lust och barnafödande. Föredrag från nordiska tvärvetenskapliga symposier i Århus aug. 1985 och Visby sept. 1987, ed. by Hedda Gunneng, Beata Losman, Bodil Møller Knudsen and Helle Reinholdt. Skriftserie från Centrum för kvinnoforskning ved Stockholms Universitet, no. 1 (Stockholm, 1989).

Fokus på kvinner i middelalderkilder. Rapport fra symposiet "Kilder til kvinnehistoriske studier i nordisk middelalder", Isegran, september 1990, ed. by Berit Jansen Sellevold, Else Mundal, Gro Steinsland (Skara: Viktoria Bokförlag, 1992).

Kirkehistorier: Rapport fra et middelaldersymposium, ed. by Nanna Damsholt, Grethe Jacobsen, Niels Henrik Holmqvist-Larsen. (København: Museum Tusculanums Forlag, Københavns Universitet, 1996).

5

Gendering work: reflections on home, skill, and status in Europe, 1750–1820

Deborah Simonton

INTRODUCTORY

Throughout Europe, shifting concepts of work, skill and gender shaped women's work. The relationship between woman and her labour is mediated by a number of issues. Some, such as the nature of the work available, its urban or rural character, and the work process, affect men as well. In addition for women, key issues concern family and the female life cycle. But work is mediated also by ideology and by concepts of gender, status, and power in particular. These are less concerned with labour as such than with the relationships and psycho-social needs which work fills above and beyond its economic role. Work as a concept is historically specific and relative to the context and value systems in operation at a particular time. The division of labour along sexual lines came into operation not simply because it was a "practical" way of working, nor was it only about protecting jobs from cheap unskilled labour. It was about power, status, position, and masculinity. Gendered notions of place and work are, of course, variable over time and space. Different cultures at different times redefine them, as other factors, like demography, technology, and economic structure, come into play. Capitalistic challenges, as well as shifting attitudes toward women, meant that women came to be targets of specific interdictions and redefinitions of work. In fact, the need to define skill and redefine work probably contributed to reshaping femininity. When society has needed women as workers, it has always been adept at redefining their character to fit new demands.

The period between about 1750 and 1820 is of particular importance because the concept of work itself was being redefined. Europe witnessed significant shifts in commercial activity and new processes in the manufacture of goods. In pockets of Europe – such as some parts of Scotland – this meant the beginnings of large-scale concentrated industrialisation, but for much of Europe – including most of Scotland – the key development was in domestic industry. Agriculture too was in flux, with older-style, semi-feudal peasant practices operating alongside newer commercial agriculture. Whilst the timing, and indeed the pattern, of change varied regionally, these developments contributed to shaping the meaning of work for both men and women. The most obvious changes were that work was increasingly defined as waged labour, that the location of work changed for large numbers of people, and that the structuring and use of time were altered. In conjunction with these shifts, the meaning of work changed so that skill and status took on new meanings.

Shifting notions of gender at work can be demonstrated by the ways that "skill" was defined and used to redefine working patterns – the sexual division of labour in particular. Recent historical, sociological, and feminist literature associates skill with capitalism and gender to explain the character of work, women's relative position in the labour market, and the sexual division of labour. Skill has been defined in terms of strength, training, intelligence, custom, and control, while terms like technology, skill, and expertise regularly appear. Eighteenth-century usages and implications of the English word "skill", or the Scottish "skeel", were different from our current concepts. "Skeely" entered the language in the late eighteenth century to mean "experienced" or "practised" and, like skill, was synonymous with "airt" or "art". Commonly, in the early modern world, skill denoted possession of discrimination or knowledge, and described the "capability of accomplishing something with precision and certainty". Additionally it could be construed to mean "practical knowledge in combination with ability" or "cleverness, expertness". To be skilled was to be possessed of "skill or knowledge, properly trained or experienced", while a "skeely wife was credited with great or supernatural healing powers". Thus, the notion of skill carried with it a sense of knowledge, but also described an ability to accomplish something: i.e. a sense of not only *knowing* but being able to *do* something.[2] This was not limited to a practical or technological sense, and paid heed to both experience and training as ways of knowing. Interestingly, skill, technique, and expertness do not appear in the language of apprenticeship by and large. Instead indenture documents, and writers like Adam Smith, invoked "mystery" rather than skill, referring to the secret or the unknowable and to "an action or practice about which there is, or is supposed to be, some secrecy; a 'secret' or highly technical operation in a trade or art". Whilst mystery encompassed technical operation and trade, it also included art, and the sense of usage had far more to do with trade secrets than technical skill.

French workers referred to work in a personal way, instead of talking about tasks, so that the proficiency of the worker and the qualities of the work were relatively indistinguishable. They acknowledged respect for each other as *le plus fort* or *le plus gros*, thus ascribing the quality of the work to the worth of the individual. Sonenscher has stressed the importance and usage of this language to assert position within the workplace and to establish status. His discussion of the *compagnonnages* identifies the importance of rituals in creating symbolic inequalities in order to establish barriers which protected workers' fragile claims to the work that they did. In a world that relied on relatively homogeneous skills and a similar range of abilities, rituals and ascription of status or honour were important to defend the worker's place. They also allowed masters a means of controlling work and journeymen.[3] These usages illustrate the importance of the language of skill as a device to claim and maintain control and exclusivity in the workplace. The idea that there was a secret to maintain, that there were rituals to go through, and even that strength or size were aspects of the ascription of status and skill are of significance if we are to understand the position of women with regard to the workplace. Similarly Rule has shown how the property of skill in the period of manufacture was at the centre of workers' self-evaluation and how it spilled far beyond the workplace to enter more generally the vocabulary of labour – with its own rights and dignity.[4]

Patterns of women's work overlapped, and the same tasks could be done within or outside of guild structures; in an urban or rural setting; part time or full time; and with or without formal training. In many industries and activities, women's work could be seen as supplementary, or complementary to that of men; their position depended on their relationship to a male worker. In this way, women's participation was interpreted as subordinate. Because their work was subsidiary, it was also cheap; women could be perceived as casual, part-time workers – a concept which ignored the totality of their household contribution. Specifically these interpretations became more important as definitions of work changed, and as men sought to protect their position in circumstances that meant that many men's independent work status was threatened and, with it, their personal status and value. Thus it became important to define skill and status not only *vis à vis* other men, who were seen as poachers, but also against women.

This development drew on the importance in the Germanic world of the distinction between "honourable" and "dishonourable" work, so that disesteemed and "unskilled" rural industry came to be identified as "women's work". Equally important was the assurance that persons who learned a trade in a household would not be admitted to guilds.[5] By denigrating the productive strength of the rural household, guildsmen came to equate village work with women's work. Thus the increasingly closed world of the guild began to use gender as a fundamental determinant of work roles and their valuation.[6] At the same time, the notion that status attaches to the workers and not to the work became explicit in the identity of male workers in the *compagnonnages* and implicit in reworking notions of skill when gender is at stake. Thus "skilled" work in guild shops was increasingly defined as men's work, and craft mysteries as things which were not to be shared with women. In this way, artisanal practice identified productive work as properly male and household activities as properly female. These concepts were especially important in towns like Aberdeen or Württemberg, where corporate controls remained important in establishing status and defining workers.[7] Significant in this practice was the association of women with work which was perceived as unskilled.

DOMESTIC ROLES, FAMILY ISSUES, AND WOMEN'S WORK

Women's roles in the family and in the household shaped their attitudes to work. They also conditioned the ideas of those around them, including employers, about their work. For rural women, work centred on a responsibility for the farmyard, small animals, and the house itself. For urban women, the tasks of the house and the shop constituted much of their responsibility. For both, contribution to the trade of the household, and the provision of food and often clothing for all, including workmen, fell to them. Almost always the duties required to run a household have been regarded as a normal part of women's tasks. During the eighteenth century, domestic chores had not yet evolved into a notion of "housework" nor did they have the connotation of "domesticity". They were simply a part of, and frequently the primary part of, women's work. Not only were domestic tasks important to the household, they were important to women. They helped to define their scope and space, and gave value to much of their work. If earning money became necessary, women, whether single or married, were expected to take on paid work for whatever period was required. The woman's skill was based on her household responsibilities and "her property in the virtue of her person".[8] Her identity rested in the home. Shifts in the view of the family, deriving in part from Enlightenment thought, and a sublimation of these archetypes into newer, highly gendered views of the family, contributed to creating a model of women and work which were mutually exclusive. The early formulation of domesticity was grounded in this period. It stressed the significance of woman's place in the home and of her moral responsibility for it, for the upbringing of the children, and for the conduct of a range of domestic tasks in ways which could enhance a family's standing and respectability. Perceptions of working women were influenced by such views. Women were seen as dependants, subject to control, reliant on men. Thus, by the nineteenth century, men were usually defined by the work they did, and women by their domestic status as single or married, daughter or mother. There is no doubt that contemporary rhetoric reflected the idea that men had a basic *right* to work, and that women did not; women had a *duty* to the home which might include earning.

Language helps to illustrate not only how meanings and usages changed, but also how ascription and status shifted. In French, *ménagère*, which has come to mean housework, formerly covered the entire farm administration. Where it once carried the sense of managing with "masculine" connotations, these were lost – and the "feminine" meaning of "household tasks" was maintained. A similar shift can be seen in German and British experience. The English term housewifery (sometimes "huswifery") was used throughout the eighteenth century. Along with the masculine form, husbandry (sometimes "housebandry"), it referred to household maintenance. The German *Hausmutter* shared responsibility for the household (*ganzes Haus*) with the *Hausvater*: "The household was their joint domain and every task carried out – whether by the *Hausvater* or the *Hausmutter* – was important and indispensable for the farm's prosperity." As Johann Heinrich Zedler's 1735 *Universal-Lexikon* indicated, "because the wife, as housemother, has also to help her husband administer and supervise the household, some authority can be ascribed to her". But as with the meanings of femininity and masculinity, housewifery became narrowly defined household tasks. The *Hausmutter* became a *Hausfrau*.[9]

The persistence among historians of an idea of "family strategies", in which all members of a household contribute to its survival, also underpins much thinking on women's work. However, a view of "family strategies" which argues that families operate to maximise income, making decisions about deployment of family members based on economic considerations, tends to overlook the power of the ideological arguments, which had great potency during the period. Thus Nardinelli wrote that "division between market production and household production for any given member of the household does not depend on attitudes, affections, customs, sexual stereotypes or outside coercion; it depends only on relative productivities".[10] Pure economic considerations would suggest that in times of difficulty it was always preferable to send women rather than children out to work, given that women could usually bring in a greater income. And yet such was the power of domestic arguments that often children were sent to work before women.[11] A range of other variables could also be present, such as the type of work available and obligations around the house, but the importance of gendered notions of women and the role played by views of women's place must be recognised.

The concept of the family economy was also imbedded in an economic system based on agricultural trades and a domestic system of production. Work, family, and household were integrally related ideas. Decisions about household formation, fertility, and economic survival, while not completely within an individual's control, were undoubtedly coloured by the economic need to survive, and by love, sentiment, and affection. Knowing a woman's relationship to her home and its membership, on affective, demographic, and economic terms, is crucial to understanding her place within society. Used sensitively, the family economy model remains useful in highlighting the importance of strategies to a household and in stressing the interdependence of household members, and the centrality of women and children – and their labour – to a household's response to economic conditions.

TASKS AND TIME

Underlying numerous accounts of women's work is the assumption that because work was located in the home, women could do it, and work away from home was not available to them. There are two aspects to this way of thinking. One is the obvious one that women, particularly married women, normally had to stay at home in order to fulfil their female role. The second is that women required work which did not depend on time discipline – their work, whether for market or family, had to be flexible and based on tasks so that it could be fitted in to the interstices of their domestic duty. William Reddy observes that:

> for whatever reason, women's work usually included a bundle of tasks that could easily be combined and carried on simultaneously within the household.... Women often were the specialists in task-combining, a fact that helps explain their prominence in certain kinds of proto-industrial manufacturing. [12]

Indeed, for Scotland, Whyte says that:

> There was little problem with spinning which was done almost entirely by women and could be fitted into slack periods of virtually any household or farm economy. [13]

Or as the minister of Keith-Hall said, a woman could knit "and do some little things about her house at the same time. Or she can work at her stocking while feeding her cows". [14] Encapsulating their strategies in such a way, however, undervalues their work, and simply does not reflect the variety of approaches women employed to balance obligations. Also, a single female's experience and availability was different from that of a married woman; an argument based on domestic roles tends to overlook her position in the labour force.

Even though certain types of work seem to have remained immutably in the hands of women – such as spinning, sewing, lace making, laundering, and silk working – this cannot be explained simply by the need for women's work to be fitted around household and maternal responsibilities. Although certainly a great deal of women's work did fit into a task-oriented model, reliant on flexible use of time, it should be remembered that a large proportion of artisanal work was task oriented. Certainly the fact that a woman bore children influenced the kind of work she did, but it did not restrict her to a specific set of tasks, nor did it exclude her from productive activity. Because much of married women's

[69]

household work was task-oriented, employment which was centred on tasks rather than on time was easier to take up. Single women were not so constrained; and restrictions did not always operate on married women either. The extent of compatibility depended on the character of the work, and on the economic cycle, as well as on the woman's status and position in the life cycle. International markets brought spells of highly intensive labour followed by phases of unemployment. Such erratic demands made it even more difficult to integrate the demands of housework and childcare with paid labour. The degree to which paid work could be merged with other responsibilities varied enormously by region, by industry, and over time. The experience of a spinner or nail maker was not the same as that of a pottery worker or button maker; a flax spinner in Aberdeenshire could experience work differently from one from in Saxony.[15]

Work discipline and the value placed on industrial time could be significant for women. Scotswoman Dorothea Maria Ogilvy of Clova captured the situation of most women, the spinners of Europe:

Sittin spinnin, sittin spinnin
   A' the lea-lang day
Hearin the bit burnie rinnin,
   And the bairns at play.
I'm sweirr to get my leg loose.
To do a turn aboot the hoose;
Oh, amna I a waeful wife
To spin awa my thread of life?
Spinnin, spinnin, ever spinnin,
never ending, aye beginnin;
Hard at wark wi hant and fuit,
Oh, the weary spinnin o't![16]

Such a combination of productive work and domestic role were regarded as inevitable. To assume that women had "an imperfect sense of time", embedded in a pre-modern world in which "task-orientation" operated in relation to "natural work-rhythms" instead of time discipline, distorts women's strategies.[17] Women endured the time discipline imposed by market dates, raw material delivery times, and putting-out networks – a discipline greatly amplified by the intensification of labour driving down piece rates. Both single and married women – whether working at home, in workshops, or in small factories – were increasingly tied to forms of work that structured the use of their time, rather than allowing them to fit it in between other tasks of domestic life.

Ideologically, however, the notion of women's work as task-oriented made it appear as though they were "part-time", supplementing the "real" work of men. It lent credence to the idea of women as casual, non-essential labour, although quite the opposite was true. Certainly mothers and housewives "respond[ed] to different rhythms than those dictated by the clock, and a working week". In that respect, so did most proto-industrial workers. But women's patterns were not "casual", they were

> orientated to care for others. The rhythm of life and work of housewives is not just task-orientated; it is governed by a strict day by day and week by week time discipline, and continuous thinking of the future.... Not only is time disciplined; it is spent on others in different ways, leaving virtually none of it for the housewife to "waste" on herself. [18]

The tempo of work and the tempo of domestic life cut across each other. Where industrial work was regulated for all workers by factors such as the delivery times of raw materials, the dates of markets or fairs, the time patterns of other social and income-earning activities, or the availability of assistants whose time economy might vary, time discipline mattered to the proto-industrial world.[19] Where agricultural seasons and the demands of nature dictated tasks, time also mattered. It also mattered to women. To reconstruct it as a casual world, made up of tasks to be picked up and put down, with industrial activities seen as by-employments to women's "real" work, belies the structure and meaning of women's lives. Reddy identifies a similar view of the actions of spinners who did not engage in distinct entrepreneurial, labour, or consumer functions; they were all of these at once. "They were not trying to max-imise purchasing power as consumers or minimise labour time as labour-ers."[20] In their daily lives, they reconciled conflicts between diverse functions, such as a desire for earnings against a desire for leisure, in terms of an idea of a way of life which they sought to achieve. Time and work discipline imposed as much pressure on women as did the location of work.

Many women experienced work as an intermittent part of their life, with regular waged work more likely during their single years, and peri-odic and part-time work more likely during the years of marriage and child-rearing. This archetypal pattern helped to reinforce ideology. It is misleading, however, to adopt the view that men usually worked in a single occupation throughout their working life, while women experienced interrupted and temporary work in a range of occupations. These models do not adequately express the variety of patterns experienced by men or women. Some women had stable "careers" gaining skill and status in what they did; others worked for much of their lives in the same or similar jobs. Many men, on the other hand, had the kind of variable and peripatetic experience more usually associated with women. Representing "the skilled craftsman as the exemplary 'worker' ... repressed differences of training, job stability, and tenure among male workers and thus also similar patterns of irregular and changing employment for male and female workers".[21] Married women also worked at a full range of activities, often continuing at the same job they did before marriage. Others found new ones, as, for example, did some domestic servants who had lived in the homes of others and, on marriage, turned to laundering or charring. Silk workers frequently worked much as they had before, and so did many female agricultural labourers. Women did not necessarily leave factories or workshops on marriage or at the birth of children. The decision they made depended on their circumstances and on their perception of them.

LOCATIONS AND ORGANISATIONAL STRUCTURES

Another way in which the home influenced ideas about women's work was through the belief that "Industrialisation affected women most profoundly through the separation of work and home."[22] For this to have been significant, it had to clash with their other perceived roles. Movement of work away from home had to be coupled with other factors – such as what other roles were expected of women, and the time discipline associated with the newer form of work. Industrialisation in a literal sense brought work into the home. Factories and large-scale workplaces were, of course, largely distinct from home, but they were of less relevance until later in the nineteenth century.

Underpinning all this is the argument that women's domestic duties prevented them from following paid work out of the home. But a fundamental flaw here lies in the assumption that work in previous periods had been located at home, giving women equal access to it. Few historians today accept such a simplistic reading of the pre- or proto-industrial period: the complementarity and mutual dependence of men's and women's activities did not mean that the sexes were "equal" in the workplace. It is also patently obvious that not all work was in the home. Women's status in the workplace was not necessarily determined by the degree or nature of their access to it, nor their participation in it, but rather by the gendered meanings attached to work. In short, work which was located in the home did not gain status for women which was then eroded by removal of work from the home.

There is an important ideological aspect to the separation of home and work, however, which carries a semi-veiled reference to the public/private dichotomy. As waged and salaried employment came to be seen as proper work for men, and family maintenance, housework, and childcare as the proper province for women, an ideological separation of home and work took place. Whilst this was first generated as an ideal – initially a bourgeois ideal – it was also supported by actual changes in the location of work. It is important, however, to ask how such ideological thinking contributed to the way those changes took place, and in particular to the exclusion of women from certain kinds of workplaces. Although women's activities could be described as "domestic" in recognition of their responsibility for home management, for food production and preparation, and for child-bearing and child-rearing, this belies the extent of their non-family, non-domestic activities. In that male work also contributed to household maintenance, the distinction between public and private was blurred. Much of women's work was performed outside the domestic setting, and not always in clothing and food activities associated with females – as is demonstrated by the numbers in mining and metal trades. Similarly family maintenance or household management frequently involved women in negotiations in the so-called public sphere. Marketing was the most obvious, and at times it led to popular protest, often bread riots. But women also acted as intermediaries between husbands and employers, negotiating working and financial arrangements; and they managed the financial affairs of both business and household in many settings. In both the rural and urban world, women were central to the networking of the neighbourhood and community. Much of their life was played out in the neighbourhood and street. These variations illustrate the divergence between the reality and the ideology of women as domestic creatures.

Clearly, women left home to work in agriculture, industry, and commerce. The migration of single women was a noteworthy feature of the rural-urban nexus. In Scotland, for example, Highland girls went to Lothian farms, and rural spinners to Lanarkshire factories. In many parts of Europe the countryside simply could not support all of its growing population, and the migration of girls to towns, either temporarily or permanently, was common. These girls were largely unaffected by shifts in the location of industrial concerns. Married women also left home to work, either locally or at longer distances. Sometimes they migrated temporarily with their children or as a part of a family migration. Examples of this phenonemon can be seen amongst those who sought work in the early factories of Rouen. [23]

Under some circumstances, the development of industrial capitalism did create a physical separation of home and work, but this could be experienced in different degrees. There were great variations in the transformation of the processes of manufacture, and there was no uniform effect on the location of waged labour. The dramatic changes brought by factory working in some areas sometimes obscured the fact that it never was the occupation of the majority; much industrial organisation continued to centre on the small workshop even into the twentieth century. For many decades domestic industries expanded alongside mechanised, factory-based branches of the industry concerned – a route followed in most of Scotland.[24] And local and small-scale workshops might not be very different from the home, in terms of work and time discipline. Throughout Europe, much of the rural countryside remained dedicated to farming, where women continued to work on farms either as family members or servants. Women as hired day labourers remained fairly unusual until after the Napoleonic wars. They continued to be employed primarily in their own homes or on land and in workshops virtually contiguous to their home, where their economic and domestic roles merged, or in the homes of others as servants and labourers. Thus only a small proportion of people, male and female, were affected by the separation of home from work during this period. New technologies, the concentration of some industries, and commercial farming provided work for some groups of women, but these developments disadvantaged others.

A more useful approach is to recognise that the shift was "not from work at home to work away from home, but from one kind of workplace to another". Industrialisation and commercialisation did not create a division between home and workplace, nor did it create for the first time some of the pressures on childcare and domestic duties which are often cited. Women had always had to make arrangements for childcare. Changing ideas of housework and Enlightenment views of motherhood created as much pressure on the married woman and mother to concentrate on childcare and housework as did the changing workplace. In any case, the impact of any separation was delayed, for the most part, until the second part of the nineteenth century. "If there were problems associated with this move – a new time discipline, noisy machinery, wages dependent on market conditions and economic cycles, profit-driven employers – they nonetheless were not caused by the removal of women from their own home and family settings." Joan Scott argues that the story of separation of home and work contributed to the creation of the "woman worker" as a problem – legitimising terms and expressions which minimised continuities with the past, assumed the sameness of women's experience, and stressed differences between women and men. [25]

Organisational structures were important in determining the extent to which work in commercial manufacturing translated into independent incomes, new status, or freedoms for women. The concentration of labour was useful to merchants, and this strategy was used to take advantage of existing female skills. Some early small mills were set up in the countryside to take advantage of skilled female labour, an example being the Courtaulds' decision to transfer silk work from Spitalfields to Essex. Many early mills were simply large workshops which brought together many of the activities of domestic industry under one roof – Wedgwood's, for example. Even the earliest cotton mills were little more than a collection of large jennies, such as the one at Spinningdale in Scotland. In the Caux, Rouen merchants similarly moved jennies to the countryside to expand the spinning potential of rural domestic workers. However, it was far more efficient to set up factories in Rouen, so that women had to migrate if they wished to retain the work.[26] So by the early nineteenth century, women in certain industries faced a significant transition in the character of their work, which was as much technologically induced as geographically or structurally generated.

Even in domestic industries, women worked under varying organisational structures. They could work directly for a putting-out merchant, could be sub-contracted by husbands, or could be part of a household production unit. Much of women's market work appeared supplementary or complementary to that of a man. For example, the woman would be engaged in carding and spinning while the man wove. The rate paid for the finished product, in this case cloth, represented the whole effort. In this process, women's participation was interpreted as supplementary and subordinate. Because their work was subsidiary, it was cheap. Although their status in domestic industry was perhaps an improvement to that in the agrarian world, "their labour was still far cheaper than ... in workshops or early factories".[27] As families turned more and more to waged activities, males continued to draw the equivalent of the family wage while women were regularly paid less. The relative invisibility of their work thus disadvantaged many women once there was a growing

[75]

reliance on wages, which made it difficult for them to support themselves or a family. An important exception is identified by Pamela Sharpe writing about spinsters in Colyton, where employment opportunities favoured women and suggest a pattern for women in other parts of Europe:

> Women's work was not a corollary of men's, nor a complement, as the current "family economy" theory suggests. It was, rather, separate and different in terms of the type of job involved, the wages earned, and the amount of time spent in employment. The type of domestic industry carried out in Colyton did not require a family unit as the typical proto-industrial model suggests. Rather, it promoted the independence of women as wage earners in their own right.[28]

At the same time, although women were able to support themselves and live independently, there is little evidence that their position was enhanced or that their quality of life was significantly different from that of women in other regions. The woman working in her own right did have a better chance of an independent living, but usually her wages were too low to allow this, particularly in the countryside.

This exposes one of the key difficulties with the "separation of home and work" perspective: it can obliterate the differences between women. It emphasises the situation of married women, especially those with children, and overlooks single women who made up the majority of the visible workforce. Single women found different sets of choices as economies became more commercialised. On the one hand, large numbers worked in homes as domestic servants, so that work and "home" were not any more separate for them than for their predecessors. On the other hand, the majority of factory workers were single women who preferred the work, which paid better than many alternatives, and through which they gained a semblance of independence. Arguably all work structures were patriarchal, and women were affected by the way each system imposed patriarchy. The corporate structures of the community at large ensured that women's opportunities in terms of independence, status, and income did not improve in a proto-industrial economy. Married women or widows could work under a husband's licence, as could daughters and servants. However, the work of all women could be regulated simply because they were women.[29] There is also widespread evidence that single women were rigidly controlled throughout European society, with attempts being made to keep them within a male-headed household and thus to support patriarchal control in society as a whole. Although widows were under many of the same disabilities as other women, they were also more able to establish themselves in their own right. Wherever the small family business structure predominated, a potential route was available for widows to exploit: they could use their skill and initiative to establish themselves in high status work. [30]

WOMAN'S SKILLS; WOMAN AS WORKER

Women's role in household maintenance made them eminently suitable as a workforce for domestic industry. Their domestic role led to their industrial role insofar as they already had skills to transfer to the industrial labour market. Almost all women were engaged in making things for the household – bread, drink, clothing which required spinning, weaving, sewing, knitting. An important shift came with making things for the market, and initially products for sale were indistinguishable from those made for household consumption. Precisely this close association between domestic manufacture and the home led to a long struggle by workers in central Europe to establish that their artisanal work was distinct from, and more esteemed than, the domestic production which came to be defined as women's work.[31] As hiring workers for wages became more the norm, attitudes to women workers were shaped by notions of womanhood and sexuality on the one hand, and by the needs of capitalism and working-class families for paid labour on the other. As female employment – "women for hire" – became more visible, and as its existence clashed with emergent notions of domesticity, it became grounds for debate. In many eyes, women were not workers: the terms were mutually exclusive. This view shaped the context of women's work and contributed to perceptions of women as casual and temporary employees, who could and should be treated differently from men, and who should not be paid the same.

Berg argues that during the early stages of industrialisation it was assumed that female and child labour was the key workforce to be targeted, so that machines and processes were designed with them in mind. New processes in calico printing and spinning were prime examples. Calico printing was broken down into a series of steps, performed best by teenage girls who had learned manual dexterity at home in needlecrafts. If girls were seen as more suitable, it was because the work was planned to take advantage of their cheapness and the skills they were expected to have learned from their mothers. The development of spinning machines and power looms required someone to re-attach broken threads precisely and swiftly, a task thought suitable for women who were seen as dexterous. In fact the major prerequisites were sharp eyes and, in the case of looms, sufficient height. Thus in central and northern Italy, as in Scotland, women were thought be most adept at this task, "because their fingers are supple and they learn the skills more easily".[32] A commentator on Italy noted that the "working of silk requires little physical force and our women, as befits this most delicate of arts, have good eyes and swift fingers".[33] Employers of Saint Chamond emphasised how well machine-tending suited women because it did not require physical exertion, although they undercut their own argument by establishing twelve-hour shifts around the clock.[34] With the need to provide a cheap labour force, the suspicion arises, employers adopted that part of the feminine ideal which matched their needs, describing women's "delicacy" in terms which justified employing them. Association of women with delicate fabrics and soft textiles carried this allusion further.

Such gendered descriptions of jobs appeared throughout contemporary literature, helping to create a category of women's work. As Scott says

> Often employers described their jobs as having inherently gendered qualities. Tasks requiring delicate, nimble fingers, patience, and endurance were marked as feminine, while muscular strength, speed, and skill signified masculinity, although none of these descriptions was used consistently across the range and variety of jobs offered and, in fact, they were the subject of intense disagreement and debate.[35]

These debates centred on different perceptions of male and female, and were highly class dependent. The feminine ideal could hardly have applied in the same way to working-class women as to the bourgeoisie, but the battleground centred on the *nature* of the female and male. At the same time workers were needed, so adapting the nature of work helped resolve the issue. The views of colliers are revealing: girls were said to work harder than boys; play around less; be fitter and more supple; be more attentive to their work; be more punctual; and be easier to control. They were also praised for knowing their place:

> they make better drawers than lads. They are more steady.... A lass never expects to be a coal-getter and that keeps her steady.[36]

Women were seen as docile, malleable creatures, subject to a well-established patriarchal regime, subordinate to men and masters, and their natural steadiness and docility were cited as key factors in making them better employees. Again miners claimed that:

Females submit to work in places where no man, or even lad could be got to labour in. They work in bad roads, up to their knees in water, in a posture nearly double. [37]

The feminisation of the Lombard silk industry was said to be the result of women providing a more pliable workforce than men. They had no mutual aid societies, very few strikes, no union-organised stoppages, nor any other open manifestation of discontent.[38] Similarly the capitalists of the spinning mills considered females to be more docile workers than males, arguing that they were less prone to collective action, less likely to cause work slow-downs or stoppages.

Two thoughts occur here. First, if women were accustomed to a patriarchal world in which male authority ruled, it is not too surprising that they behaved in an obedient way. Second, if a woman needed work, she was unlikely to be so disruptive as to risk losing it, especially if there were no obvious alternatives. Arguments about female self-exploitation suggest that a woman with few alternatives would take whatever pay and conditions existed in order to feed herself and her children. At the same time women were largely excluded from collective action, particularly as organised men came to believe more and more that their interests were not necessarily the same.

The issues in domestic industry were not distinct from those in artisanal trades, except that the character of control and the perceptions of place, skill, and status usually were not as overtly expressed. There is little doubt that women's work was central to many rural industries. As regards technical abilities and manual dexterity, there is also no doubt that these stages in production required "know-how" or "knack" which had to be learned or acquired. Many stages of production were essentially female trades, especially spinning. Significantly, when there was pressure for more spinners, men did not turn to spinning. The response was to bring in more women rather than expect men to do it. When rural spinning fell off, however, women took up weaving. Nevertheless, in the Caux women were allowed to take up only calico weaving, while men continued to weave heavy fabrics. Retaining this sexual division of labour enabled male weavers to maintain their craft superiority, and, since the fabrics required relatively little expertise, relegating women to calico weaving was intended to retain the same pecking order of the household which had existed when men wove and women spun.

Male weavers quickly came to see the new division of labour as based on natural differences between the sexes that went far beyond physical strength, and therefore as proof of their own superiority.[39]

As one weaver said, women

> make the articles that are the most easily made and consequently the least lucrative, *because* they are more suited to their [weaker] physical strength and their inferior intelligence.... [Men] are *naturally* inclined toward the articles whose construction is more laborious and difficult because they procure higher *benefits*. [40]

The appeal to male attributes, such as strength and supposed superior intelligence, is common in the debates about skill, and operated to maintain the low status of women as workers. Such was the case of the introduction of the scythe into agriculture.

Berg's exploration of female skills and female technologies underlines the extent to which the sexual division between trades was mirrored within technologies when male workers could restrict entry – women tended to be confined to less efficient and more labour intensive technologies.[41] Although notions of skill underpinned these distinctions, the very definitions of skilled and unskilled had at their root gender distinctions far more significant than those attached to technical attributes. The skills which women had, such as dexterity and deftness, were seldom regarded as skills. They were seen as "natural" and feminine and therefore not given the credit which "expertise" carried with it. Also, many so-called female skills were not acquired through a recognised, and controlled, training. They were learned working side-by-side with other women. They were the wisdom and practices passed from mother to daughter. In this way they lacked the status which apprenticeship gave to many "male" skills learnt in the same way.

Despite the fact that most women worked most of the time, their work was unreported in many accounts and was considered casual and part time. Often it was piecework and was low paid. The concept of skill was blurred by the association of women with homework and casual work. Their work was not considered real. Eugène Buret in 1840 summed up woman's dilemma:

> Woman is industrially speaking, an imperfect worker. If a man doesn't add his earnings to the insufficient wage of his partner, sex alone constitutes for her the cause of misery. [42]

Contemporary views thus denied *the fact* of women as workers as well as their *identity* as workers. But within such constraints, women strove to create their own meaning and a sense of their own identity out of their labour. Credit for their work and ability remained largely, as Natalie Zemon Davis has shown, within their own world, "their street, their commérage, their tavern, their kin – unpublished and unsung". [43]

NOTES

(1). A fuller exploration of the issues summarised in this paper is in Deborah Simonton, *A History of European Women's Work* (London, 1998).

2. Mairi Robinson, *The Concise Scots Dictionary* (Aberdeen, 1985); *Compact Oxford English Dictionary* (London, 1979).

3. Michael Sonenscher, "Mythical work: workshop production and the *compagnonnages* of eighteenth-century France", in Patrick Joyce (ed.), *Historical Meanings of Work* (Cambridge, 1989), p. 50.

4. See John Rule, "The property of skill in the period of manufacture", in Joyce, *Historical Meanings*, pp. 99–118.

5. Jean Quataert, "The shaping of women's work in manufacturing guilds, households and the state in central Europe, 1648–1870", *American Historical Review*, 90 (1985), pp. 1126–1127.

6. Quataert, "Shaping of women's work", pp. 1134–1135.

7. See Ian D. Whyte, "Proto-industrialisation in Scotland", in Pat Hudson (ed.), *Regions and Industries: a perspective on the Industrial Revolution in Britain* (Cambridge, 1989), p. 234; and Shelagh Ogilvie, "Women and proto-industrialisation", in Pat Hudson and W. R. Lee (eds), *Women's Work and the Family Economy in Historical Perspective* (Manchester, 1990).

8. Sally Alexander, "Women, class and sexual difference", *History Workshop*, no. 17 (spring 1984), p. 139.

9. Martine Segalen, *Love and Power in the Peasant Family: rural France in the nineteenth century* (Oxford, 1983), p. 9; Ute Frevert, *Women in German History: from bourgeois emancipation to sexual liberation* (Oxford, 1988), p. 23, and quotation from p. 24; Ruth Schwartz Cowan, *More Work for Mother: the ironies of household technology from the open hearth to the microwave* (London, 1989), pp. 16–18; *Compact Oxford English Dictionary*.

10. Clark Nardinelli, *Child Labour and the Industrial Revolution* (Bloomington, 1990), p. 59.

11. I am grateful for the comments of Hugh Cunningham on this line of thought.

12. William Reddy, "Proto-entrepreneurship, the inadequacy of numerical measurement in the study of eighteenth-century household manufacturing", unpublished paper presented to a conference on Custom and Commerce (University of Warwick, 1987), p. 16.

13. Whyte, "Proto-industrialisation in Scotland", p. 246.
14. John Sinclair, *Statistical Account of Scotland*, vol. IX (reprinted in Wakefield, England, 1982), p. 469.
15. Hudson and Lee, *Women's Work*, p. 16; Maxine Berg, "Women's work and mechanisation", in Joyce, *Historical Meanings*, p. 76
16. In Catherine Kerrigan (ed.), *An Anthology of Scottish Women Poets* (Edinburgh, 1991), p. 188.
17. See E. P. Thompson, "Time, work-discipline", in M. W. Flinn and T. C. Smout (eds), *Essays in Social History* (Oxford, 1974), pp. 42–43, 55.
18. Maxine Berg, Pat Hudson and Michael Sonenscher (eds), *Manufacture in Town and Country before the Factory*, (Cambridge, 1983), p. 10. See Thompson, "Time, work-discipline", pp. 42–55.
19. Berg, Hudson and Sonenscher, *Manufacture in Town and Country*, pp. 9–10.
20. William Reddy, *The Rise of Market Culture, the Textile Trade and French Society, 1750–1900* (Cambridge, 1984), p. 33.
21. Joan Scott, "The woman worker", in Geneviève Fraisse and Michelle Perrot (eds), *A History of Women in the West*, vol. IV: *Emerging feminism from revolution to World War*, (Cambridge, Mass., 1993), p. 401.
22. Theresa McBride, "The long road home: women's work and industrialization", in Renate Bridenthal and Claudia Koonz (eds), *Becoming Visible: women in European history* (Boston, 1977), p. 283.
23. Gay Gullickson, "The sexual division of labor in cottage industry and agriculture in the Pays de Caux, 1750–1850", *French Historical Studies*, vol. 12 (1981), p. 188; Elizabeth Fox-Genovese, "Women and work", in Samia Spencer (ed.), *French Women and the Enlightenment*, (Bloomington, 1984), p. 120–121; Olwen Hufton, "Women, work and marriage in eighteenth-century France", in R. B. Outhwaite (ed.), *Marriage and Society: studies in the social history of marriage* (London, 1981), pp. 190–194; and "Women and the family economy in eighteenth-century France", *French Historical Studies*, vol. 9 (1975), pp. 19–22.
24. See the discussion of alternative forms of industrial organisation in Maxine Berg, *The Age of Manufactures: industry, innovation and work, 1700–1820*, (London, 1994), pp. 66–76.
25. Scott, "The woman worker", pp. 400–401, 404–405.
26. Gullickson, "Sexual division of labour", p. 188.
27. Berg, *Age of Manufactures*, p. 160.
28. Pamela Sharpe, "Literally spinsters: a new interpretation of the local economy and demography in Colyton in the seventeenth and eighteenth centuries", *Economic History Review*, vol. XLIV, no. 1 (February 1991), p. 55.
29. Ogilvie, "Women and proto-industrialisation", pp. 86–93.
30. Leonore Davidoff and Catherine Hall, *Family Fortunes: men and women of the English middle class* (London, 1987), pp. 250–251.
31. Quataert, "Shaping of women's work", pp. 1125–1127.

32. Quoted in Maxine Berg, "What difference did women's work make to the Industrial Revolution?", *History Workshop Journal*, no. 35 (spring 1993), p. 34.

33. Vittorio Ellena, quoted in Simonetta Cammarosano, "Labouring women in northern and central Italy in the nineteenth century", in John A. Davis and Paul Ginsborg (eds), *Society and Politics in the Age of the Risorgimento: essays in honour of Denis Mack Smith* (Cambridge, 1991), p. 165.

34. Elinor Accampo, *Industrialization, Family Life and Class Relations: Saint Chamond, 1815–1914* (Berkeley, 1989), p. 82.

35. Scott, "The woman worker", p. 413.

36. Parliamentary Papers (PP), 1842, vol. xv, p. 27; vol. xvi, p. 283; vol. xvii, p. 202.

37. PP, 1842, vol. xv, p. 24.

38. Anna Cento Bull, "Lombard silk-spinners in the nineteenth century: an industrial workforce in a rural setting", in Zygmut Baranski and Shirley Vinall (eds), *Women and Italy: essays on gender, culture and history* (London, 1991), pp. 24, 31.

39. Gay Gullickson, "Women and proto-industrialisation: a review of the literature and the case of the Caux", unpublished paper presented to a conference on Custom and Commerce (Warwick, 1987), pp. 15–16.

40. Gullickson, "Women and proto-industrialisation", p. 17

41. Berg, *Age of Manufactures*, pp. 154–155.

42. Eugène Buret, *The Misery of the Working Classes* (1840), cited in Joan W. Scott, "L'ouvrière! Mot impie, sordide ...: women workers in the discourse of French political economy, 1840–1860", in Joyce, *Historical Meanings*, pp. 125–126.

43. Natalie Zemon Davis, "Women in the arts mécaniques of sixteenth-century Lyon", *Mélanges Richard Gascon* (Lyon, 1979).

6

A gendered approach to the history of the welfare state: reflections on a study of the fight against tuberculosis in Norway

Ida Blom

In 1885, the French feminist Hubertine Auclert formulated a two-sided theory of the state. She maintained that it could be seen either as a Minotaur (*état minautaure*) which, through war, devoured its own children, or as a mother (*état maternel*) helping her children to peaceful production and good health. This was clearly a gendered conceptual division,[1] and in this chapter I ask if the analogy with motherhood is useful in our attempts to understand the early evolution of the welfare state between the 1890s and the inter-war years. I begin with some remarks on theories of state-construction, particularly with reference to the welfare state in Norway.[2]

I

We are used to thinking of the public and the private as dichotomous concepts. And Leonore Davidoff, amongst others, has shown that the conceptualisation of the state as public and of civil society as private, throughout the nineteenth century, clearly had gender implications.[3] Politics, the market, economics, and science were activities seen as demanding what were perceived as masculine qualities of independence: the capacity to own property; rationality; and individuality. The state became the single legitimate arena for the use of force and the military was a masculine preserve. On the other hand, civil society – the home and the family, and the world of voluntary organisations – were either feminine preserves, or in some cases gender-mixed arenas with masculine leadership.

Seen in this light, the transition from the nineteenth-century, *laissez-faire*, liberal state to the interventionist welfare state – a transition which began in Norway in the 1890s – can appear as a change in the gendered character of the concept of the state. The main objectives of the liberal state were to secure peace and order and to defend the national territory, objectives understood as male responsibilities. Distribution of wealth and advantages were left to the free play of market forces. National responsibilities for the well-being of needy individuals were regarded as minimal. What Hubertine Auclert saw as feminine fields of responsibility – helping individuals to peaceful production and good health – were not matters of concern for the liberal state.

Changes set in with the construction of the early welfare state. From 1894 national legislation began creating a safety net under the economically active part of the population. Insurances against accidents at work and against sickness (1909), and public assistance to trade-union unemployment funds (1906), also signalled a philosophy of caring that might be seen as an expression of what Hubertine Auclert had called "l'état maternel". So too did a law on tuberculosis, enacted in Norway in 1900, in an attempt to curb the then number-one killer disease. There was an interruption during the inter-war years, but in general the idea of a socially active state – the instrumental side of the concept "state" – gradually evolved to cover ever wider fields of need, helping people to peaceful production and good health, until the fully fledged welfare state was born in the decades following World War II.[4]

However, if the instrumental aspect of the state gradually acquired a somewhat maternal face, what the state *was* – the institutional aspect of the early welfare state – remained clearly masculine. Until female suffrage was obtained (a gradual process from 1901 to 1913), the state operated as an exclusively masculine arena. Nor, in this respect, did female suffrage make much change. As late as the 1970s, for example, only a small percentage of MPs were women: in 1945 it was 5 per cent; in 1965, 8 per cent; and, in 1973, still only 16 per cent. An institutionally masculine state, therefore, was capable of demonstrating instrumentally feminine qualities. This suggests the need to beware drawing easy conclusions from an attempt to analyse the state in terms of gender dichotomies.

As with most writing on welfare-state problems, what has been said so far takes it for granted that the producer of welfare was the state. Historians, and (probably even more clearly) social scientists, for long saw the public arena as the one where political actions shaped welfare. It was generally agreed that, in the area of meeting fundamental needs, there had been an historical development from private to public initiative. It was also taken for granted that, in making this division, between the public and the private, it was the public arena which was worthy of scientific investigation.[5]

During the 1980s, however, historians expanded their definition of the public sector, and began to investigate municipal welfare measures. They argued – and rightly so – that early welfare measures, such as old age pensions and mothers' allowance, were, in many instances, inaugurated at the municipal level long before they were enacted nationally. By World War I, welfare measures already consisted of a mixture of national and municipal projects. The "public" was deconstructed into *different* public arenas, and the concept of the welfare municipality was created. Then historians discovered the significance of the private sector. In the early 1980s the importance of voluntary organisations in constructing the early welfare state was emphasised by Anne-Lise Seip.[6] The assumption of a dichotomy between public and private was challenged when, in 1991, Seip suggested a triangular model for understanding changes in how responsibilities for welfare measures were met. In two of the corners of the triangle were the state and the municipality (the public arena) and in the third corner was the voluntary sector (the private arena). According to this model, the welfare state was created in a complicated interaction of initiatives emanating from all three corners. Patterns of collaboration and conflict changed over time, both with regard to the degree of responsibility and the distribution of responsibilities for different activities.[7]

At the same time as Seip's work was appearing, others were applying gender analysis both to the public and the private arenas of welfare production. These historians were analysing women's work in the family and in the household, as well as in public welfare institutions such as hospitals and schools. They also highlighted women's activities within voluntary organisations. Questions were raised about how the consequences of the growth of the welfare state might be understood from a gendered point of view and about how far the creation of the welfare state had depended on gendered contributions. [8]

It was pointed out that the criteria for being included in social security insurances were having waged work and paying a certain contribution oneself. This made the safety net available to men to a much higher degree than to women. Women would mostly be included indirectly, through fathers or husbands; widows and unmarried mothers might, until 1964, be left with no such national protection at all. On the other hand, researchers found that, at the municipal level, lone mothers were in some instances supported economically outside the poor law system. What was also demonstrated was the importance of women's activities through voluntary organisations (and, indeed, through political parties) to make special provisions for mothers, such as maternity clinics; mothers' centres, sometimes with advice on contraception; and eventually, after a long fight by women, a national scheme of child allowances. [9]

The earliest contributions within this paradigm, especially from social scientists analysing the fully developed welfare state, applied theories of patriarchy. The welfare state was seen as yet another form of men's control over women. As welfare was moved from the private to the public arena, so women were moved from a family patriarchy to a public patriarchy, remaining dependent on men, both as clients and as employees of the welfare state. Gender still located power with men, not with women.[10]

Gradually, however, more sophisticated understandings of gender emerged. Helga Hernes in the late 1980s launched the theory of the woman-friendly welfare state, of what she termed "state feminism", where women in politically influential positions would cooperate with less powerful women in creating a woman-friendly state.[11] Such ideas are in line with Hubertine Auclert's *état maternel*. In my view, however, the theories of the Danish researcher, Birthe Siim, which have also been welcomed in Norway, are more interesting. Responding to Helga Hernes, Siim has maintained that the welfare state embodied channels of empowerment for women. Public support might ease women's economic dependence on a husband or father. As clients as well as employees, women had the possibility of organising around common interests, and, by networking, of gaining the support of liberal and social-democratic men. Siim has advanced a theory of the welfare state as a complicated partnership, in which conflicting interests are expressed and in which gender as an analytical category must be seen as interacting with other categories, such as class, profession, and bureaucracy.[12]

These theories, as well as the results of empirical research both in history and social science, challenge both the concept of a clear dichotomy between the public and the private in general and in particular the idea of the public as a masculine, the private as a feminine arena. They dismantle the model of *public man/private woman* and open the way for a multifaceted understanding of the construction of welfare states.

II

With this point of departure, I now turn to an outline of my latest research project. The object is to analyse the fight against tuberculosis from the particular perspective of the town of Bergen between about 1900 and the 1960s.[13] By the latter decade, the fight was won. This theme, in my view, takes us into one of the most fundamental contributions made to the creation of the welfare state. It centres on the elimination of a feared and vicious disease, which both stigmatised and isolated those who suffered from it, and, all too often, resulted in death. Tuberculosis was, through the centuries, a well-known and dreaded disease with very high mortality. During the nineteenth century, it decreased in some areas of Europe, but grew in intensity in others. The fall started in England in the 1830s, but in Scotland not until the 1870s, when tuberculosis receded in many other countries too. Norway and Ireland, however, experienced a steady growth in incidence and mortality, reaching a climax around 1900. The significance of the systematic fight to curb the disease should in no way be played down. It does have to be noted, however, that it started receding before this fight took off.[14]

In my study I apply a gendered model of four care systems, introduced by a political scientist, and originating in a British discussion during the 1970s on the role of voluntary organisations.[15] I shall begin by describing the four systems.

First, the *public care system* consists of initiatives taken by the state and/or by municipal authorities. This system constituted a mainly masculine arena. The law on tuberculosis of 1900 is a central example of public care, involving, as it did, municipal health authorities.[16] The law allowed these authorities to move individuals suffering from tuberculosis, even against their will, from their homes to hospitals and sanatoriums. This was harsh compared to actions taken in most other countries, where compulsory notification of cases of tuberculosis was usually as far as the government went. Denmark introduced compulsory notification in

1905, as was done in parts of the USA about the same time. In Britain it was introduced at the local level, rather than by national legislation, starting with Sheffield in 1903 and then some parts of Scotland in 1906. The same year, the Local Government Board Act for Scotland stated that tuberculosis was an infectious disease within the meaning of the Public Health Act of 1897. This gave local authorities statutory powers to deal with pulmonary tuberculosis along with other infectious diseases and started off local provision of beds for treatment. [17]

The conferring on local health boards of the power to institutionalise people suffering from tuberculosis may be perceived as the politics of a masculine monster state, attempting to protect the healthy against contamination. Analysis of how this strategy was implemented at the local level, however, reveals careful and reluctant application of the law, especially during its first decade. Gradually, a rising percentage of people with tuberculosis were sent to hospitals and sanatoriums – in the late 1930s about half of all new cases, or about seventy to eighty people each year. But it seems that the application of the law had more to do with economic consideration than a real desire to force people to leave their homes, since municipal authorities were reimbursed four-fifths of the expenses incurred in hospitalising people. The sources show no examples of resistance. Although this certainly does not necessarily mean that everybody accepted being removed to a hospital or sanatorium, most probably did not resist being institutionalised because they hoped to be cured and had been told that remaining at home would imperil the health of the rest of the family.

Another early example of the workings of the public care system is the municipal tuberculosis clinic, started in Bergen in 1908, and developed, in the inter-war period, into a fully fledged dispensary. Here people could turn for advice and diagnosis. They would receive home calls from a specially trained nurse who would explain the complicated household procedures needed to avoid contamination. A similar scheme worked in many other countries. Best known in Scotland – indeed world-famous – was the anti-tuberculosis scheme introduced in Edinburgh in 1887 by Sir Robert Philips, which embraced institutional treatment and aftercare. [18]

Second, the *voluntary care system* was made up of those voluntary organisations which dedicated all, or important parts, of their resources to the fight against tuberculosis. The main examples dealt with in my project are the Norwegian Women's Sanitary Organisation, a women-only organisation and the National Association for the Fight against Tuberculosis, which was gender-mixed but headed by medical men and other prominent males. The Bergen branches of these two organisations started their activities in 1900 and 1912 respectively. Their main activities consisted in assisting, by practical and economic measures, families threatened or already infected by tuberculosis. I am looking at these two bodies, as representative of the voluntary care system, from the point of view of cooperation and conflict between them and also from that of co-operation and conflict between both of them and the public care system, comparing what happened locally with developments at the national level.

Third, there is the *informal care system*, which has in the main been neglected in previous research. It comprises the family, friends, and neighbourhood. This system is gender-mixed, but usually regarded in the sources either as a feminine or as an ungendered arena. The material I have lends itself particularly to studies of the gendered responsibilities and activities of the family and of relations between family care and the two other care systems.

The fourth system, the *commercial care system*, operating with a philosophy of profit, has played a minor role in the construction of the Norwegian welfare state generally. This is also the case in the fight against tuberculosis.

Previous research by a social scientist has discussed the problem without gender analysis, and mainly at the national level.[19] My focus is, first, on assessing the importance of gender and, second, on investigating whether new insights may be gained by a closer observation of interactions at the local level. In the second respect, I conclude that many of results of the research at the national level will also obtain – but only in part – at the local level.

Theories based on the idea that there was interaction between the public and the private creators of welfare, applied to Bergen, hold true at the municipal level. Interaction between the public agents (the municipal council) and private agents (the two voluntary organisations) was clear from the start, in 1900; and there were few controversies. The main tendency, though this did not emerge with full force until the 1930s, was for the public authority to take over the most expensive responsibilities. Voluntary associations, however, never ceased to contribute decisively. It is also possible to discern a gendered dichotomy between a powerful public sector and more dependent private sector.

A gendered understanding may also be fruitful when it comes to studying relations between the two voluntary organisations involved. Looking for a moment at the national level, the Norwegian Women's

Sanitary Organisation was established in 1896, and it embarked on the fight against tuberculosis two years later. The National Association against Tuberculosis, established in 1910, followed suit. Previous research, as well as research in progress, into what happened at the national level indicates a rather fierce battle over resources between these two organisations – one an all female organisation, the other gender-mixed but headed by medical men and other prominent males – until they gradually reached an understanding of how to coexist and cooperate without too much conflict.[20]

Conforming to their gendered identities, the leaders of the National Association saw their organisation as the controlling agent, guiding and regulating local activities, and interacting with government and parliament. They preferred to have the Women's Sanitary Organisation work more at the local level with clearly defined tasks. The Women's Sanitary Organisation, however, was headed by strong women, who at the same time were vigorously involved in the fight for the vote. They protested against this division of labour. Refusing to give up their independent organisational status, they fought successfully for public resources to be divided equally between the two organisations, and insisted on keeping control of their own local branches.

Although the gender dimension is very clear in this picture, it has not been highlighted until very recently. Neither has emphasis been placed on the historical context of the early twentieth century in explaining the conditions in which cooperative relations had to be established. The period was marked by fierce discussions over female suffrage and over women's access to certain professions, as well as by controversies within the welfare professions such as doctors and nurses. Gender conflicts in the political public sphere, as well as within the world of health professions, provided important elements in the background to the controversies between the two organisations. It is clearly necessary to deconstruct the private agencies (the voluntary organisations) into their masculine and feminine elements if we are to grasp this complicated picture at the national level as well.

At the local level, which is where my own research project comes in, it seems at first sight that, from 1912, the National Association, headed by a doctor, took over and dominated activities up to then initiated and carried on by the local Women's Sanitary Organisation. In Bergen, the female voluntary association seemed quickly to give up leadership to the male association. A closer look, however, reveals that very close cooperation between medical men and the local Women's Sanitary Organisation was not new; it had been the rule from the very beginning. Further, the doctor heading the local branch of the National Association was a woman. She had also been, and continued to be, head of the Women's Sanitary Organisation. At the local level, to a great degree, the same people worked within both organisations. Finally, the activities started by the Women's Sanitary Organisation were continued under the cloak of the National Association, while the Women's Sanitary Organisation started new activities against tuberculosis.

What therefore happened at the local level – and this was different from the national situation – may be understood as the Women's Sanitary Organisation absorbing the National Association, broadening its field of action, and continuing earlier cooperation with the medical profession, as well as with local politicians. This strategy seemed as successful as the head-on-collision politics occurring at the national level.

These findings should warn us against easy conclusions as to the gendered character of organisations, as well as of strategies. They also show the importance of researching beyond the institutional level, of studying individual actors, and of mapping their participation in different arenas. The linking peoples between the public and the voluntary care systems were often medical men (and a few medical women), which highlights the importance of the concept "profession" as well as of "gender".

This also indicates, it need hardly be said, that class was decisive in determining who was involved in the fight against tuberculosis. The researcher's expectation that middle-class women and men would be found at the forefront proved right. However, in 1911, working-class women formed their own voluntary association, the Working Class Women's Nursing and Tuberculosis Organisation. They worked in exactly the same way as middle-class women within the Sanitary Organisation, funding their activities through bazaars, etc., and focusing on offering children and housewives opportunities of short stays in healthy surroundings during the summer period. Further research might show whether the Bergen Working Class Women's Nursing and Tuberculosis Organisation was an exception that proves the rule of middle-class dominance within the voluntary care system or if working-class women also organised elsewhere for this, or any similar, purpose.

Research so far has concentrated exclusively on the public and/or the voluntary care systems. It will, however, be important, if possible, to include the *informal care system* and to keep the *commercial care system* in mind. Returning to Seip's triangular model, and having categorised the voluntary, the informal, and the commercial care systems as the component parts of the private sphere, one might also say that the third corner of the triangular model needs to be split into three groups of actors: voluntary organisations, the family, and commercial groups. I concentrate here on the informal care system, looking at the home and the family as active producers of welfare. I argue that, without looking into the activities in the homes, a full understanding of the fight against tuberculosis – and of the production of welfare at large – is impossible.

It should be remembered that despite the growth of sanatoriums, health homes, and hospitals, the home was where most of those suffering from tuberculosis spent their many years as patients. There are abundant sources which point to the importance of the home front in this battle. Annual reports from the municipal health board meticulously chart the housing problems of families where one or more members were infected with tuberculosis. Small unhealthy flats dominated the picture. Between 1916 and 1920, more than half of the people registered in Bergen as suffering from tuberculosis shared their bed with another person. As late as the years 1936 to 1940, this was still the case for one in four. In such circumstances, complying with the directions given by the medical experts must have been a great problem. Doctors admonished housewives to maintain a very high level of cleanliness; to produce nourishing food; and to supply warm and clean clothes, bedclothes, etc. Pages and pages were written giving housewives detailed instructions – for instance on how to wash bedclothes and destroy contaminated expectorations, not to speak of how to fight the evil habit of spitting (incidentally a predominantly male habit). As late as 1931, housewives' work was praised by doctors as "work done without much ado and little noticed ... but of the utmost importance when it comes to curbing tuberculosis".[21] It was, however, medical expertise from the late 1930s on – in the form of x-rays, Pirquet-tests, and finally, in the 1940s BCG-vaccination – which dealt the *coup de grâce* to tuberculosis. But by then mortality rates had been reduced to less than a quarter of the level at the turn of the century and morbidity rates had been more than halved. The work of countless housewives was an important, but forgotten, contribution to this success.

Focusing on women's contributions to welfare through their daily work in the home, however, should not make us forget the other side of the gender dimension. The possibilities of achieving good results from this work were also determined by what resources the provider could muster. The masculine role of providing for the family was decisive for the class aspect of private welfare. A husband's income would set the limits within which the housewife had to work. Dismantling the walls of

silence surrounding women's work in the home and family is as necessary to a full understanding of the construction of the early welfare state,
as is the deconstruction of the private care system into different, and
sometimes competing, voluntary organisations.

Applying gender analysis to the construction of the early welfare state,
then, highlights not only the gendered meaning of the different care systems, and the uneven distribution of power within these systems, it also
warns against making too sharp a dichotomy between the public and the
voluntary care system, and between those two systems and the informal
care system. The main objective of the early fight against tuberculosis
was to strengthen the informal care system. The provision of information
to, and the education of, individuals – especially housewives – so that
they understood the importance of cleanliness and antiseptic habits,
coupled with some economic assistance to needy families, were important means to this end. And they were the tasks undertaken especially by
voluntary associations, though with the support of public authorities.
Both voluntary organisations and public authorities engaged in establishing and running hospitals, sanitariums for people suffering from
tuberculosis. All these measures may be seen as an expression of Hubertine Auclert's *état maternel*, helping individuals to good health.

It is also important to note that some people acted *at one moment* as representatives of the public care system, *at another* as representatives of
voluntary organisations. And some simultaneously took their part of the
burden of the informal care system. There were, therefore, obvious link-
ages between the three systems. Professional people, doctors certainly
but also nurses, are time and time again to be found in linkage positions.

III

The roots of the welfare state cannot be seen as a clear-cut change from a
liberal monster state to a maternal welfare state. The early manifestations
of the welfare state were neither yet another expression of patriarchal
power over women nor the start of a woman-friendly state. Rather, they
were the product of a complicated partnership, involving both conflicts
and cooperation between different care systems. Although, in the final
analysis, the decisive power, in the form of economic strength as well as
medical expertise, was represented by the public care system, the feminine informal care system was the prime arena in which disease was com-
batted. The fact that the public and the voluntary systems have left much
more ample source material should not blind the historian to the need to

highlight the informal care system in order to gain a full understanding of the roots of the welfare state. Death rates as well as rates of incidence were seriously reduced before the public care system, with its increased medical expertise and higher standards of living, was able to finally conquer the fight against tuberculosis in the post-war years. Without diminishing the importance of the public care system, a reappraisal of the informal care system is therefore needed.

The final defeat of tuberculosis came from the public care system when, from the 1940s on, mass screenings and vaccinations put an end to the threatening disease. By the time that end came, around 1960, the contributions of the informal as well as of the voluntary care system were all but forgotten. The private "mothers" of the welfare state were eclipsed, the public fathers prevailed. But the liberal monster state had vanished.

However, for all the importance attached to the informal care system, it should not be forgotten that the need for informal care, in the form of women's unwaged work in the home, was one of many obstacles to women's self-determination and to gender equality. Neither should the historian forget that voluntary organisations, be they women's organisations or organisations of medical men, often demonstrated a condescending attitude to clients, highlighting class hierarchies. Finally, the concept of public welfare as a right, not as a stigmatising last resort, has, and with reason, been seen as a development into a better, more just, and equal society. The strengthening of the public care system was, therefore, in the long run, a *sine qua non* for what has been termed social citizenship, and for opening the public arena to women. Without the comprehensive public care system of the fully fledged welfare state, the gendered dichotomy of the public and private would have been much sharper.

From the case I have been describing here, it can be shown how a gendered approach to the history of welfare states – while it, by itself, does not explain everything, and certainly must be an aid to rather than a substitute for empirical research – can add to our understanding in important ways. The lessons that can be learned, it is also worth saying, may have practical as well as academic implications, since, during the past few years, tuberculosis has again showed its ugly face in Bergen and in other urban centres; and this time, the resistance of the bacilli to medical treatment has made it a new threat.

NOTES

1. Hubertine Auclert, "Programme electoral des femmes", in *La Citoyenne*, August 1885, cited from Seth Coven and Sonya Michel, "Womenly duties, maternalist politics and the origins of welfare states in France, Germany, Great Britain and the United States, 1880–1920", *American Historical Review*, 95, 4 (October 1990), p. 1077.
2. For a further working-through of the ideas about the state presented in this chapter, see Ida Blom, "Refleksjoner over kjønn og stat", in Anne-Hilde Nagel (ed.), K *Kjønn og verferdsstat* (Bergen, 1998), pp. 24–49.
3. Leonore Davidoff, *Worlds Between: historical perspectives on gender and class* (Cambridge, 1995), pp. 227–264.
4. For a brief account of Norwegian history (without a gender perspective), see Rolf Danielsen et al., *Norway: a history from the Vikings to our own times* (Oslo, 1995).
5. Eirinn Larsen, "Gender and the Welfare State: maternalism – a new historical concept?", unpublished cand. philol. thesis, Department of History, University of Bergen, spring 1996; Eirinn Larsen, "The American introduction of 'maternalism' as a historical concept", in *NORA, Nordic Journal of Women's Studies*, vol. 5, no. 1 (1997), pp. 14–25.
6. Anne-Hilde Nagel (ed.), *Velferdskommunen: kommunenes rolle i utviklingen av velferdsstaten* (Bergen, 1991); Anne-Lise Seip, *Sosialhelfstaten blir til Norsk sosialpolitikk 1740–1920* (Oslo, 1983), p. 12.
7. Anne-Lise Seip, "Velferdskommunen og velferdstrekanten – et tilbakeblikk", in Nagel, *Velferdskommunen*, pp. 24–42.
8. Larsen, "Gender and the welfare state".
9. See for instance Harriet Holter (ed.), *Patriarchy in a Welfare Society* (1984); Ida Blom, *Barnebegrensning – svnd eller sunn fornuft?* (Bergen, 1980); Anne-Lise Seip and Hilde Ibsen, "Family welfare, which policy? Norway's road to child allowances", in Gisela Bock and Pat Thane (eds), *Maternity and Gender Policies: women and the rise of the European welfare states 1880s – 1950s* (London and New York, 1991), pp. 40–65; Ida Blom, "Widowhood: from the Poor Law society to the welfare society – the case of Norway, 1875–1964", *Journal of Women's History*, vol. 4, no. 2 (autumn 1992), pp. 50–81; Vind Bjornson and Elisabeth Haavet, *Langsomt ble landet et velferdssamfunn* (Oslo, 1996), pp. 203–228.
10. Helga Maria Hernes, *Staten: kvinner ingen adgang?* Universitetsforlaget (1982); Holter, *Patriarchy*.
11. Helga Maria Hernes, *Welfare States and Woman Power: essays in state feminism* (Oslo, 1987).
12. Birthe Siim, "Towards a feminist rethinking of the welfare state", in Kathleen B. Jones and Anna G. Jonasdottir (eds), *The Political Interests of Gender: developing theory and research with a feminist face* (SAGE Publications, 1988),

pp. 160–187; Birthe Siim, "The gendered Scandinavian welfare states: the interplay between women's roles as mothers, workers and citizens in Denmark", in Jane Lewis (ed.), *Women and Social Policies in Europe* (Hants, 1993), pp. 25–48.

13. [Ida Blom writes (6 April 1998): "As for reporting new findings from my project – which in January this year has resulted in a small book – I could write pages. But I do not think it necessary, since the main *idea* of this paper has not been changed by the fascinating research I have been doing since we met in Aberdeen...." Editors' note.] See Ida Blom, *Tre omsorgssystemer I kampen mot tuberkulose, 1900–1960* (Bergen, 1998).

14. F. B. Smith, *The Retreat of Tuberculosis*, Oxford, 1988, pp. 4 and 220–237.

15. Per Arne Hestetun and Gunnar Onarheim, "Velferdsekspansjon og organisasjonsendring: organisasjonar og staten I kamp mot tuberkulosen", in Stein Kuhnle and Per Stelle (eds), *Frivillig Organisert Velferd – Alternativ til Offentlig?* (Alma Mater forlag, Bergen, 1990), pp. 29–49; *The Future of Voluntary Organisations: report of the Wolfenden committee* (Croom Helm, 1978), pp. 15–30.

16. The following is based on Ida Blom, *Feberens Vilde Rose: kampen mit tiberkulose I Bergen, 1900–1960* (work in progress).

17. Linda Bryder, *Below the Magic Mountain: a social history of tuberculosis in twentieth-century Britain* (Oxford, 1988), pp. 29 and 42.

18. Bryder, *Below the Magic Mountain*, pp. 74 and 91.

19. Hestetun and Onarheim, "Velderdsekspansjon og organisasjonsendring". This article contains a summary of Hestetun's unpublished master's thesis, Department of Comparative Politics, University of Bergen, 1985.

20. Sofie Rogstad, "Kampen iom eiendomsretten til tiberkulosesaken. Om å søke næring av tæring", *Historisk tidskrift*, no. 1 (1997), pp. 87–116; Hestetun and Onarheim, "Velferdsekpansjon og organisasjonsendring".

21. Theodor Frølich, *Meddelelser fra Nationalforeningen for Folkehelsen* (1931).

7

Literature and history: women and the city in early twentieth-century Scottish fiction

Margery Palmer McCulloch

Historians *have traditionally been wary* of putting too much faith in literature and the arts as primary source material. And probably justifiably so. The artist inevitably has a dual agenda in which formal, aesthetic considerations balance content, and can in the end transform that content or modify our perception of it. Art is not the actuality of life however much it may spring from the experiences of life.

On the other hand, when we come to the question of women's history we find that we are entering an area of "uncharted lives".[1] So much information relating to women's lives has not been publicly documented in a "proper" manner that we find ourselves of necessity researching not only personal diaries, letters, and other autobiographical writings, but also artistic sources such as paintings, poetry, and – especially – fiction by women authors. This chapter will therefore look at the experience of Scottish women in the city in the early years of the twentieth century as it is presented in fiction by women authors writing in the 1920s and 1930s.

In addition, it will make reference to the findings of Liz Heron, a Scottish writer now domiciled in London, whose *Streets of Desire*, an anthology of writing about the city by twentieth-century English, American, and European women, was published by Virago in 1993.

In passing, I would mention that when we met at a graduate summer school at Université Stendhal, Grenoble, in 1995, Liz Heron told me that she had not included any excerpts from Scottish women writers in her anthology, firstly, because she did not find that Glasgow, the largest city in Scotland, functioned as a metropolis in the way that London, New York, and Paris did and, secondly, because she could not find Scottish women writers who wrote about the city in a way comparable to English, American and European authors. Recent research into the work of Scottish women writers from the inter-war period, however, has demonstrated that there *are* Scottish female writers who can take their place on Heron's streets of desire. In particular, my own investigations for *A History of Scottish Women's Writing* (1997) demonstrate a similarity between the freedoms experienced in the cities of Europe and America by the women in the Heron anthology and those experienced by women in early twentieth-century Scottish fiction.[2] And although one could not claim Glasgow as a true metropolis, my investigations suggest that a city such as Glasgow can appear to be a "local metropolis" for the immigrants from small towns and the countryside who flock to it, so that it functions for them in a way not dissimilar to that of Paris or New York or London in relation to intellectual and artistic groups of international emigrés.

The city experience was central in early twentieth-century modernism. In Scotland, however, while the literary Scottish Renaissance movement – initiated in the immediate post-1918 period by the poet Hugh Mac-Diarmid – shared some of the characteristics of European modernism, there were also significant differences. As with modernism generally, the Scottish Renaissance was male-dominated. There was little direct involvement in it by the women writers who were working contemporaneously alongside it and who were therefore more readily marginalised and forgotten – falling victim to what Germaine Greer has called "the phenomenon of the transience of female literary fame".[3] Unlike modernism generally, however, the male Scottish Renaissance, although intellectually motivated, took its impulse not from city life but from the experiences of writers whose formative years were spent in rural, small-town, or sea-coast and island areas. In the years immediately before and after World War I, Glasgow was still perceived as the "second city of the empire", and was in addition exhibiting all the after-effects of industrialisation. Despite its intellectuality and modernistic formal method, Mac-Diarmid's *A Drunk Man Looks at the Thistle*, published in 1926, is rooted in the imagery and language of his Borders childhood and of the ballads and traditional Scottish culture. Glasgow and the urban scene have no part in the Drunk Man's quest for regeneration. Edwin Muir's poetry, furthermore, looks towards Orkney as an ideal community, while Neil M. Gunn and Lewis Grassic Gibbon set their most successful fiction in the Highland context of the crofting and fishing villages of Caithness and in the Mearns farming country of north-eastern Scotland. While the city experience in the early twentieth century was becoming the dominant experience for an increasing number of Scots, it did not feature to any extent in the writings of the foremost male authors of the time. And this is where my neglected women writers of the 1920s and 1930s enter the scene.

Although there are many women writers from this period whose work is now being rediscovered and reassessed, my interest here is limited to four authors who set their fictions in the city: Catherine Carswell, Dot Allan, Catherine Gavin, and Mary Cleland. The most significant and stylistically most sophisticated of these writers is Catherine Carswell, whose first novel *Open the Door!* won the Melrose prize for fiction when it was published in 1920, but was described somewhat patronisingly by MacDiarmid (in his *Contemporary Scottish Studies*) as "a deft but superficial study in personalities".[4] Carswell followed *Open the Door!* with *The Camomile* in 1922, but after a time both novels went out of print and were forgotten until the American-inspired feminist initiative to recover and re-present neglected women authors resulted in their being reprinted by Virago in the mid-1980s.[5]

Catherine Carswell's was a genuinely new voice in Scottish fiction, superseding both the rural and Highland settings of much nineteenth-century writing, and the religious conflicts, Jacobite scenarios and supernatural resonances which so often provided a central theme in that fiction. In addition, her two novels were published *before* MacDiarmid's Scots-language lyrics and *A Drunk Man Looks at the Thistle* launched the literary revival. In herself, therefore, Carswell heralded a renaissance with a different agenda. Carswell's principal setting is middle-class Glasgow in the pre-1914 period – the West-End Glasgow of the art school and university, of Kelvingrove Park and the Park Circus terraces, of Sauchiehall Street and Renfrew Street and the steep streets which link them. To Joanna, heroine of *Open the Door!*, the South Side, over the river, is alien territory – as, indeed, it still is for many West Enders and Northerners in the city today. And equally alien for Joanna are the living patterns of the South-Side dwellers, the well-off shopkeepers and trades-people who make their money from commerce in the city, as opposed to the professional classes of the West End.

What is strikingly new about Carswell's depiction of the city is the sense of at-one-ness, at-home-ness one finds in it, and the ease with which she takes up the city theme. There is no modernist angst here in relation to a metropolis which can be as alienating and disorientating as it can be intellectually and imaginatively stimulating. In this urban con-geniality, *Open the Door!* reminds one of Virginia Woolf's *Mrs Dalloway* (1925), where Clarissa Dalloway wears the city like one of her fashionable evening gowns as she progresses through Westminster to order flowers for her party, noticing with appreciation every detail of the city life around her. Westminster is Clarissa's place just as West-End Glasgow is Joanna's.

This sense of female at-one-ness with the city is one of the principal findings in Liz Heron's *Streets of Desire*, which includes excerpts from Woolf's *Dalloway* novel, and from Dorothy Richardson's *Pilgrimage* – whose heroine talks of "the lovely, strange, unconscious life of London" (*SD*, p. 1). The metropolis of Paris also was both a real city and a city of the imagination for early twentieth-century women writers and artists – many of them expatriate Americans. Djuna Barnes of Greenwich Village, and a writer much admired by T. S. Eliot, lived there, as did Gertrude Stein and Sylvia Beach, who published James Joyce's *Ulysses* in 1922. The Norwegian painter and novelist Cora Sandel, excerpts from whose auto-biographical novel *Alberta and Freedom* are included in the Heron antho-logy, lived in Paris both before and after 1914 and depicted in her fiction the freedom women artists like herself found there. For many women, in reality and in fiction, the city provided a stage where they could be both anonymous and visible, where they could watch themselves in the glass of the shop windows as they walked down the streets, creating for them-selves a new identity. It was an identity unhampered by the gaze of local acquaintances who had already allotted them a fixed, unchangeable role within a fixed set of possibilities. "I'm free – I've got free – nothing can ever alter that", Miriam, the heroine of *Pilgrimage,* repeats to herself as she sits by the fire in a London coffee house:

> A strength was piling up within her. She would go out unregret-fully at closing time and up through wonderful unknown streets, not her own streets, till she found Holborn and then up and round through the squares (*SD*, p. 43).

To stress this celebration of freedom is not to say that the sense of belonging experienced in the city by these authors and their fictional heroines was without its down side. Cora Sandel's artist heroines experience
poverty and unsatisfactory living conditions as well as the freedom to
create new selves. In Woolf's *Mrs Dalloway*, Clarissa's enjoyment of the
city scene and her sense that even beyond death her spirit would survive
in the flow of life in the London streets are opposed by her feeling of
being trapped by her *place* in that city life, despite her privileged social
position. For Clarissa, however, this relates to her awareness of the loss of
her own individual identity as a woman – she is now not "Clarissa" but
"Mrs Richard Dalloway", wife of a member of Parliament and exquisite
hostess to his fellow members and friends. Her memories bring to us her
sense of loss, as she recollects the girl she once was and the feelings she
had as that girl. Despite this subtext, which has little to do with the city
experience *per se*, it is the sense of belonging in the city which predomin-
ates in Woolf's text.

Returning to the Scottish context, Catherine Carswell's ease in her depiction of the city scene in *Open the Door!* is tempered by her communication of the impatience felt by her heroine Joanna for the familiar city of
Glasgow. And it is here, perhaps, that Liz Heron's comment about Glasgow not being a metropolis becomes relevant. For Joanna is not intellectually at ease with Glasgow. Having grown up in the upper social strata
of the city, she finds Glasgow stifling, almost like a village or small town
in the way that family and family friends intrude into her life and try to
involve her in her mother's religious concerns. Joanna's first attempt to
flee is through her impetuous marriage with the Italian, Mario, but when
she returns to Glasgow after her husband's unexpected death, she again
finds that this Scottish city cannot satisfy her. Her sense of the city as a
parochial cultural milieu is endorsed by her new lover, the painter Louis
Pender – a visiting artist from London modelled on Maurice Greiffen-
hagen, who came to Glasgow School of Art in 1906 as professor of the life
class and with whom Carswell had a passionate love affair. Glasgow is
no cultural metropolis to the southerner Louis: "A month ago he would
not have believed it possible to find himself so charmed in this dismal
hole of a place called Glasgow".

> And here am I [he tells Joanna], as bucked as if I were a pavement
> artist at being rather reluctantly asked to add my daub to the
> other daubs in that ghastly chocolate-coloured building you
> Glasgow people are so proud of (*OD*, p. 203).

His reference is to the City Chambers, the dominant building in Glasgow's central George Square, and as she answers him Joanna

remembered the rich and splendid vision it had been to her as a child when her father had taken them all to receptions up its alabaster staircase (*OD*, p. 207).

Here as elsewhere in the novel, Joanna's – and perhaps her author's – responses to her home city are ambivalent. Because she is of the city herself, having its life as a formative part of her growth to adulthood, Glasgow cannot provide a new beginning for Joanna, and having trained as a designer she follows her lover to London, a true metropolis.

Carswell's heroine Ellen in *The Camomile* is a musician who, like her author, has studied at the Frankfurt conservatoire. She has ambitions to be a writer and similarly finds herself frustrated by Glasgow – with its rigid religious and social mores and what she believes to be its predilection for the less than first-rate in culture. She had gone to Frankfurt "because I loved all the arts and had to get away from Glasgow" (*C*, p. 13). Although Ellen recognises her "*hübsches Talent*" for the small musical talent it is, this love of the arts and the need to get away from what is perceived as the parochial home city is an impulse perhaps not so different from that which drove artists and intellectuals from European and American cities into the Paris of the late nineteenth and early twentieth centuries. For Ellen, and the earlier Joanna Glasgow, despite being a very large city, is also an intensely personal milieu where neither can escape sufficiently to be herself. Ellen writes to her London friend, Ruby, in terms which relate to the experiences of women in the Heron anthology:

How splendid it must be in London where it is really quite unlikely, when you go out, that you will meet any one you know! To be able to walk in the crowded street, secure in the knowledge that you need have no companion but your own thrilling thoughts! I'm sure I should welcome that, even if just at first I sometimes missed the other from habit (*C*, p. 20).

For the women represented in these early-twentieth-century novels, Scottish and non-Scottish, one of the most significant freedoms offered by the city is sexual freedom. The portrayal of women in Scottish fiction by male authors has throughout the centuries been stereotypical, even archetypal in nature, and the male writers of the early-twentieth-century renaissance did not prove to be an exception in this regard. Scottish fictional heroines have tended to be colourless, but good, god-fearing and dutiful. The Victorian stereotype of the "Angel in the House" and the opposition of madonna and magdalen are still to be found, for example, in the Highland novels of Neil M. Gunn. In *The Shadow*, the heroine and her aunt are said to be "sitting at the bottom of the well of the world ... with the something that is missing in our hearts";[6] while Gunn's characters who have city connections are portrayed negatively – as promiscuous and disruptive of local values. It has recently been argued by a male scholar that Lewis Grassic Gibbon has given a feminist representation of Chris Guthrie in his 1932 novel *Sunset Song*, on the grounds that he has portrayed her as a sexually active young woman, rejoicing in her own sexuality.[7] While this is to a certain extent true, Chris Guthrie is also deeply identified with the land in *Sunset Song* – in particular with her sense of belonging to the land, and with her sense of the peasant people who have lived and worked that land throughout the ages. It might be argued that Chris, although she is given personalised qualities, is less a sexually active *modern* woman than an archetypal earth-goddess, a fertility symbol in a dying agrarian way of life.

Catherine Carswell's novels of the early 1920s depart from this stereotype, or archetype, in relation to the representation of women. Joanna in *Open the Door!* is recognisably a modern woman, a sexual being depicted from within female experience. Her first stirrings of sexuality are experienced – felt but not understood – in relation to an adult cousin as she watches him skin a chaffinch for stuffing at the family's holiday home in Perthshire. Later as a young adult in Glasgow, Joanna is the one to take the initiative with her first boyfriend, Bob. Female sexuality is openly presented by Carswell, although, when she embarks on her first attempt to flee her home with the Italian Mario, Joanna is aware that nothing in her upbringing has prepared her for what marriage entails. On her honeymoon, she ponders her new relationship and feelings as she ascends with Mario in the funicular to Vallombrosa:

> But was it right? Did all wives feel and behave like this? She thought of her mother, of Mrs Boyd, of Aunt Georgina, of the teaching and the traditions on which she had been nourished. Which was right – those traditions or this abandonment? It seemed impossible that both could be right, yet could anything be wrong which gave such release, such harmony with the golden world and the violet heavens?... She no longer jarred on herself (*OD*, p. 109).

At this point in the novel it is not the city, but the exotic foreign landscape and the foreign husband which are associated with Joanna's sense of sexual freedom. Nonetheless, this is an entirely new depiction of a city-bred woman in the Scottish novel, told from the inside. And it is told in a way which makes one aware of the changes which were taking place in the lives of women in the early years of the century, changes which could take place more readily in the city environment. For it was that environment with its increased opportunities for social contact which had enabled Joanna to meet the foreign Mario, a man from outside her usual circle of family and friends, and to marry and to leave for Italy with him.

After Mario's death, Joanna eventually finds that the anonymity offered by the metropolis of London gives her greater freedom to pursue her second sexual relationship, with the English painter Louis. But for the heroines of other Scottish city-based novels of the 1920s and 1930s, Glasgow itself offers the possibility of sexual freedom. In Dot Allan's *Makeshift*, published in 1928 and set in the period immediately after World War I, the heroine Jacqueline goes from a small country town to work as a typist in a city office. Like some of the heroines in Liz Heron's *Streets of Desire*, she encounters the sexual dangers as well as the freedoms awaiting the innocent in the city. She eventually forms a relationship with a well-off and much-travelled explorer, the kind of man who would have been outside her social circle and therefore beyond the bounds of a possible marriage relationship in her small country town. But before she meets him she has to fight off the unwanted attentions of her male employer, who thinks he can own her body as well as her typing skills. There is a similar scenario in Catherine Gavin's *Clyde Valley*, published ten years later in 1938. These ten years have made a difference, however, in that the later heroine, Lenny, comes to the city from her crofting home in the Clyde valley to study at Glasgow University. She is an ambitious girl and her degree leads to a job as personal assistant in a large Glasgow company and to her meeting and falling in love with the politician owner of the company, a married man. Lenny therefore moves in more elevated circles that Dot Allan's Jacqueline, but again the city offers her the freedom to make relationships with men far above her in status – relationships which she could not hope to have had, and remain respectable, in her home village. Yet, Lenny differs from many of the more sexually sophisticated "new women" in *Streets of Desire* in that she fights hard with herself to hold on to her virtue. And just at the point where she has cast off her scruples about living with her employer, her author, somewhat melodramatically, contrives an accident for her, followed by the death of her prospective lover.

Whether or not this kind of plot development can be put down to the continuing influence of the Scottish religious tradition, one notices that these novels of freedom in the city by Scottish women writers are still moral novels – despite their counter-narrative attributes. They may question stultified conventions and break the sexual rules, as Carswell's heroines most clearly do, but they seek to reconstruct a moral context of their own. The three sections of Carswell's *Open the Door!* have, as epigraphs, quotations from the Bible with a text of "making things new". Carswell's heroine in *The Camomile*, Ellen, has no patience with the denial of sexuality evident in a woman-friend's attitude to marriage, finding this a false, life-destroying approach to a relationship. She has no patience either with her own fiancé's insistence on the conventional set period of engagement before marriage – even when he is called back unexpectedly to his Indian civil service post, and so must leave her behind to prepare for a wedding some months ahead. Ellen questions the hypocrisy of social conventions, including the taboo on sexual relations before marriage; she tries to persuade her fiancé that they can find a more honest and satisfying way to begin their life together. These Scottish heroines do not appear to pursue sexual freedom for its own sake, as we find in some of the scenarios in *Streets of Desire*. Nor is marriage necessarily cast aside. Even for Carswell's Joanna, sexual freedom eventually leads to marriage – with a man she has known from her early Glasgow days – when she finds her role as mistress increasingly empty. Marriage is a problem in these novels only when society insists on it as the sole route to maturity and identity for a woman.

It is interesting that this insistence on the domestic role is most uncompromising in the attitudes of the mothers or mother-substitutes in the novels. In Mary Cleland's 1923 novel *The Sure Traveller*, set in the middle-class South Side at the turn of the century, the mother refuses even to consider the possibility of her daughter's going to university, despite her intellectual achievements at an English boarding school. Her view is that "the men don't like college-bred women for wives, and if you got left later on, you'd be blaming me in your heart" (*ST*, p. 19). The uncle of Jacqueline in *Makeshift* similarly urges marriage on her because "there's too many women wanting homes of their own these days" (*M*, p. 189). These novels also demonstrate that fears about a life without marriage in a society where marriage is the designated role for a woman are not fears without foundation. *Makeshift* depicts Jacqueline visiting the bedsitter of a middle-aged typist colleague, who has an alcohol-dependency problem and has become ill. Jacqueline's male companion cannot hide his distaste:

"'God!' he said, 'What a hole! the typical home of the surplus woman'" (*M*, p. 132). Here we are reminded that for many women in the aftermath of World War I, there was no possibility of the traditional domestic role, even if they wanted to pursue it. The potential husbands were no longer there. They were indeed "surplus women".

One of the principal achievements of these city novels by Scottish women writers, then, is that, written as they are from a female perspective and thus from an insider's point of view, they are able to portray with understanding the attitudes and actions of both convention breakers and of those women who wish to hold to the old ways, despite the fact that they themselves have been damaged by them. Catherine's mother in *The Sure Traveller* has been married for her father's business connection, not for love; Joanna's mother, Juley, in *Open the Door!* – who is an interesting female study in herself – has never been fulfilled sexually, her religious husband having suppressed his emotions and she herself having been conditioned to be ashamed of her passionate feelings. In Carswell's fiction we have several spinster aunts and visiting female acquaintances who have become, like Joanna's mother, addicted to religion and church-going – without, however, having the satisfaction of playing a recognised public or professional role in that religious sphere. Unlike the Roman Catholic church, with its female religious orders, the Scottish Presbyterian tradition could not at that time offer women a public role. Within these novels, therefore, what is developed is not only the story-line detail of their heroines' lives but also a wider discourse about the roles open to women in society and about the distortions and unhappiness caused by the lack of a freer, more equal social structure in relation to gender.

In addition to the opportunities offered by the city for sexual freedom, there is depicted the related economic freedom made possible through work opportunities in the city. Mary Cleland's middle-class Glasgow heroine is not allowed by her parents to take up paid work of any kind. Carswell's and Dot Allan's heroines, however, train for work – as does the later Lenny in Catherine Gavin's *Clyde Valley*. All manage to support themselves. Carswell's Joanna and her sister Georgie grow to adulthhood in the period before the outbreak of World War I, and are encouraged by their mother to train for employment. Since her husband has died leaving only a small inheritance for his children, she is concerned that her daughters should be able to support themselves if necessary. In this respect, if not in others, Juley is a forward-looking mother. It is interesting to note, however, that both sisters train for artistic careers, something considered suitable for young women of their time and social status.

They do not, like the lower-class Jacqueline in *Makeshift*, go to work as typists in offices. Georgie goes abroad to study music, but gives it up for marriage to an up-and-coming Jewish member of Parliament when she realises that her talent will not take her to the top of the musical profession. It is, however, that musical profession and residence in the metropolis of London which opens up the possibility of an elevated marriage. Joanna studies at Glasgow School of Art, but she trains as a designer, not a painter like her lover Louis, and she eventually makes a living as a fashion designer, sketching the costumes of theatre-goers in London.

For all her innovative qualities in other respects, Carswell does not here break the stereotype of the woman in the *minor* or performing art forms. Nor does she succeed in giving a convincing picture of Joanna in the world of work in her novel. This is especially the case when the setting moves to London where we are expected to believe that Joanna supports herself through selling her designs and sketches. We never see her, however, interacting with design studios or magazine editors or with other aspects of the world of work. The focus remains on her affair with her lover and on the domestic details of her flat and neighbours, although descriptions of the London street scene do play their part in establishing an atmosphere of metropolitan anonymity and freedom of movement. Carswell did support herself and a young child as a journalist in both Glasgow and London – indeed she was dismissed by the *Glasgow Herald* for slipping a review of D. H. Lawrence's *The Rainbow* into the paper without the knowledge of the literary editor – so she must have had both factual knowledge and experience of the world of work. For whatever reason, however, the plot of *Open the Door!* banishes this world to the periphery of the action, making the novel a not particularly useful source of information in that area.

Another surprising absence in all these Scottish authors, given their feminist perspectives and the time-setting of the plots, is the suffrage movement. I cannot explain this, and am intrigued by it. Nor, in Carswell, is there any mention of World War I, although part at least of Joanna's young adulthood must have been contemporaneous with this event.

Work experience is much more convincingly handled in Dot Allan's *Makeshift* and in Catherine Gavin's *Clyde Valley*. In *Makeshift* Allan presents both the negative and positive sides of economic freedom through work in the city. Jacqueline, employed as a typist in a Glasgow office, finds all too soon that far from starting out on a career with prospects, "she was a cog in the wheel of commerce that whirs unceasingly from the granite steeps of Maryhill to the many-storied buildings that cluster round the Clyde" (*M*, p. 32). For a woman, work is seen merely as a way of putting in time until marriage.

One occupation which recurs in these novels, and one which causes the greatest conflict between women characters and their families and acquaintances, is that of being a writer. This is an interesting piece of social evidence in relation to the increase in female authorship which took place in the post-1918 period. As mentioned earlier, all too many of these novels of the 1920s and 1930s, although demonstrating the new higher profile of women authors at that time, fell out of print, and were forgotten as the years passed. They had the proverbial butterfly existence, being superseded by other equally short-lived texts, so that a female tradition of writing, with attendant support systems, was difficult to establish. In addition, the conflicts depicted in the novels over the ambition to be a writer demonstrate how hard it must have been for the authors themselves to pursue their chosen vocations. The classic text in this area is, of course, Virginia Woolf's *A Room of One's Own* (1929), where she insists that a woman who has an ambition to be a writer needs two things: a room of her own and £500 a year. Even before Woolf's book was published, Catherine Carswell had begun the practice of renting a room which she kept secret from family and friends, so that she could have privacy to write. This is a policy followed also by Ellen in *The Camomile*, who is not so successful, however, in keeping her working place secret. In addition, Ellen has to fight against the knowledge that her mother had become insane apparently through her struggles to be a writer – a fact of which her family never ceases to remind her. The stigma of "insanity" has often been levelled by a patriarchal society against "idiosyncratic" women who want to write. When Ellen prepares to go to India with her fiancé, Duncan, she is disturbed by his hostility to her writing ambitions, despite her proven success. He warns her not "to speak of anything abstract or 'superior' or of 'high-brow works of art'" in front of his Anglo-Indian colleagues, in case she is regarded as "a bore and a bluestocking". In Duncan's estimation,

"life ... is a bigger affair than books, and life is pre-eminently your business. Wait till your hands are full of life, and I doubt if you will have the time or the wish to add to the mass of feminine writings already in the world." (*C*, pp. 236, 250.)

Jacqueline's fiancé in *Makeshift* shows similar hostility when she encounters by chance the author who had encouraged her early writing ambitions:

> What the blazes did the man mean jawing away about Jacqueline's poetry, puffing up the poor kid she could write?... Didn't he realise she was going to be married – married? Wasn't that a sight more worth talking about than this "modern movement", this "rhythmic feeling" and all the rest? (*M*, p. 215.)

Both these heroines break their engagements and the novels end with their departure for London to pursue their writing ambitions in the anonymity of the metropolis.

The representation of women and their lives in these Scottish city novels is so convincing, and so mutually supportive, that one feels that the novels do provide a reliable and useful basis for further investigation of women's social history in the early years of this century. As with the English, American, and European life-styles in *Streets of Desire*, one has the sense of Scottish authors and their characters rewriting female scenarios and, in so doing, pointing with understanding to the changes occurring in women's lives. In addition, these women authors show that the city was not a "literary no-go area", as it has appeared to be in canonical accounts of early twentieth-century Scottish writing. As in the international scene, women authors in Scotland were not only writing themselves, they were also writing the city as a place where they could find a truer way to be themselves.

BIBLIOGRAHY

Page references for quotations from the principal books discussed are given, along with title abbreviation, in parenthesis after the quotation in the text. Abbreviations and publication details are as follows:

C   Catherine Carswell, *The Camomile* (London: Melrose, 1922; reprinted, London: Virago, 1987).

CV   Catherine Gavin, *Clyde Valley* (London: Arthur Barker, 1928).

M   Dot Allan, *Makeshift* (London: Melrose, 1928).

OD   Catherine Carswell, *Open the Door!* (London, Melrose, 1920; reprinted, London: Virago, 1986; and Edinburgh: Canongate, 1996).

SD   Liz Heron, *Streets of Desire* (London: Virago, 1993).

ST   Mary Cleland, *The Sure Traveller* (London: Hodder and Stoughton, 1923).

NOTES

1. See Glasgow Women's Studies Group, *Uncharted Lives: extracts from Scottish women's experiences 1850–1982* (Glasgow, 1983).
2. Margery Palmer McCulloch, "Fictions of development 1920–1970", in Douglas Gifford and Dorothy Macmillan (eds), *A History of Scottish Women's Writing* (Edinburgh, 1997), pp. 360–372.
3. Germaine Greer, "Flying pigs and double standards", *Times Literary Supplement*, 26 July 1975, p. 784.
4. C. M. Grieve (Hugh MacDiarmid), *Contemporary Scottish Studies* (London, 1926; reprinted, Manchester, 1995), p.311.
5. In addition to its reprint of *Open the Door!* (1996), the Edinburgh publisher, Canongate, has reprinted Carswell's *The Life of Robert Burns* (1990), and her unfinished autobiography *Lying Awake*, (1997).
6. Neil M. Gunn, *The Shadow* (London, 1948; reprinted, Glasgow, 1989), p. 222.
7. See Keith Dixon, "Rough edges: the feminist representation of women in the writing of Lewis Grassic Gibbon", in Joachim Schwend and Horst Drescher (eds), *Studies in Scottish Fiction: twentieth century* (Berlin, 1990), pp. 289–301.

8

Rethinking narratives in European women's history: motherhood, identities and female agency in early twentieth-century Spain

Mary Nash

The chapters in this book range from the Mediterranean to the Nordic countries and draw attention to the shared experience of women's history – despite its unequal visibility and influence on mainstream history in different countries. The use of common, though debated, analytical categories, and most significantly the capacity of women's history to generate new questions and to critically re-engage with traditional issues, continue to challenge traditional forms of historical narrative. Writing women's history by now is a complex world-wide endeavour with several decades of history behind it.[1] Because of their greater consolidation, resources, development, and domestic influence, women's history and women's studies in the United States have undoubtedly shaped the analytical tools, the interpretative frameworks, and even the identification of the historical issues examined in this world context. But it is becoming increasingly important to focus on the European situation.

EUROPEAN WOMEN'S HISTORY: RETHINKING NARRATIVES

The Scottish-western European dimension of this volume make it a good place to raise comparative issues in a European context. A fully comprehensive view of European women's history has yet to be established. North/south, periphery/centre divides still persist in existing perceptions of the subject. Meta-narratives identified as being representative of European women's history, but based on a selective reading of British or French studies, are still accepted as representative of a "European" discourse.[2] Rethinking traditional narratives through women's history implies challenging false universalities and opening up the discussion on the terms of reference of the very concept of "European" when applied to women's history. The recognition of the specificity of historical contexts is crucial to the advance of women's history, as is also the need to be attentive to the dangers of excessive generalisations and the use of undifferentiated categories.

To my understanding, the notions of diversity and specificity need to be further addressed and problematised. Rewriting women's history, be it in the mode of gender or the other analytical categories – discussed for example by Siân Reynolds in chapter one – still remains crucial to rethinking the standard paradigms and analytical frameworks of national histories. This raises the issue of reconciling the notion of common cross-national histories with that of diversity. And the implications of discussing the diverse expressions of women's historical experience include the need to give a voice to the multiple expressions of women's lives and history, even within territorially defined national contexts. Although this question is not discussed directly in the body of this book, it is clear that women's history in a European context has to confront the problem of writing historical narratives which engage with national or regional cultural diversities within countries. Thus, for example, it can be argued that there is a need to recognise the heterogeneity of expressions of women's historical trajectories in the case of Scotland or Catalonia in a way which does not subordinate this task to the categories of mainstream history – whether this means national histories, or even women's history itself. Identifying common themes, and differences, in women's historical experience can, for instance, illuminate our understanding of the complex interaction of female agency, and collective subjectivity, in the contexts of Scottish/British or Catalan/Spanish women's history. Recognising multiple diversity, complex historical trajectories, and the politics of location, however, does not imply losing sight of common patterns in women's collective historical experience.

One of the challenges of women's history today is to provide a gendered understanding of nation building and national histories. In her chapter, "Feminists – citizens – mothers: citizenship, national identity, and motherhood in nineteenth-century Germany", Lynn Abrams points to the continuity of the notion, in most approaches to national histories, that the politics of nation-forming are gender-neutral. But, as narratives of national construction and nationalism in Europe move to incorporate the category of identity politics as a key construct in nation-building, the relationship between national identities and gender identities opens up crucial issues for a socio-cultural-political understanding of national politics and for the construction of citizenship.[3] Although studies on nationalism in western Europe over the past decade have explored the cultural construction of nationalism, and the historical creation of what Benedict Anderson has called "imagined communities", the signs of cultural identity are often seen as gender-neutral.[4] Over a decade ago, George Mosse stressed the significance of the cultural construction of sexuality and sexual identity in the development of national identities in western Europe.[5] But, despite this pioneer work, mainstream historians generally fail to engage with a gendered reading of the cultural and political construction of nationalism, national identities, and state construction. It can be argued, however, that this perspective is crucial to the understanding of contemporary European history.

As Partha Chatterjee has demonstrated in the case of India, the re-creation of a new patriarchal order, and a new model of gender identity for women, based on modernity but also incorporating signs of national tradition, were crucial in the construction of nationalist imagination and identity in the development of the nationalist movement, and of the national state itself, both in the colonial and post-colonial period.[6] A rereading of the political genealogy of first-wave feminism in Spain and Catalonia also reveals the reinvention of new models of gender identity, the setting of a political agenda that emphasised *either* Spanish nationalist components *or* Catalan nationalist identity. It is in this sense that I have argued elsewhere that "politics and the State are at the core of the formulation of gender identity and the women's struggle in Spain."[7] In the case of Catalan women, the specific expression of the women's movement was shaped by their integration into the Catalan nationalist movement, which structured their collective expectations and moulded the way they expressed their feminism, while also providing a gendered reading of Catalan nationalism. In the case of the Spanish women's movement, central-state politics shaped many Spanish feminisms, some of which rejected any regional nationalist claims. In this sense, it is highly significant that nationalist discourse in the sense of Spanish nationalism was a core element of the *Asociación Nacional de Mujeres Españolas*, one of most combative feminist organisations in Spain in the 1920s. The patriotism of the *Asociación* was clearly expressed in its programme as its first stated goal was to "oppose, by whatever means available to the Association, any act or manifestation that threatens the integrity of the national territory".[8] Opposition to the nationalisms of the periphery and the defence of the central state were key features of this form of Spanish feminism – in opposition to the nationalisms of the Catalan and Basque women's movements.[9]

It is clear, indeed, that political diversity, central-state national construction, and nationalist cultural identity can be considered crucial in working towards a gendered reading of state politics and, indeed, for the articulation of the diverse strands of the women's movement in many countries. Further cross-European comparative perspectives on gendered readings of national identities and nation building could set an agenda to explore the significance of gender and the development of national identities in state construction. Other contributions to this volume suggest that gender-identity politics, motherhood, and maternalism are key features in the understanding of national histories and politics. This points to the fact that there are significant issues to be explored, which include the implications of the gender identity of motherhood in the process of nationalist construction in states with fractured or weak national identities – such as nineteenth-century Spain or Germany – and the significance of gender discourse in peripheral nationalisms – for example, in Scotland or Catalonia. The development of a discussion on these questions can contribute to a cross-European comparative approach, as also can the further exploration of the part to be played by gender-analysis in understanding the construction of concepts of citizenship and the welfare state.[10]

MOTHERHOOD AND IDENTITIES IN EARLY TWENTIETH-CENTURY SPAIN

In the course of nineteenth- and twentieth-century history in Spain and in western Europe, motherhood, reproduction, and the shaping of gender identities became a contested terrain. It can also be contended that collective gender identity became crucial in the development of the women's movement and in the generation of women's agency. It has been argued that the new social movements of recent decades have relied on identity politics, and submerged networking, for their development and consolidation.[11] In the same way it can be suggested that, in their evolution as a social phenonemon in the early twentieth century, feminism and the women's movement also relied on a common collective gender identity. The rest of this chapter will raise a set of questions about motherhood, collective identity, and female agency in the context of early twentieth-century Spain. Its purpose is to sketch briefly a number of issues that may be useful for a more general discussion of comparative European women's history.

My understanding is that motherhood has been the core defining feature of women's collective identity in development of contemporary Spanish society. Within this framework, I see gender identity as a key factor, not only in explaining women's collective agency but also the modernisation and political construction of modern Spanish society. Rereading motherhood can provide insights into the gendered construction of citizenship, into political subjectivity, and, indeed, into the process of democratisation of modern Spanish society. My argument is that, in order to understand the paths Spanish women took in the public arena, it is necessary to address the development of gender discourse in Spain and to re-examine the meanings of gender identity in shaping women's agency in society. Contestation and conformity in Spanish women's lives can be better grasped if they are seen through the lens of gender-identity politics. Moreover, I have contended elsewhere that gender identity can be interpreted as the collective legitimisation of a significant stream of Spanish feminism[12] and that the discourse about it defined a significant forum for a social and political apprenticeship which shaped women's challenges and their political agenda. I am arguing that this experience was decisive in shaping the gendered democratisation of society during the Second Republic and also in defining women's role and collective agency during the Spanish Civil War. In the latter context, the political strength of gender identity can illustrate the redefinition of motherhood as a prime mobilising force in the fight of women against fascism.

Despite traditional attempts to understand the historical experience of Spanish women through the lens of "Black Spain" and the predominance of inquisitorial, religious, conservative, traditional cultural values, it can be argued that, on the contrary, gender culture was based primarily on the prevalent Western ideology of domesticity.[13] Moreover, by the early twentieth century, this traditional model of good mothering and demure acquiesce to housewifely duties – commonly known as the *Angel del Hogar* (Angel of the Hearth) – had become modernised in some parts of Spain to the familiar gender model of the *Nueva Mujer Moderna* (new, modern woman). The transition to modernity in the early twentieth century also entailed the transformation of cultural modes and values that, in turn, generated a different ideological discourse about women. The shift to the innovative "modern woman" allowed women to adjust to the process of modernity by adapting more restrictive, traditional gender roles towards the new needs of a modern labour market and society. The new modernised gender model challenged women's total restriction to the home, and enhanced women's personal and professional options and their subjective experience *as women*. But despite its modernising effect, it must be stressed that the new model maintained the core of traditional gender identity: it redefined women, but essentially as mothers and child-bearers – thus continuing to restrict women's role in society.

The modern redefinition of gender discourse shifted from religious legitimisation to a secular one, founded on medical and scientific authority. I want now to focus on the implications of the medical redefinition of motherhood in particular. First, it continued to be based on a bio-social legitimisation that defined motherhood as the biological destiny of women. Biological essentialism continued to be a core feature in this modern rereading of motherhood. But a second point must be stressed. This modernised version of motherhood had an innovative approach as it also sanctioned a wider political – and, therefore, public – reading of motherhood. In the mid-1920s, the emerging voices of authority – those of doctors, lawyers, and scientists – redefined motherhood as a common good, thus transcending women's individual rights as persons.

This shift in the understanding of a "public" motherhood was highly significant in the legitimisation of a differential notion of citizenship. As has been argued for other Western countries, it can also be contended for Spain that maternalist politics and gender discourse established the basis for a gender-differential in the definition of citizenship.[14] Since the concession of a universal male franchise in 1891, political views held that men were active political subjects with a right to the exercise of full political citizenship. An idea of social citizenship founded on human reproduction, but also on public social motherhood, was the ground for the gradual political integration of women into the public arena. This political framework legitimated women's access to some spaces within the public arena, while guaranteeing that others remained out of bounds. However, although motherhood was in many ways to be crafted around a more political reading – linked with the notion of differential citizenship in the process of modernisation of Spanish society – it still revolved around a traditional, biological notion of motherhood. Here, in my view, lies the strength of modern Spanish gender discourse, as it continued to be based on bio-social thought and on the naturalisation of cultural gendered discourse.

GENDER IDENTITY AND WOMEN'S RIGHTS

Despite the constraints of gender discourse as an effective mechanism of social control, changes in the models of femininity and gender roles also responded to contestation by women and were redefined by them to justify women's agency in society. In this sense, in the 1920s and 1930s, the gender model of the "new modern woman" was liberating for many Spanish women, while gender identity was intentionally used by many women in their emancipatory struggle to legitimate their claims to public spaces, to new experiences, and to freedom. Until the 1930s, it can be argued, the experience of their common gender identity and the bonds of the cultural experience of motherhood were the grounds for the development of a strong women's movement and for the shaping of a collective feminist agenda in Spain.

In my interpretation of Spanish and of Catalan feminism, I have contended that activists did not focus primarily on demands for women's suffrage and political rights.[15] With some differences, both developed a stream of social feminism that was based not on the paradigm of equal political rights but rather on the political foundations of the acknowledgement of gender difference. It must also be stressed that the influence of the predominant political culture in Spain was crucial in shaping demands for women's rights. Until the 1930s, with the development of political reform under the democratic Second Republic, the achievement of individual political rights was not the key factor in the Spanish liberal and democratic tradition as it sought political and social advance. In the scenario of a political culture disenchanted, in a context of widespread political corruption, with notions of individual political rights, women also did not focus on political rights and enfranchisement. Feminists claimed civil and social rights in the fields of work and education. They championed the causes of paid work and quality education for women. They fought for improved social status and for the right of women to be active in many socio-cultural fields. In this way they challenged the boundaries that imposed gender norms on female activity, restricting women to the private sphere. They created new spaces for women that were socially defined through gender roles. Within the canons of gender discourse, feminists took on board the widely proclaimed idea of "social motherhood" – and, thus, the idea of a gendered social citizenship for women.

This undoubtedly legitimated women's claims to be active in the public arena, but at the same time, it redefined the gendered boundaries of "the public". In this sense this redefinition of "the public" was articulated on the ground of an acknowledgement of difference and of the gender basis of women's social and political agency. This, however, raises the general issue of the political significance of a feminist agenda based on the gender identity of motherhood; it also leads to questions about the implications of its role in social apprenticeship and in the promotion of a specific political culture in the development of female political subjectivity.

The inauguration of the democratic regime of the Second Republic in 1931 forced a redefinition of citizenship within the paradigm of equality and political rights.[16] It can, however, be argued that a traditional reading of sexual difference still prevailed in the way citizenship was conceptualised during the suffrage debate in 1931 – when male politicians, across the political divide of left and right, still claimed a gender-differentiated citizenship. The major Spanish suffragist, lawyer Clara Campoamor, a member of the Radical Party, was an exception in espousing the defence of women's suffrage on the grounds of equality, freedom, and individual rights.[17] In the hostile climate of the parliamentary debate on the concession of women's suffrage in the autumn of 1931, she brilliantly defended the notion of political citizenship without any gender restrictions and argued for gender equality in the new constitution. By placing the legitimacy of the young democracy on the foundations of equality, Campoamor established universal political citizenship as the basic tenet of the new republic. The universal principle of citizenship could not admit any exclusions, or a gender differential in the understanding of the notion of citizenship, as had been current in Spanish politics. Together with a liberal and democratic political rationale, the suffragist leader also based her arguments on feminist politics. She openly claimed that if the constitution did not admit the principle of equal political rights, the newly established republic would be disqualified as a democratic system and exposed as a patriarchal social order exclusively defending male interests, and thus violating the principle of the sovereignty of the people:

The first article of the constitution could say that Spain is a democratic republic and that all its power emanates from the people; to
me, to women, to men who esteem democratic principles as
mandatory, this article would state only one thing: Spain is an
aristocratic republic of male privilege. All its rights emanate exclusively from men.[18]

Campoamor's clear espousal of equality and universal individual political rights was quite exceptional in this period, which was characterised
by the ambiguities of both left and right regarding female enfranchisement. The principle and practice of political equality was not espoused
by many Spanish politicians. The parliamentary discussion in the autumn
of 1931 illustrates the legacy of the notion of differential, gendered citizenship and the continued legitimacy of traditional gender discourse.
Most arguments rejecting women's suffrage, and their capacity as active
citizens, were founded on political expediency and the supposed political
alignment of women with conservative forces. This argument was
founded on the traditional premise of women's dependency and lack of
political judgement. In this case, women's lack of autonomy and political
subjectivity was based on the dual assumption of male authority within
the family (Spanish women would vote in whatever way a husband or
father told them), and on male religious authority (Spanish women
would vote on the dictates of the priests).

It is beyond the scope of this chapter to explore the debate on female
enfranchisement. The point to be stressed here is that a reading of sexual
difference was still clear in the prevalent conceptualisation of citizenship,
in which differential, gender citizenship was claimed by male politicians
across a political divide of left and right. The argument of biological determinism was used to claim unequal capacities between men and
women. One republican deputy, Dr. Novoa Santos, disqualified women
as capable of acting as active political subjects with the argument that
hysteria was an essential component of the female character. He argued
that enfranchising women would signify handing over the new republic
to female hysteria. Sexual difference and specific female attributes were
also invoked by Professor Manuel Ayuso, of the Republican Federal
Party, whose bio-social definition of women led him to state that women
should not be given the vote until the age of forty-five as they did not
achieve psychological equilibrium, mental maturity, or control of their
will, until that age; males, on the other hand, attained all these attributes
at the age of twenty-three. Biological essentialism – this time defined as

the end of the female reproductive cycle – thus justified the limitation of women's rights as political subjects.

Even more progressive deputies such as the socialist, Dr. César Juarros Ortega, had recourse to bio-social reasoning – though, in this case, to justify the concession of the vote to women. Social motherhood was a key component of his line of argument, which stressed the need for women's active presence in the world of politics as

> women represented a sentiment of motherhood that man cannot even conceive. Women's psychology is different from men. [19]

Juarros Ortega justified women's right to vote on the familiar grounds of the modernised version of gender discourse which contended that men and women were complementary. He claimed that women's experience of motherhood created a differential perception of citizenship and political agency. The recognition of gender difference through motherhood continued to be a tenacious feature in justifying a complementary view of women's political subjectivity – one defined as centring on the defence of more humane morals and political values, understood by women because of their experience of maternity.

The notion of motherhood as the defining feature of women's identity thus figured openly in the debate on the new democratic constitution. Although Juarros Ortega's argument, based on a gendered idea of political agency, was constructed with the aim of achieving democratic cohesion, it paved the way for the admission of the practice of differential citizenship during the Second Republic, despite the egalitarian principles finally established in the new constitution in 1931.

COMBATANT MOTHERHOOD AND WOMEN'S AGENCY IN THE CIVIL WAR

During the Civil War (1936–1939) women's strategies and choices in the fight against fascism must also be understood in the context of their historical apprenticeship and their gender identity. The Civil War brought about one of the greatest mass political and social mobilisations of women in Spanish history.[20] Women's fight against fascism was channelled through a number of organisations that became instrumental in promoting a new, mass female movement in villages, towns, and cities throughout unoccupied Republican Spain. Women's agency was crucial in undertaking new social, economic, and military activities in the anti-fascist resistance.[21]

Some women also challenged conventional gender roles by undertaking an active part in warfare as *milicianas* (militia-women).[22] They assumed a ground-breaking definition of female citizenship by claiming women's right to bear arms – a role hitherto reserved, in an exclusively male definition of citizenship in contemporary European liberal and democratic traditions, for men. The *milicianas* fought at the front, as well as providing necessary auxiliary services for the soldiers. At first they symbolised the "good fight" against fascism and were an inspiration for anti-fascist resistance and revolution. The heroic figure of a woman in arms became the symbol of the courage and bravery of the Spanish people struggling against fascism. The belligerent image of the woman combatant in her blue *mono* (overalls) was predominant in the war posters that aggressively urged men to enlist in the popular militias. For example, one well-known poster by artist Arteche shows a *miliciana* dressed in a blue *mono*, a gun in her uplifted hand as revolutionary *militians* march with their flags in the background. The *miliciana* in the poster persuasively asserts: "The militia needs you".[23] Other posters show *mono*-clad militia-women calling on people to fight and to join the revolutionary struggle or posing among male *militians* in combat positions.[24] Such images had undoubted impact precisely because they broke with tradition. They portrayed women in a militaristic, revolutionary, and aggressive light. This revolutionary image of women figured extensively in war posters and played a key role in collective imagery, and in the symbolic representation of the anti-fascist cause. However, the *milicianas'* courage, tenacity, and dedication were insufficient to gain the general acceptance of women in the military role: their reputation in this respect was gradually discredited. As citizens of the Second Republic under fascist attack, the mobilisation of women in the anti-fascist resistance apparently did not entitle them to carry arms.

Despite the initial prevalence of the cultural representation of the *miliciana* as the model for women's role in the Civil War, it is my contention that, on the contrary, the politics of gender identity through motherhood continued to define differential gender roles in the war and revolution. In a very short time, the subversive heroine, the *miliciana*, was quickly discredited on the grounds of sexual transgression. There were allegations of prostitution at the front, leading to the dissemination of venereal diseases.[25] The symbolic *miliciana* was replaced by a more traditional model, the "Combatant Mother", the "Heroine of the Home Front", who embodied traditional gender virtues and roles. The politics of motherhood quickly became one of the core organising principles of the war. Women's role in anti-fascist resistance and revolutionary change was defined not as that of a combatant-in-arms but rather as that of a dedicated mother, housewife, nurturer, healer, factory worker, educator, and social worker at the home front. War rhetoric and imagery insisted on clearly gender-differentiated areas of activity in the war effort.

The women's organisations of different political tendencies incorporated the symbol of motherhood into their diverse strategies. The myth of motherhood was powerful, and one with which Spanish women collectively identified. Motherhood transcended the wide political polarisation in Republican Spain and provided a common collective identity for women in the fight against Franco. The bonds of motherhood were intentionally used to build coalitions among women who were deeply divided politically – as anarchists, communists, socialists, dissident Marxists, or Catholic republicans. Women were constantly addressed in public rhetoric as mothers, and, as such, exhorted to participate in the war effort. They were to fight against fascism in order to protect their children. Motherhood was the lens through which it was claimed that women could perceive their subjectivity as actors in the war against fascism.[26] The narrative of maternal service, in other words, was a key feature in Republican anti-fascist discourse.

On another level, the universal cultural representation of women's collective identity through motherhood transcended national boundaries. The idea of combatant motherhood against fascism[27] had a universal, comprehensive, dimension, which could reach women all over the world. The sacrifice, pain and courage of Spanish women was projected in a way which embraced all of suffering humankind, particularly people living under other fascist regimes. Female resistance was envisioned, through the radical subjectivity of pain, as a collective experience of mothers whose children were lost or threatened through fascism. The embodiment and representation of pain through the loss of sons in war was perceived as a collective female subjectivity transcending political and territorial boundaries, uniting all women in a common goal against fascism.

The defence of the Republic against fascist aggression was conceived not only as a commitment with immediate benefit for Spanish offspring, but one with positive consequences for the children of all the mothers of the world. Motherhood was the basis for world appeals for solidarity in support of the anti-fascist cause. A text of a war poster of the time clearly illuminates this view:

Mothers and Women of the World! Our children have to be saved from this strife, our children who do not belong to us mothers, but who are also the hope of humankind. [28]

Women were evoked as an invincible "vanguard of mothers" committed to defeat fascism through a collective, universal identity generated through the notion of combatant motherhood:

Women in the Basque Country today form part of a vanguard. It is the vanguard of mothers – those who have given the generous gift of lives to others and those who share the feeling of motherhood. This vanguard is invincible. Neither life nor death will stop us.... We are committed to defeat fascism, to crush it like a violent animal caught in a snare. And we will carry it out. [29]

The common gender identity of Spanish women as mothers, forged in gender discourse in former decades, was a powerful collective experience with which women identified – thus shaping their more militant collective identity in times of war and revolution.

"Motherhood" evoked not only courage and bravery but also sacrifice. While initially understood as a symbol of passive defence against fascist aggression, it acquired significant belligerent and combative connotations. Combatant motherhood forged a common military identity for Spanish women, as maternity implied not only protection but also the need to sacrifice one's sons for a greater cause. Female heroism was equated with maternal sacrifice: women able to engage their sons in military resistance were heroic. Women's role in the anti-fascist fight was gendered and perceived as an indirect contribution to the war through the sacrifice of their sons and husbands. Combatant motherhood not only implied the active participation of mothers in the war effort, it also gave them the moral authority, and even compulsion, to oblige their sons to fight. The vital role of women was not as combatants-in-arms at the front, but as mothers who urged their sons to participate in trench warfare. [30]

By 1937 as the Republican front faced increasing difficulties, the war rhetoric insisted that mothers provide soldiers for the defence of the Republic. Paradoxically, then, while mothers were urged to reinforce their maternal role, they were also told to risk the lives of their sons. Mothers were perceived as being inherently proud of their sons, but they were to be even prouder when the moment came for them to fight "in defence of a just cause". According to a popular communist view, victory depended on the attitudes of mothers:

Victory ... will be forged by the sacrifice of those sons whom you had such difficulty bearing, and for whom you have so much hope. This blood which flows so generously is yours; it is the blood of the most generous of our women.... To you, then, to your blood, to your flesh, we will owe victory.[31]

This idea of sacrifice, generously borne by mothers, also presaged far-reaching effects in the future. The sons mothers bore would, in turn, determine the fate of future generations. Maternal service was seen as the equivalent as male military service. Militarist policies addressed to women were strictly gender-defined and held to traditional definitions of masculinity such as honour, courage and virility. Lack of such gendered masculine characteristics were to be rejected as shameful by women.[32] As the much voiced slogan by communist leader, Dolores Ibárruri – Pasionaria – proclaimed: "Better be the widows of heroes than the wives of cowards".

The experience of the war brought a new dimension to the traditional role of mother, housewife, and nurturer, as women's duties were projected on to the larger community beyond the bounds of the immediate family, embracing the civilian population as a whole. This collective dimension of women's nurturing role broke new ground and accurately reflected the blurring of the boundaries of public and private at the Republican home front. The social drive towards women's new role in community nurturing challenged the traditional restrictions of female activity to the home. It thus legitimised women's access to the public sphere, albeit through supportive activities. It must be stressed that civil resistance and everyday survival during the years of the war was only feasible because of the agency and initiative of women. However, even at this time of war and revolutionary changes, women's previous collective historical experience, and social apprenticeship through the gender identity of motherhood, continued to shape their social responses and strategies for change. The redefinition of social motherhood in terms of combatant motherhood provided maternal services to the community and guaranteed civil resistance. It widened the range of women's activities. But, once again, it did so by way of a clearly gendered definition of women's role and space – this time in a war situation.

CONCLUSION

This brief sketch of a number of possible rereadings of motherhood opens up the discussion on the implications of gender identity, and of the many meanings of motherhood, in the construction of the social and political history of contemporary Spain. It also raises the issue of how historical experience in gender identity shaped women's choices as social actors, while women's agency also shaped resistance strategies within this framework. In the Spanish case, gender identity and motherhood can be seen through the double filter of contestation and conformity. The meanings of motherhood varied according to changing historical circumstances and to the nature of women's social apprenticeship. The protean nature of motherhood, and the malleability of the rhetoric of "social motherhood", points to different usages of the social construction of motherhood by women and other social actors. My understanding is that the scope, range, and transformation of "motherhood" not only illuminates the specific significance of gender, but also provides another lens through which to develop further our understanding of the gendered construction of contemporary Spanish society. Finally, there remains to be answered – and the fifth Mackie conference began at least to furnish one sort of answer – the question of how rethinking specific narratives through the categories of women's history in a Mediterranean country such as Spain can be mutually fruitful within the wider perspective of a comparative western European women's history. And such a comparative history must embrace Scotland too.

NOTES

1. See Karen Offen, Ruth Roach Pierson and Jane Rendall (eds), *Writing Women's History: international perspectives* (London, 1991).
2. Aware of this problem, the Spanish version of Charles Duby and Michelle Perrot (eds), *Histoire des Femmes Occident* (Paris, 5 vols, 1988–92), translated into English as *A History of Women in the West* (Cambridge, Mass., 1992) incorporated several chapters on Spain in each volume: see *Historia de las Mujeres en Occidente* (Madrid, 1992–93).
3. Ernest Gellner, *Nations and Nationalism* (Oxford, 1983); Josep A. Llobera, *The God of Modernity: the development of nationism in Western Europe* (Oxford, 1994).
4. Benedict Anderson, *Imagined Communities: reflections on the origin and spread of nationalism* (London, 1983).
5. George Mosse, *Nationalism and Sexuality: middle-class morality and sexual norms in modern Europe* (Madison, 1985).
6. Partha Chaterjee, *The Nation and its Fragments: colonial and postcolonial histories* (Princeton, 1993).

7. Mary Nash, "Political culture, Catalan nationalism and the women's movement in early twentieth-century Spain", *Women's Studies International Forum*, special issue entitled "Links Across Differences: gender, ethnicity and nationalism", vol. 19, nos 1/2 (January-April 1996).

8. Aguado et al., *Textos para la historia de las mujeres en España* (Madrid, 1994), p. 398.

9. Mercedes Ugalde Solano, *Mujeres y Nacionalismo Vasco: génesis y desarrollo de Emakume Abertzale Batza (1906-1936)* (Bilbao, 1993).

10. Gisela Bock and Pat Thane, *Maternity, Visions of Gender and the Rise of the European Welfare States, 1890-1950* (London, 1991); G. Bonacchi and A. Groppi, *Il Dilemma della Cittadinanza: diritti e doveri delle donne* (Rome, 1993); Seth Koven and Sonya Michel, *Mothers of a New World: maternalist politics and the origins of welfare states* (London, 1993).

11. Alberto Melucci, "The symbolic challenge of contemporary movements", *Social Research*, vol. 52 (1985); and *Nomads of the Present: social movements and individual needs in contemporary society* (Philadelphia, 1989).

12. Mary Nash, "Experiencia y aprendizaje: la formación de los feminismos en España", *Historia Social*, no. 20 (1995).

13. See Mary Nash, "Un/contested identities: motherhood, sex reform and the modernization of gender identity in early twentieth-century Spain", in Victoria Enders and Pamela Radcliff (eds), *Contested Identities: women in contemporary Spanish society* (New York, forthcoming).

14. Mary Nash, "Género y ciudadanía", in Juliá Santos (ed.), *Política en la Segunda República. Ayer*, no. 20 (1995).

15. Nash, "Political culture, Catalan nationalism".

16. Nash, "Género y ciudadanía".

17. On the suffrage debate see: Rosa M. Capel, *El sufragio femenino en la Segunda República española*, (Granada, 1975; Madrid, 1992); Geraldine Scanlon, *La polémica feminista en la España contemporánea (1868-1974)*, (Madrid, 1976; 1986); M. Gloria Núñez Pérez, *Madrid. 1931: mujeres entre la permanencia y el cambio* (Madrid, 1993).

18. Clara Campoamor, *Mi pecado mortal: el voto femenino y yo* (Barcelona, 1981), p. 61. See too C. Fagoaga and P. Saavedra, *Clara Campoamor: La sufragista española* (Madrid, 1981).

19. Cited in Campoamor, *Mi pecado mortal*, p. 116.

20. Mary Nash, *Defying Male Civilisation: women in the Spanish Civil War* (Denver, 1995).

21. Martha A. Ackelsberg, *Free Women of Spain: anarchism and the struggle for the emancipation of women* (Bloomington, 1991); Carmen Alcalde, *La mujer en la guerra civil española* (Madrid, 1976); Mary Nash, *Las mujeres en la Guerra Civil* (Madrid, 1989).

22. Mary Nash, "Milicianas and homefront heroines: images of women in war and revolution 1936-1939", *History of European Ideas*, vol. 11 (1989); and

"Women in war: milicianas and armed combat in revolutionary Spain, 1936–1939", *The International History Review*, vol. XV, no. 2 (May 1993).

23. Arteche (1936), 144 x 100 cm, Fundación Figueras, Centro de Estudios de Historia Contemporánea, Universidad de Barcelona.

24. See the collection of war posters at the Fundación Figueras and the Centre d'Estudis Històrics Internacionals, University of Barcelona; Carmen Grimau, *El cartel republicano en la Guerra Civil* (Madrid, 1979); Inmaculada Julián, *Les avantguardes pictòriques a Catalunya* (Barcelona, 1986), pp. 57–75.

25. For a discussion of these allegations, see Nash, *Defying Male Civilization*, chapter 4.

26. Membership card of the *Agrupación de Mujeres Antifascistas*.

27. See Maxine Molyneux on combative motherhood in the context of Nicaragua in her "Mobilization without emancipation? Women's interests, the state and revolution in Nicaragua", *Feminist Studies* vol. 11, no. 2 (summer 1985).

28. "¡Madres y mujeres del mundo! Un llamamiento de las mujeres de España", *Frente Rojo*, 26 October 1938.

29. El Comité, "Pedimos un puesto en la lucha contra el fascismo", *Mujeres* (Edición de Bilbao, March 1937).

30. "La incorporación de la mujer a la industria de guerra. Necesidad de escuelas de capacitación", *Mundo Obrero* (Edición para los frentes, 29 October 1937).

31. "Missió de la mare a l'avantguarda i de la futura mare a la reraguarda", *Treball* (12 January 1937).

32. "Dones antifeixistes de Catalunya!", *Treball* (27 April 1938).

And they lived happily ever after? Medieval queenship and marriage in Scotland, 1424–1449

Fiona Downie

Most medieval kings were trained from birth to rule. The queens of fifteenth-century Scotland, however, were not born to be queens. They were made into queens later in life and crowned following marriage to a king. The source of a queen's power was therefore her marriage, which also played an important role in defining the scope of her role as a queen. In the cases of Joan Beaufort (d. 1445) and Mary of Guelders (d. 1463), queens of James I and James II respectively, their marriages – like other royal marriages in the fifteenth century – were arranged to meet the political, economic, and social goals of the families of the bride and groom.[1] As foreign brides, their marriages symbolised the creation of treaties of political and economic alliance and, in the case of Joan Beaufort, the achievement of peace and unity between warring kingdoms. It is quite clear, however, that while an international royal marriage could symbolise peace, it could not actually end a war and that, even in the case of a political or economic alliance between friendly kingdoms, a marriage could not ensure the continued success of that alliance. Despite the apparent inability of foreign marriages to guarantee peace and friendship, medieval royal governments continued to emphasise their potential to do so, and invested a great deal of effort in establishing marriage alliances. The continuing interest in what appears to be an unsuccessful policy suggests that such alliances held other, less obvious, benefits. It could be argued that the real purpose of a marriage alliance was to create communication networks based on family ties which would continue to operate regardless of the success or otherwise of the political or economic alliance it represented.

The marriage of James I and Joan Beaufort in 1424 illustrates the role of marriage within a political alliance and the broader aim of creating a family network. The marriage was arranged as part of English plans to release James, captured in 1406, in order to win Scotland away from her alliance with France, secure an Anglo-Scottish truce, and raise money to continue fighting the Hundred Years' War.[2] The Scottish king's release was secured in exchange for a truce and a £40,000 ransom, but the plans contained a major flaw. As a prisoner, James had been forced to accept unfavourable terms, but as a free man, he could not be forced to uphold these terms: the agreements depended upon James' co-operation, and if he chose to stop paying the ransom and to renege on the English alliance by renewing the French alliance there was no way to stop him. The English council hoped it could rely on James' goodwill following his release, a goodwill that had been carefully nurtured during his long years of captivity. His inclusion in court life while in England did not arise from simple generosity: it was hoped that James would feel at home in the English court and establish relationships with the royal family and nobility, perhaps through marriage, that could be of use in the future. But all of this depended on James' goodwill. An English wife, on the other hand, would create a link between the two kingdoms even if James managed to forget his other friends in the south. With these thoughts in mind, the English council raised the possibility of marriage in 1423, at the same time as discussing the issues of a truce and James' release. The role of the marriage within the overall truce is made quite clear in the instructions issued to the English ambassadors in July 1423 which state that "pro majori Amicitia nutrienda et conservanda" between the two allies, the Scottish king might wish to marry a "Nobilem Mulierem Regni Angliae".[3]

The bride chosen for James was Joan Beaufort, a cousin of the English king and niece of a key figure on the English council, Henry Beaufort, bishop of Winchester and later cardinal of St Eusebius. Joan's marriage was celebrated by the bishop in his church of St Mary Overy in February 1424. After the celebrations, James and his bride set out for Scotland, stopping at Durham to seal a seven-year truce between England and Scotland; James was then once again a free man. James' marriage was therefore secondary to the immediate requirements of English foreign policy and was designed to counteract the effects of his release in the long-term by establishing communication networks between the two kingdoms which would operate via his wife if James reneged. The English council later used these personal ties to open negotiations with James. Joan Beaufort's uncle, Thomas, duke of Exeter, was sent on an embassy to Scotland in 1426; Cardinal Beaufort had private talks with James in 1429; and Joan's brother Edmund, count of Mortain, was despatched to Scotland in 1433.[4]

The marriages of six of James' seven children followed a similar pattern.[5] The French king, Charles VII, sent an embassy to Scotland in 1428 to request Scottish military assistance in exchange for the marriage of the dauphin to James' daughter, Margaret, a marriage which finally took place in 1436.[6] The French marriage alliance brought Scotland into contact with other powers in the French sphere of influence, a political change in alliance which coincided with a dynastic accident. James had five other daughters to marry, who as sisters-in-law of the dauphin were now more valuable on the marriage market than they had been simply as daughters of James I of Scotland. Their new status raised the possibility of establishing an alliance with France through a marriage alliance with Scotland, as the duke of Brittany recognised in his attempts to secure a Scottish marriage for his son. The first Breton proposal of 1437 was rejected by the Scots, but the second offer of 1441 was accepted and resulted in the marriage of Isabella Stewart and Duke Francis I of Brittany in 1442.[7] These two marriages were followed by intense diplomacy leading to the departure of the remaining four unmarried Stewart princesses for the continent in 1444–45, beginning with the marriage of Mary Stewart to a Burgundian noble, Wolfaert van Borselen, son of the lord of Veere, in 1444. Circumstantial evidence suggests that the duke of Burgundy was involved in the arrangements for Mary's marriage, and both he and the French king approved of and supported the betrothal in December of the same year of Mary's sister Annabella to Louis, count of Geneva, son of the duke of Savoy.[8] Annabella left Scotland for Savoy in the summer of 1445 and was soon followed by her sisters Eleanor and Johanna who travelled to the French court where Charles VII negotiated

Eleanor's marriage to Archduke Sigismund of Austria-Tirol in 1448.[9] The negotiations for the Austrian marriage coincided with James II's search, conducted with the assistance of both Charles VII and the duke of Burgundy, for a suitable bride.[10] Although James claimed to be seeking either a French or Burgundian wife, the surviving evidence makes it clear that he preferred the latter, perhaps to widen his alliances or to protect Scottish trading interests in the Low Countries, and he married Mary of Guelders, great-niece of the duke of Burgundy, in 1449. The only one of James I's children not to be included in this network of alliances was Johanna, who had accompanied Eleanor to France in 1445. She remained in France before returning to Scotland in 1458 to marry James Douglas, earl of Morton, after failing to secure a foreign match, perhaps because she is reported to have been deaf and dumb.

Several patterns emerge from this series of marriage alliances. In the first place, these marriages were part of a network of European alliances revolving around France and Burgundy. The complexities of European politics in this period, and the growth in power of the French king and of the duke of Burgundy, encouraged lesser rulers to maintain links with both men and provided them both with the opportunity to negotiate marriages that would secure those links.[11] The Stewarts, following Margaret's marriage, were known and available, and could be offered in marriage to advance French and Burgundian interests. The ability of Charles VII and the duke of Burgundy to use the Stewart marriages in this way was increased by the murder of James I and by the changes in domestic politics during the minority of James II. There was no difficult father who might make awkward demands or delay his child's marriage, as, in the case of Margaret's marriage, James I had done for eight years while he continued negotiations with England – negotiations which twice included the discussion of an Anglo-Scottish royal marriage.

The second pattern is the creation of a complex and active network of family relationships. Annabella's betrothal, for example, was supported by the French king, her brother-in-law the dauphin, and the duke of Burgundy. Another brother-in-law, the duke of Brittany, was included in the marriage contract, and Annabella stayed in the household of her Veere in-laws en route to her new home in Savoy in 1445.[12] Eleanor was invited to France by the duchess of Burgundy at the instigation of Eleanor's sister, Margaret, and the arrangements for her marriage required the agreement of James II, the duke of Brittany, and the duke of Savoy before the ceremony took place in the presence of the king and queen of France.[13] The treaty of alliance accompanying the marriage of James II and Mary of Guelders incorporated Scotland, Burgundy, Guelders, and Brittany.[14] The duke of Brittany's involvement in the marriages is partly explained by the fact that he was married to the second eldest princess and became, with his wife, James' heir after Margaret's death in 1445. But this does not explain his part in Annabella's betrothal in December 1444, nor does it account for the interest of other Stewart in-laws in the other marriages.[15] The involvement of the in-laws in the Stewart marriages is indicative of the way in which these marriages, regardless of their initial diplomatic purpose, created one family which continued to take an interest in its members in the long term. Even in the case of Mary Stewart's marriage to Wolfaert van Borselen, for which there is little surviving evidence, there were long-term family relationships at work. Annabella lived in the Veere household in 1445, and Mary's father-in-law was present at James II's marriage to Mary of Guelders in 1449. At the other extreme, the excellent collection of letters to Eleanor Stewart – it includes letters from her sister Isabella and Isabella's daughter, from her half-brother, James Stewart, earl of Buchan, and from her nephew, James III – provides detailed evidence of the operation of the Stewart family network.[16]

The third pattern to note is that in creating this family network, it was the women who left one family to join another. At the same time, for the network to function effectively, these women had to maintain links with their own family, which in turn prevented them from losing their outsider status in their new family. A royal bride was thus a liminal figure, partially included in two families and mediating between them. This liminal status meant that the wife did not represent too much of a threat to her new family's homogeneity, and ensured that her own family did not lose any honour and could even derive some benefit from her new role. This split identity of foreign wives is highlighted in their titles. In a letter expressing her consent to her daughter's marriage, Isabella Stewart calls herself "Ysabeau fille de Roy descoce duchesse de bretaigne", a description also used by her Breton subjects in a debate on the same matter.[17] She is referred to simply as "ysabeau descosse" by Charles VII.[18] James II referred to his wife as "domicella Marie de Gelris", while the duke of Burgundy called her his "nepte marye de gheldres Royne descosse".[19] The *Auchinleck Chronicle* described Mary as the "Queen of Scotland, the Duke of gillerlandis dochter".[20] This recognition of multiple ties is also shown in pictures of foreign brides, in which they display either their family arms alone or in combination with those of their husbands' families. Several pictures in a book of hours belonging to Isabella

Stewart incorporate the Scottish and Breton arms, including two of Isabella at prayer wearing a dress decorated with both sets of arms. [21]

The foreign bride was therefore a focus for the communication networks of at least two families. A great deal of effort and expense was invested in creating these networks, but their success largely depended on the bride's ability to manage her role as focus of communication. To manage her duties effectively, a foreign bride had to attempt to overcome her status as an outsider at court and to establish ties with that court. Without these personal relationships she could not possibly appreciate problems or exert influence. The bride's ability to establish these ties was sometimes hindered by a lack of knowledge of language or local customs, as well as by the suspicion of court and family of her foreign origins. In trying to establish ties with the court a bride might go too far, and risk being accused of vulgarity, or of not going far enough, making her appear arrogant. She might link herself to the wrong people or spend too much time with her own people. In short, although her marriage made her a symbol of unity and alliance, her presence at court could make her a focus of tension and dispute. The court was a centre of gossip and intrigue, containing many traps for the newcomer but also providing many opportunities. It is unlikely that royal families would have pursued long-term marriage policies which rested largely on the abilities of their daughters without also training them for their future roles.[22] What form did this training take?

Royal and noble women in the fifteenth century did not receive a formal education, but many of them were taught to read and were able to learn much from books.[23] The books available to women tended to be of a religious or moral nature, but the ideals preached in these works did have some practical use. Books of hours, for example, contained pictures of saints that might provide examples of virtuous behaviour as well as of those that might be of local or national significance, which were particularly useful to a foreign bride trying to learn about her new home. One of the books of hours belonging to Isabella Stewart, duchess of Brittany, contains separate portraits of the duke and duchess with their patron saint, Francis, in addition to pictures of other saints, with particular emphasis on the Madonna and child, a crucial image of virtue and motherhood.[24] Several of these illuminations include the combined arms of Brittany and Scotland – evidence that the contents of the book were designed specifically for its recipient.[25] It is easy to assume that the book is yet another example of ideals that were imposed, and that it had little practical purpose, but Isabella's active interest in the book is shown by her signature at the bottom of almost half of the pictures, presumably those of the saints she found most comforting.[26] Books of hours could also provide more specific advice for young brides, as is shown by the prayer for young girls found in another book of hours owned by Isabella.[27] The prayer advises girls to think always of God and their souls, and to always be aware of their thoughts, words, and deeds – advice of considerable importance in the very public world of the court. As women were the focus of gossip and suspicion, it was essential that they gave at least the appearance of living a virtuous life and did not do anything that might give rise to rumour and speculation.

The same moral instruction is the basis of Christine de Pizan's *The Treasure of the City of Ladies*, written in 1405 for Margaret of Burgundy on the occasion of her marriage to the dauphin.[28] The first chapter tells "great queens, ladies, and princesses" that their first duty is "to love and fear God". It is followed by six chapters explaining how this love and fear will help these women to avoid temptations and to live a virtuous life. Christine then proceeds to explain the duties and qualities required of a princess, beginning with chapter eight, entitled "How the good and wise princess will make every effort to restore peace between the prince and the barons if there is any discord." Other advice includes how the good princess should deal with her husband and children, how she should control her court and finances, and how to perform acts of charity and extend largesse. Perhaps the most important chapters are those in which she explains how the good princess should conduct herself towards her husband's family and friends; how she should win and maintain the goodwill of her subjects; and "how to maintain a discreet manner towards those who do not like her and are envious of her." The princess was not only to act as a focus of communication between families and courts, she had also to facilitate communication within the court itself. Christine's interpretation of the duties of a princess were based on her own experiences of the French court, experiences which made her fully aware of the problems facing Margaret of Burgundy in her new home and of the kind of strategies needed to manage her potentially conflicting loyalties and responsibilities. Margaret's father, John the Fearless, who had a vested interest in ensuring that his daughter was able to manage her dual loyalties to Burgundian advantage, approved of the advice and generously rewarded Christine de Pizan following her presentation of the book. His patronage ensured that the work achieved a wider popularity, as shown by the copies in the libraries of the Cleves and Bourbons, in addition to the many surviving paper manuscripts.[29]

For most royal and noble women, however, training for their future role was most likely to take the form of a kind of apprenticeship. James II's queen, Mary of Guelders, was effectively apprenticed to Isabel of Portugal, duchess of Burgundy, one of the most powerful women of the fifteenth century. The duke of Burgundy had no daughters of his own and arranged the marriages of his sisters' children, including Mary, to Burgundian advantage.[30] This policy was assisted by the practice of having the eligible brides live in the duchess's household as illustrated by the constant presence of the "damoiselles destampes de bourbon et de guelres" in the household accounts between 1446 and 1449.[31] This practice meant that the young women learned about court, established relationships with people of importance, and were able to see at close quarters the ways in which the duchess of Burgundy managed her responsibilities.

The Burgundian expectation that women would play an active public role, and the varied activities of individual duchesses, meant that these young women were learning from experts. Isabel of Portugal, duchess at the time of Mary of Guelders' residence at the Burgundian court, was an active and successful diplomat and negotiated on matters such as marriages, treaties, ransoms, and trade.[32] She was nominated by her husband to deal with the English king in diplomatic negotiations on a number of occasions, partly because of her skills, and partly because she was cousin to Henry VI and had visited the English court. These links were behind her nomination to act as mediator, with Cardinal Beaufort, between England and France at Calais in 1439.[33] She and the cardinal were to choose dates for talks, decide how many people could attend these talks, and preside over them. Negotiations took place in the duchess's tent. She was present, along with her niece, the Princess of Navarre, and ten other ladies. The duchess was therefore closely involved in all stages of what has traditionally been seen as male-dominated high politics and was also concerned to train other women to work successfully in this sphere. The duchess did not confine herself to the formal world of high politics, but also adopted other, less formal, methods of communication and mediation, often following both strategies simultaneously. This was the case when she acted as the duke's representative at the conference of Chalons in 1445, convened to address disputes between France and Burgundy. On that occasion she discussed diplomatic matters with representatives from France, Savoy, Milan, Castile, England, and the Empire. Perhaps more importantly, in her two months at the French court, Isabel established close ties with Marie of Anjou, queen of France, and Margaret Stewart.[34]

These informal ties could maintain communications between diplomatic meetings, and perhaps also when diplomatic relations became strained. They were made even more significant by the fact that her husband, the duke, never met his nephew, Charles VII, himself. [35]

Mary of Guelders spent three years in Isabel's household before her marriage to James II, learning these skills and meeting many of the people of importance that Isabel negotiated with and entertained. The accounts of the duke's household show that he often invited the ladies of his wife's household to banquets with the intention of introducing them to visiting dignitaries and advertising their qualities and skills to potential suitors. Two such banquets involving Mary and her colleagues were held for the Scottish ambassadors in August and September 1448.[36] At this point, Mary's father still seems to have intended marrying her to the duke of Austria, but the Scots were obviously still trying to promote James II as a potential husband. The large dower they eventually offered made the Scottish suit more attractive, but it was also recognition of Mary's worth, enhanced by years of training at the Burgundian court. The variety of skills and experiences acquired by young women in this kind of apprenticeship formed the basis of future international relationships and justified the expense of keeping them at court for long periods.

The practice of apprenticing a prospective bride at court was most fully developed in cases in which the couple were betrothed as children. This meant that the bride could be brought up in the particular court she would one day run. The experience of Margaret Stewart provides an example. At the time of their betrothal in 1428, Margaret was three and Louis, the French dauphin, was five. The marriage contract specified that Margaret was to sail to France before February 1430, by which time she would have been five. The terms of the marriage therefore specified that the French king was to treat her as his daughter until the marriage could be formally concluded when the couple had reached the canonical ages for marriage – that is, twelve for girls and fourteen for boys. The marriage did not take place until 1436, and in the final round of negotiations the issue of Margaret's upbringing was again raised. Her father, perhaps out of a genuine concern for her welfare, asked that, upon her arrival in France, Margaret be accommodated in her own household with her own people, but conceded that she might stay with the French king and queen when they desired it. While he wanted her to have her own people about her, he recognised that the king and queen would select French gentlemen and gentlewomen to teach Margaret behaviour fitting to her station.[37] Charles refused these requests, saying that before her marriage

Margaret should live with the French queen as her daughter, in order to learn "les estaz et manieres de france". It was not convenient for her to live elsewhere.[38] He later specified that while Margaret could travel with as many Scots as James wished, only one or two women and the same number of men could remain with her in France, because, if she were surrounded by "gens de sa nation", "elle ne apprandra voluntiers francoys ne lestat de ce Royaulme".[39] It was presumably for a similar reason that Margaret's sister, Annabella, spent over ten years at the court of Savoy before her betrothal was broken off in 1456, while the residence of Eleanor and Johanna at the French court would have prepared them for life in the courts of those princes within the French sphere of influence. It is possible that these arrangements reflect fears that Scottish princesses were not civilised enough to become queen of France or ladies of continental courts, but the practice of bringing up child-brides in their future courts does seem to have been fairly widespread.[40] Regardless of her origins, it was essential that the future lady of the court learned about that court and its subjects.

Royal families therefore invested a great deal of time and money in the design and execution of their marriage plans, and this investment reflected the importance they placed on the role of their daughters within those marriages. This role was one of communication, of influence, of persuasion, of mediation, and it was a role that these women were expected to play throughout their married life. It was also a role that was essential to the smooth operation of the court and of foreign policy – as the women themselves recognised in their pursuit of their own marriage policies within the court and beyond. While the importance of this role gave women real power, it is necessary to differentiate between this power and the official and formal authority of their husbands. In other words, queens had power, but there was no office of queenship. They could not act in their own right, but only as assistants to, or deputies of, kings. The expectation that they would act on behalf of the king should the need arise indicates that contemporaries believed that queens were in theory capable of acting in their own right, as both Joan Beaufort and Mary of Guelders proved, following their husbands' deaths. While she may have been capable of acting in her own right, a fifteenth-century queen was prevented from doing so. A queen-consort had constantly to acknowledge her husband's superior power and to remain in the background. This was an important part of Christine de Pizan's advice to queens and princesses. She constantly emphasised women's abilities; she also advised them to remain modest, to persuade, and to influence, rather than to act. A fifteenth-century queen-consort could not forget that, as queen, she was primarily a wife. And as a wife she ought to be obedient to her husband and to ignore her own priorities in favour of those of her family.

NOTES

1. For a general discussion of the importance of royal marriage decisions, see A. Crawford, "The king's burden? - the consequences of royal marriage in fifteenth-century England", in R. A. Griffiths (ed.), *Patronage, the Crown and the Provinces in Later Medieval England* (Stroud, 1981), pp. 33–56.
2. For more details of the negotiations, see E. W. M. Balfour-Melville, "The later captivity and release of James I", *Scottish Historical Review*, vol. xxi (1924), pp. 89–100.
3. T. Rymer (ed.), *Foedera, Conventiones, Litterae et Cuiuscunque Generis Acta Publica* (original edition, London, 1704–35), pp. x, 295.
4. M. Brown, *James I* (Edinburgh, 1994), pp. 110, 152; *Foedera*, pp. x, 358.
5. The marriages of James I's children are discussed in Brown, *James I*, pp. 110, 162–163; A. I. Dunlop, *The Life and Times of James Kennedy, Bishop of St Andrews* (Edinburgh, 1950), pp. 66–67, 84–96, 99–103, 179–182; and C. McGladdery, *James II* (Edinburgh, 1990), pp. 41–46. The reasons for this apparently sudden foreign interest in Scottish marriages have never been examined in depth, partly because the series of marriages has never been the subject of a detailed study making use of the sources available in continental archives. The marriages of Margaret, Isabella, Eleanor, and James II have been discussed in some detail in individual studies (see notes below), but, while these studies explore the reasons behind each marriage from both a Scottish and a continental perspective, they do not attempt to explain the interest in Scottish marriages overall, nor do they link the marriages to each other. Studies of more than one marriage have only been made in general works about fifteenth-century Scotland, and focus on the importance of the Stewart marriages to Scotland rather than their allies. For a study of the marriages as a series, see Fiona Downie, "'Sche is but a Womman': the queen and princess in Scotland, 1424–63" (unpublished PhD thesis, University of Aberdeen, 1998), pp. 61–124.
6. For a detailed discussion of the negotiations and marriage, see L. A. Barbé, *Margaret of Scotland and the Dauphin Louis* (London, 1917).
7. A short account of Isabella's life and marriage can be found in L. A. Barbé, "A Stuart duchess of Brittany", in L. A. Barbé, *Sidelights on the History, Industries and Social Life of Scotland* (London, 1919), pp. 1–45.
8. Annabella's European marital career is examined in F. Downie, "'La voie quelle menace tenir': Annabella Stewart, Scotland and the European marriage market, 1445–1455", *Scottish Historical Review* (forthcoming).

[139]

9. The most detailed account of Eleanor's life is found in M. Köfler, "Eleonore von Schottland", in M. Köfler and S. Caramelle, *Die Beiden Frauen des Erzerhogs Sigmund von Österreich-Tirol* (Innsbruck, 1982), pp. 15–114.

10. See D. Ditchburn, "The place of Guelders in Scottish foreign policy, c. 1449–c. 1542", in G. G. Simpson (ed.), *Scotland and the Low Countries, 1124–1994* (East Linton, 1996), pp. 59–75. The article by J. H. Baxter, "The marriage of James II", *Scottish Historical Review*, vol. xxv (1928), pp. 69–72, is a list of some of the sources available in the Lille archives rather than a discussion of the marriage itself.

11. See G. du Fresne Beaucourt, *Histoire de Charles VII* (Paris, 1881–91), vol. iv; and R. Vaughan, *Philip the Good* (London, 1970), pp. 98–126.

12. Turin, Archivio di Stato, Inv. 16 Reg. 93, ff. 370–394, Inv. 102 Mazzo 12/3.

13. Dunlop, *Life and Times*, p. 85; Beaucourt, *Charles VII*, pp. 366–370.

14. Ditchburn, "Place of Guelders", pp. 63–65.

15. Edinburgh, Scottish Record Office, SP7/13.

16. These letters are held in the Landesregierungsarchiv für Tirol in Innsbruck, Sigm. IVa/181.

17. Nantes, Archives Departmentales de Loire Atlantique (ADLA), E12/15, E5/11.

18. Nantes, ADLA, E13/1.

19. Lille, Archives Departmentales du Nord (ADN), B427/15877, 15877 bis, 15877 quater, 15882 bis.

20. McGladdery, *James II*, p. 169.

21. Paris, Bibliotheque Nationale (BN), MS. n.a. Latin 588, f. 33v.; MS. Latin 1369, f. 55r.

22. For a full discussion of this point, see J. C. Parsons, "Mothers, daughters, marriage, power: some Plantagenet evidence, 1150–1500", in J. C. Parsons (ed.), *Medieval Queenship* (Stroud, 1994), pp. 63–78.

23. On female education in the Middle Ages, see J. M. Ferrante, "The education of women in the Middle Ages in theory, fact and fantasy", in P. H. Labalme (ed.), *Beyond Their Sex: learned women of the European past* (New York, 1980), pp. 9–43.

24. Paris BN, MS. Latin 1369, ff. 38, 39, 55, 135, 320, 362.

25. Paris BN, MS. Latin 1369, ff. 38, 39, 55, 135, 189.

26. Paris BN, MS. Latin 1369, ff. 299, 301, 303, 305, 307, 312, 316, 318, 320, 339, 346, 348, 379, 382.

27. Paris BN, MS. n.a. Latin 588, ff. 206r.–213r.

28. C. de Pizan, *The Treasure of the City of Ladies or the Book of the Three Virtues*, trans. S. Lawson (Harmondsworth, 1985), p. 20.

29. C. C. Willard, "A 15th century view of woman's role in medieval society: Christine de Pizan's *Livre des Trois Vertus*", in R. T. Morewedge (ed.), *The Role of Woman in the Middle Ages* (London, 1975), pp. 90–120; and C. C. Willard, "The manuscript tradition of the *Livre des Trois Vertus* and Christine

de Pizan's audience", *Journal of the History of Ideas*, 27 (1966), pp. 433–444.

30. For a full discussion of Burgundian marriage policy, see C. A. J. Armstrong, "La politique matrimoniale des ducs de Bourgogne de la maison de Valois", in C. A. J. Armstrong, *England, France and Burgundy in the Fifteenth Century* (London, 1983), pp. 237–342.

31. Lille ADN, B3340, Premier compte, f. 5r; B3409–B3414.

32. C. C. Willard, "The patronage of Isabel of Portugal", in J. H. McCash (ed.), *The Cultural Patronage of Medieval Women* (Athens, Georgia, 1996), pp. 306–320; Vaughan, *Philip the Good*, pp. 107–109, 116–120.

33. The account of the negotiations at Calais on which the following discussion is based is printed in H. Nicolas (ed.), *Proceedings and Ordinances of the Privy Council of England* (London, 1837), pp. v, 334–407.

34. Vaughan, *Philip the Good*, pp. 119–120; Beaucourt, *Charles VII*, vol. iv, p. 96.

35. M. G. A. Vale, *Charles VII* (London, 1974), p. 230.

36. Lille ADN, B3340, Premier compte, f. 27v., f. 29v.

37. Paris BN, MS. Fr. 17330, f. 131r.

38. Paris BN, MS. Fr. 17330, f. 134v.

39. Paris BN, MS. Fr. 17330, f. 138v.

40. See for example J. M. Bak, "Roles and functions of queens in Arpadian and Angevin Hungary (1000–1386 AD)", in Parsons, *Medieval Queenship*, p. 17.

10

Women in Aberdeen at the end of the Middle Ages[1]

Nicholas Mayhew

On 1 June 1507 women played an unusually large part in the work of the Aberdeen Burgh Court. But though it was unusual for their testimony to loom so large on any single day, the events described were pretty typical of the time. They provide a good introduction to the lives of Scots women at the beginning of the sixteenth century. The transcript of the day's business is as follows:[2]

> The said day Isabell Cullam the relict of umquihill Alexander Homsone grauntit that she set the forbutht quhilk David Brois dwellis in to Agnes Srathachin the spous' of Andr' Gardoni for this instant zeir.
>
> The said day George Delorh' grauntit him awand ane Frensh croun of gold to the wif of Thomas Watson quhilk the burges' chargit him to pay wuthin twenty dais.
>
> The said day the bailzes assignit friday that next cu'ms to Johne Ratui to prof that William Walker tuk his houB for this zeir.
>
> The said day Bessy Sibbald deponit be hir aith' that she was

godmod' to Isabell Buchane and Androu Branch' godfadyr and hews hir ane monday befor Festernevin and she dynit that day in Alex' Thain' houB she troueit she is xij zeir' ald or allis gangand in the twelf zeir and Andro Branch' and Alexd' Thain' was baith haill & fur that tym.

Janet Kupe spous' to Alexd' Tailzour deponit be hir aitht that Isabell Buchane dourht' and ayr till umquhill Willia' Bucham burges of Aberd is alevin zeir ald & mair.

Isabell of Culla' the relict' of Alexd' Thain deponit be hir aitht she hwyss Isabell Buchan ane moinday befor Festevinevine in thesaid Alexd' Thain' hir husband' tyme she was ane zeir or he deyt that she huf neu'e baun she trowit she paB alevin zeir ald.

Alexd' Prat deponit he knavis notht hir age.

Cristiane Mortun' deponit be hir aitht that Isabell Buchan' is xii zeir ald.

Margaret Buchane said Isabell Buchane is tuelf zeir ald. She is witht berne and mitht not suer bot she tuk it one hir saule Cristiane Lilburne deponit be hir aitht that Isabell Buchan' is alevin zeir auld at Festerinevin that last was.

Johnne Culla' deponit be his aitht he trastis the wut [= wit] produsit and the ald'ma' spell is trewe.

Johnne Mow deponit be his aitht that he was bundin witht Androwe Cullane in ane obligationn' to William Buchane for his manage gudis ane zeir before zane obligationn bundin be the prior of Monymusk.

David BroiBkenny's nay thing of hir age. Johnne Cuk kenni's nay thing of hir age. Margret Kintor kenny's nay thing of hir age.

Elizabetht Mouat medwif deponit be hir aitht she cane notht tell

ye eld' of Isabell Buchane bot be hir wittin she wantit part of four zeiris before ye ded' fra sanct Katherinis day to Fest' inevin.

the wif of Andᵒ Cullane deponit be hir aitht she wat notht quhat age Isabell Buchan is bot she coud gange ett and drink lang before ye ded'.

the said day It was sufficiently prouyt that Isabell Buchane dourht and ayr till umquhill Williame Buchane burges of the said burgh is alevin zeir ald & borne of hir modir at festinevin last bigane.

Commenting on each entry, paragraph by paragraph, we may note in paragraph one that a widow confirms that she has let the forbooth which some man dwells in to another woman for a year. We do not know what became of the man, but it looks as if the forbooth was taken by a married woman in her own name, distinct from that of her living husband – probably to run as some kind of retail premises. We should note the names. As was usual in Scotland – and also in Scandinavia and Portugal and no doubt elsewhere – a widow and a wife retained their own names alongside that of their husbands. Scottish women were often referred to only as the wife or widow of some named man. But on other occasions women's names are given in full, as here: Isabell Cullam, widow of Alexander Homsone; Agnes Strathachin, wife of Andrew Gardon. It is sometimes argued that it makes little difference if a woman is named after her father or her husband, but my own instinct is that the change of name associated with marriage does touch significantly on questions of personal identity and that the Scottish practice whereby a woman retained her own name throughout her life might have made some small, but nevertheless real, contribution to her self-perception and to how other people thought about her. For the historian, it is certainly a convenience: the use of a woman's own name, especially without mention of a husband, does seem to indicate that she is appearing in her own right, whether as spinster, widow, or other temporarily independent agent.

In the second paragraph, a man admits owing a woman one French gold crown, worth about fourteen shillings Scots or four shillings sterling. The woman is named only as the wife of Thomas Watson, suggesting perhaps that the debt was incurred as part of some deal in which husband and wife Watson worked together. It seems likely that we are looking at one of the many enterprises in which wives took an active part, extending credit and clinching deals, particularly when their husbands were away. If wife Watson had been lending money, as many women did, on her own account, we might have been told her name, though that is an inference which takes us beyond what the text tells us. The question is important since it may help us to identify independent women.[3] The third paragraph concerns a rental dispute between two men – the only exclusively masculine business of the day.

The rest of the day's record was taken up with an inquest into the age of Isabel Buchan, daughter and heir of the late (umquhill) William Buchan, burgess of Aberdeen. This question had been raised on several occasions before 1 June, and witnesses had been summoned for this day to settle the matter.

Bessy Sibbald, the child's godmother made a deposition under oath that Androu Branch had been the godfather and that Isabel was "hwyssed"[4] on the Monday before Festerneven, or Shrove Tuesday. The same night, the Monday, she dined in Alexander Thain's house, and Branch and Thain were both alive and well then, so, she says, the girl is twelve or going on twelve. Several women confirmed this age – for example, Janet Kupe, spouse of Alexander Tailor, and Christine Morton. And Isabel Culla', widow of Alexander Thain, in whose house the celebration supper had occurred, confirmed the day of the birth, saying it was a year before her husband died. Several men knew nothing about it, though one remembered a debt to the girl's father. Elizabeth Mouat, the midwife, did not know the girl's age, but remembered she had been nearly four when her father had died. Another woman confirmed that Isabel could eat and drink long before this death. One woman, Margaret Buchan, said Isabel was twelve, although, unlike the others, she did not swear an oath, apparently because she was pregnant: rather she made her deposition "on her soul".

This interesting case illustrates the propensity of husbands, fathers, and godfathers to die before their womenfolk, possibly at least partly because of the tendency for older, richer men to marry younger wives. It tells us nothing about the girl's mother, who is presumably dead also, but whose death apparently did not constitute any kind of landmark. Maybe she died at the birth. It is clear that women seem to be the more active custodians of local folk memory. There is something convincing about the detail that three of the men asked knew nothing about it, while only one woman did not have something to offer. Finally, is it the case that a pregnant woman was not permitted to give sworn testimony? Or did Margaret Buchan wish to distinguish between her soul and that of her unborn child?[5] What is the difference between a statement on oath and "taking it" on your soul? The answers to these questions would throw much light on women's attitudes and belief in early sixteenth-century Scotland.

Although 1 June 1507 was a day on which women were unusually prominent in court, it is a curiosity that there was no mention that day of the sort of business which most often brought women to court. Much more often, in the Aberdeen court records, we meet women as candle makers, cake bakers, petty retailers, servants, and, above all, as brewsters.[6] Quite often women pursued more than one of these activities. Thus Canny Guthre and the wife of Johnne Symm both brewed and dealt illegally in meal; the wives of Symne Flesher, Alexander Lamyntone, and Patsy Rait all brewed and made candles.[7] It has to be said that most of these activities were pretty low-status ways of making a living. Candle making must have been a foul business, involving the boiling of tallow. (Beef tallow was cheaper than mutton tallow because it lost more weight in the boiling process. And, incidentally, the wife of Symne Flesher – that is Symne the butcher – should have been excluded from candle making as her husband's profession gave her an unfair advantage.)

Cake bakers making oat cakes were far inferior to the town's bread baxters, who took their place in the Candlemas procession with the other prestigious craftsmen. The baxters were almost exclusively men and the cake bakers exclusively women. Oat cakes were the food of those too poor to buy bread. However, women's involvement in the manufacture of cakes and ale also made them major players in the market for malt and meal. Their role in this market, so central to the life of the town, is confirmed by two startling, and contradictory, pieces of legislation. In October 1438, in the aftermath of the worst European harvest of the century, women were banned from the victual market. Then, in October 1522, the burgh court ruled that eight women, two from each of the town's quarters, should assemble together on market days and agree the day's price for malt and meal with the growers from the surrounding country.[8] Both these policies – the one banning women from the market, the other putting them in charge of it – had their origins in an awareness of the overwhelming importance of the part women played in the Aberdeen victual market. The ban was a crude attempt to reduce demand at a time of desperately short supply. It may also have reflected a belief that the retail trade in cakes and ale fuelled prices; and that, at such a time of crisis, all purchases should be limited to immediate domestic needs. On the other hand, the promotion of women to a position of control indicates that, as the dominant buyers, they knew best the state of the market and the going price. It is noteworthy that by the beginning of the seventeenth century, the fixing of the market price of corn was firmly in male hands, as it was to remain into the twentieth century.

The power of women as customers, buying malt for brewing, is one aspect of women's work as brewsters which has not been much considered, yet cumulatively the brewsters consumption of malt must have been very significant. There were about a hundred and fifty brewsters in Aberdeen at this time,[9] and concerns about malt supplies sometimes limited each woman to one celdra per week. I have estimated elsewhere that something like two hundred and sixty to three hundred and ninety pounds Scots was spent on ale each week in Aberdeen. The Edinburgh trade may have been worth three times as much.[10] This was big business, albeit business spread pretty thinly between so many brewsters.

Estimates of the size of the brewing trade in late-medieval Scotland can only be extremely approximate. Yet they may serve to direct more attention towards the mundane areas of domestic consumption and production. Historians have a tendency to exaggerate the importance of export figures and other government-generated data, failing to recognize the extremely modest proportion of GDP contributed by international trade.[11] Economic and particularly social historians have generally been quicker to understand the importance of women than political historians, but even the economists may have paid too much attention to the rather male-dominated import-export trade and not enough to primary question of sustaining life where women's role was central.

But if ale was such big business, it seems all the more surprising that it was so much in the hands of women. Why brewing should have been so much a female activity, despite its importance, and when and why men eventually did take over the industry make interesting questions. The domestic origins of commercial brewing largely explain the early dominance of women brewsters.[12] Even as early as the eleventh century brewing was women's work, as the Domesday Book entry for Hereford makes clear. Although medieval English court records do not everywhere name women as the brewers in the way that they do in Aberdeen, it would seem that when men pay brewing fines they do so on behalf of the women for whom they were held responsible.[13] It would be interesting, however, to know exactly when the women really were ousted from commercial brewing. Bennett and Goldberg both found that men increasingly moved into brewing from the fifteenth century. Both are inclined to explain this development in terms of the use of hops, which improved the keeping qualities of beer, permitting the growth of larger breweries, serving wider areas and making bigger profits. As the scale of individual businesses grew, men moved in and women were increasingly confined to domestic ale brewing or retailing commercially brewed beer.[14] In the same way at Colchester, Britnell found beer imported in the fourteenth century, but by the 1450s and 1460s beer imports were replaced by hop imports, and: "The major brewers of the fifteenth century were specifically beer men."[15]

In contrast to these developments in the south, in Aberdeen women remained firmly in charge of commercial brewing well into the sixteenth century. For Aberdeen and Edinburgh, lists of brewsters in the early sixteenth century name only women, hundreds of them. One wonders why they were able to hold on longer in the north. It is possible that the energy the authorities there devoted to holding prices down may have helped to prevent the arrival of beer, and, therefore, the displacement of ale and of ale-wives. At any rate beer was still being imported, rather than made in Aberdeen, in 1502 when John Fechat was amerced for selling it at four pence (4d.) a quart rather than three pence (3d.). Any repetition of the offence was to be punished by striking out the barrel head.[16] Again, in 1509, the assize of beer for that year stipulates that infringements be punished by the striking out of the barrel head[17] – in contrast to the customary punishment for ale infringements, which could involve the destruction of the cauldron or lede, onomatopoeically described as action to "strike and ding forth their caldron or lede bottom".[18] The contrast is between ale-making and beer-retailing equipment. The fact that John Fechat – a man – was amerced for breaking the assize of beer may or may not be significant. We cannot be sure that this is evidence of men in the beer trade, as opposed to women in ale, since in the same year John Paterson was similarly amerced on behalf of his wife.[19] However, Wat Wischewit, who was selling beer with an unrighteous pint in the same year,[20] does add further weight to the idea of men importing and selling beer while women made and sold ale.

In the case of Edinburgh, Lynch has identified 1596 as a watershed for the town's women brewsters. He has written:

> The formation in Edinburgh of the Society of Brewers in 1596, backed by merchant capital, seriously undermined a traditional domestic industry. It was the first explicit change of policy made by urban authorities towards small commodity production; it also probably did more than any single other act to undermine the economic status of women, whether as wives or widows. Protected monopolies like brewing had been an important safety net in a society where as many as 20 per cent of households were made up of single women yet where there was no compulsory poor rate.[21]

The Aberdeen Stent Roll of 1655 provides an opportunity to look again at the brewers of the mid-seventeenth century in the north-east.[22] This list names forty-eight people earning money by brewing, of whom only ten were women. The completely female preserve, indicated by the brewsters list of 1509, has been very largely taken over by men. However, most of the men had other careers. So the suspicion remains that their wives or servants may still have actually been doing the brewing, but no longer controlling the business. By 1655, the writing was on the wall for the women brewsters of Aberdeen. Thirty of the forty-eight brewers were found in Footdee. The brewing which had been home-based and widespread was becoming localised and specialised, and these were developments which will have tended to reduce the role of women. [23]

Women's opportunities were similarly becoming restricted in other fields around this time. Women no longer served as pinors (dockers) after 1636,[24] and their role in the corn market seems also to have come to an end.[25] For England, Anthony Fletcher notes the trend running against women in brewing – and also medicine[26] – around this time, but he resists the suggestion that the early modern Englishwoman enjoyed less scope than her medieval forebears, pointing to new opportunities for women in needle-work and dressmaking.[27] Others have rejected the idea of a late-medieval golden age for women, because they regard the enduring patriarchy of medieval and modern times as more significant than relatively minor changes in the degree of women's subjection.[28] My impression, however, is that demographic growth in the sixteenth and seventeenth centuries did tend to crowd women out. Wherever men found work hard to find we would expect, at least until the late-twentieth century, to find women disproportionately disadvantaged.

Scottish brewsters thus seem to have been dispossessed some hundred, or even a hundred-and-fifty, years after their English sisters. If the arrival of beer was the critical factor, why did it take so much longer to become established in Scotland? It might be suggested that as a poorer country Scotland took longer to graduate to beer, but I am not convinced of this. We know Scotland imported beer, and if poverty were really the problem it would have been cheaper to import hops and brew beer in Scotland. It may be, however, that the regulation of the industry in Scotland made for circumstances less propitious for beer making. Whereas in England brewing fines in both town and country seem often to have developed into a licensing system, less concerned to police the industry or to protect the consumer than to generate income, the evidence from Aberdeen suggests that, there, fines were genuine penalties for offences and not licences.[29] Although fines were common, and large numbers of brewsters were often fined together, in Aberdeen these look like genuine fines because first offenders were treated more leniently. Sometimes punishment was even suspended, conditional on good behaviour thereafter.[30] Exceptionally serious offences could lead to more severe punishment, such as the loss of ale, the destruction of brewing equipment, or a ban on any brewing in future.[31] Moreover, fines do not occur regularly in Aberdeen, and we never meet the charge of brewing without a licence.

[149]

One of the commonest of these brewing offences was the infringement of the price regulations. These regulations appear to have been vigorously enforced, and may have generated some fairly colourful exchanges. Despite the obvious pleasures of ale tasting, fixing the price was bound to be difficult, in the first place because prices varied legitimately from year to year – reflecting harvest fluctuations. Not surprisingly, agreeing a price for a commodity of such infinitely variable quality sometimes gave rise to hot-tempered disputes. When Gilbert Brabner's wife was fined for selling sixteen-pence (16d.) ale, and ordered to hand it over for free distribution at the market cross, she was so angry she threw it away, even though she might have guessed that she would only be fined again – the money this time being used to buy more ale for distribution.[32] Nevertheless, the authorities were not deterred by the difficulty of the task. The assize of ale researched the price of grain, both locally and further afield, to try to establish a fair price for malt. For the administration of the assize, Aberdeen was divided into quarters (Even and Crukit, the Green and Futy); and a hierarchy of baillies, serjeants, officers, and cunnars (or tasters) marched from house to house, enforcing the assize and setting lower prices for ale of insufficient strength. The cunnars were meant to taste the ale outside the house in the street – to prevent the offering or taking of inducements. The fair price was then written up outside the house.

In October 1509, Bessy Layng, the wife of John Berryhill, was convicted by a sworn assize for disobeying John Cuk, the officer in the execution of his office. She took away the ale price set by Cuk from her door and wrote up another herself.[33] Others tried to cheat with false measures.[34] In other cases formal written notice of price was served on brewsters, presumably because they sometimes tried to plead ignorance of the assize as an excuse for breaking it.[35] In the vast majority of cases, however, brewsters offended merely by charging too much for their ale. This could mean more than the assize price formerly laid down in the burgh court, or more than the lesser price at which the cunnars valued ale if it were found not strong enough for the assize price. Unfree brewsters were not permitted to brew the best ale, and the top price set for their ale was always lower than that allowed for free brewsters.[36] Around 1500, prices were set at twelve pence (12d.) per gallon for beer, and sixpence (6d.) or eight pence (8d.) a gallon for ale. There is some evidence that Aberdeen ale prices may have been set on the low side,[37] and the same is probably true of beer. Town council restraint on ale and beer prices, and profits, could well have discouraged the investment necessary for large-scale beer production. Council action may thus have delayed the arrival of beer, postponed the development of local beer brewers, and prolonged the reign of the women ale brewsters. In short, while the town council worked hard to restrain brewsters' profits, and while the short life of ale helped to keep individual businesses small, women were able to stay in control.

However, the survival of the female Scottish brewster into the sixteenth century did not protect Scots women from growing hostility in early modern European towns. Legislation limiting women's freedom in the first half of the sixteenth century is usually framed in terms of high moral concern, not so much for the well-being of the women but about the large numbers of single women in the town and the temptation which they represented. In towns all over Britain and also on the continent,[38] though widows were thought respectable, unmarried women were regarded as a problem. The authorities' attempts to stop them setting up as brewsters, hucksters, or prostitutes – or even merely setting up in rooms on their own – argues that they were in fact doing just that in some numbers. Thus legislation in Edinburgh in 1530 ordered that no brewster might hire brewing equipment, but had to possess her own – a move clearly intended to reserve brewing to more established women. Legislation also complained that as soon as serving women saved five or six merks in service, they would take a house of their own and set up as a brewster or huckster. The authorities therefore declared that no serving woman should take a house unless she were married, nor could she "pas to the bordall except scho haif license of the provest for gud rationabil causis", under pain of banishment. Anyone letting a house to unmarried women was liable to a forty-shilling fine. Only freemen, freemen's wives, widows, and honest persons admitted by the provost and baillies were to brew or tap ale. At the same time all brewsters were required to find sureties for their proper performance of the craft. Husbands stood surety for their wives, but widows and spinsters had to find other men as guarantors.[39] The outbreak of this sort of legislation is sometimes associated with the Reformation and the ascendancy of Puritan attitudes. However, the Scottish chronology, where the legislation antedates the Reformation by some thirty years, may raise doubts about this interpretation; for me it all makes better sense in a demographic context. Single women had been flocking to the towns throughout the fifteenth century, but it was only with the growth of population associated with the sixteenth century that concerns about this arose. The message seems clear: when population was low, even women were welcome, but as the world became crowded, only men need apply.

NOTES

1. Much of the original research for this chapter was undertaken with the support of the ESRC, which led to the publication of Elizabeth Gemmill and Nicholas Mayhew, *Changing Values in Medieval Scotland: a study of prices, money and weights and measures* (Cambridge, 1995). Dr Gemmill's research for this volume effectively indexed the Aberdeen Council Burgh Registers, greatly aiding the search for women. Different versions of my essay have been read at the Universities of Exeter and Bristol, as well as at the Fifth Mackie Conference; and associated articles appear in the *Review of Scottish Culture* – see note 6 below; and in *Northern Studies* – see Nicholas Mayhew, "The brewsters of Aberdeen in 1509", *Northern Studies*, no. 32, pp. 71–81.
2. *Aberdeen Burgh Court Register*, vol. VIII, pp. 705–706, 1 June 1507.
3. Sharon Krossa, a postgraduate student at the University of Aberdeen, has done a good deal of work on women mentioned in the Aberdeen Court records in their own names.
4. Which I think means "shown": see Mairi Robinson (ed.), *Concise Scots Dictionary* (Aberdeen, 1987), under "wiss".
5. I am most grateful to Lynda Gillies of the University of Bristol, and to Professor Hector MacQueen of the University of Edinburgh, for this interesting suggestion. Thanks also to Dr Tim Stretton, Clare Hall, Cambridge, for advice on this problem.
6. For an earlier consideration of Aberdeen's brewsters, from which the present study has grown, see N. J. Mayhew, "The status of women and the brewing of ale in medieval Aberdeen", *Review of Scottish Culture*, no. 10 (1996–97), pp. 16–21.
7. Compare the brewsters list of 1509 and ACR vol. VIII, pp. 888, 1028.
8. Gemmill and Mayhew, *Changing Values*, pp. 63, 78.
9. A complete list of brewsters was drawn up on 5 November 1509, ACR, vol. III, pp. 1205–09.
10. Elizabeth Ewan, *Town Life in Fourteenth-century Scotland* (Edinburgh, 1990), p. 6, suggests there were almost four hundred brewsters in Edinburgh in 1529–30.
11. I have suggested elsewhere that the booming English export trade around 1300 may have accounted for about four per cent of English GDP: see my "Modelling medieval monetisation", in B. M. S. Campbell and Richard Britnell (eds), *A Commercialising Economy: England 1086–1300* (Manchester, 1995).
12. Judith M. Bennett, "The village ale-wife: women and brewing in fourteenth-century England", in Barbara Hanawalt (ed.), *Women and Work in Pre-industrial Europe* (Bloomington, 1986), p. 22.
13. Helena Graham, "'A woman's work ...': labour and gender in the late medieval countryside", in P. J. P. Goldberg (ed.), *Woman is a Worthy Wight: women in English society c. 1200–1500* (Stroud, 1992), pp. 126–148. Kowaleski

on Exeter takes a similar view. However, Kathy Troup's work (presented at the Women's History Conference at the University of Exeter in 1996) on the brewers of Wakefield may resuscitate Bennett's idea that men who paid fines may have been brewing themselves. Troup found some variation from court to court within Wakefield, though the personnel running and recording the courts was unchanged.

14. Judith M. Bennett, "Misogyny, popular culture, and women's work", *History Workshop Journal*, no. 31 (1991), pp. 166–188; P. J. P. Goldberg, *Women, Work and Life Cycle*. See especially Bennett's analysis of Oxford brewers (pp. 168, and 181, note 15), and of the Brewers' Company of London (p. 181); and Goldberg's work on York brewing (p. 114). Goldberg also cites R. H. Britnell, *Growth and Decline in Colchester, 1300–1525* (Cambridge, 1986), pp. 196–197. In addition to this explanation of men moving into brewing as individual businesses grew big enough to attract their attention, Bennett also draws attention to the role of misogyny in the process of driving women out.

15. Richard Britnell, *Growth and Decline in Colchester*, pp. 195–196.

16. ACR, vol. VIII, p. 110.

17. ACR, vol. VIII, p. 959. The same penalty also for a beer infringement appears in Edinburgh in 1499: see *Extracts from the records of the Burgh of Edinburgh 1403–1528* (SBRS, 1869), p. 75.

18. ACR, vol. VIII, p. 337.

19. ACR, vol. VIII, p. 116.

20. ACR, vol. VIII, p. 117.

21. M. Lynch, "Continuity and change in urban society, 1500–1700", in R. A. Houston and I. D. Whyte (eds), *Scottish Society 1500–1800* (Cambridge, 1989), p. 109.

22. I am most grateful to Siobhan Convery of the City of Aberdeen Archives who kindly made her transcript of the 1655 roll available to me. Without the ready help of Judith Cripps, the City Archivist, and her staff this chapter would not have been possible.

23. R. A. Houston, "Women in the economy and society of Scotland 1500–1800", in Houston and Whyte, *Scottish Society*, p. 122, gives much reduced numbers of women brewsters in the late-seventeenth and early eighteenth century in Fife (fourteen per cent women); Edinburgh (seventeen per cent women); and Aberdeen (seven per cent women).

24. I am most grateful to Sharon Krossa for this information.

25. The jurors who set the Fiars prices for grain in Aberdeen, 1604–1900, were all men: see *Miscellany: New Spalding Club*, II (Aberdeen 1908). For a discussion of the Fiars, see T. C. Smout and A. Gibson, *Prices, Wages and Food in Scotland, 1500–1800* (Cambridge, 1995).

26. For Elizabeth Mouat, an Aberdeen midwife, see ACR, vol. VIII, p. 706.

27. Anthony Fletcher, *Gender, Sex and Subordination in England 1500–1800* (New Haven and London 1995), pp. 227–255. For the argument that women in the

later Middle Ages were less severely disadvantaged than before or after that time, see especially, Caroline M. Barron, "The 'Golden Age' of women in medieval London", in *Medieval Women in Southern England*, Reading Medieval Studies, vol. 15 (1989).

28. The classic statement of this position is by J. M. Bennett, "History that stands still", *Feminist Studies*, vol. 14 (1988), pp. 269–283.

29. Licensing did occur regularly in many English towns and manors. See Bennett, "The village ale-wife", p. 21 and note 3; and Goldberg, *Women, Work and Life Cycle*, p. 111, citing Winchester, and Colchester as well as York.

30. For first offenders, see 8 March 1406, ACR, vol. I, p. 274; 3–4 Nov. 1540, ACR vol. XVI, pp. 633, 635. For suspended sentences, see 14 Jan 1490, ACR, vol. VII, p. 160; 15 Oct. 1507, ACR vol. VIII, p. 757; 17 Oct. 1521, ACR vol. X, p. 370. On other occasions punishment failed to deter offenders: see 8–11 May 1461, ACR vol. V I, pp. 421, 438; 6 May 1482, ACR vol. VI, p. 734; 12 Feb. 1524, ACR vol. XI, p. 401.

31. "The unlaw, the lede tane up and the bodome stukkin owt vnforgevin bot ony fauour." See Sir James D. Marwick (ed.), *Extracts from the Records of the Burgh of Edinburgh* (Scottish Burgh Records Society, Edinburgh, 1869): this extract dated 1450; 15 Dec. 1451, ACR, vol. V. i, p. 134 – a wife barred from the craft.

32. Gemmill and Mayhew, *Changing Values*, p. 29.

33. ACR, vol. VIII, p. 1028. Curiously Berryhill's wife appears in the brewsters list in Androu Naughtie's quarter.

34. 20 May 1482, ACR vol. VI, p. 736: a famine year, and the time of black money. See also ACR vol. VIII, p. 561, though on this occasion their fault may have been a failure to come into line with a reform of measures rather than an attempt to defraud their customers. See Gemmill and Mayhew, *Changing Values*, p. 102.

35. 5 Nov. 1505, ACR vol. VIII, p. 515.

36. Pamela Sambrook tells me that this weaker ale would have been more difficult to make and keep than the stronger ale.

37. Gemmill and Mayhew, *Changing Values*, p. 53.

38. Houston, "Women in the economy and society", p. 133, cites cases in Dunfermline, Stirling, St Andrews, Kirkintilloch, Worcester, Manchester and Bradford. Sian Jones in "Out of the footnotes: the 16th century sisterhood of Southampton wool packers", a paper read to the Second Exeter International Gender History Conference in 1996, mentioned similar attitudes in Southampton. Also on Malmo in 1549, see Grethe Jacobsen, "Women, marriage, and magistenai Reformation: the case of Malmo, Denmark", in Kyle C. Sessions and Phillip N. Bebb (ed.), *Pietas et Societas: new trends in Reformation social history. Essays in memory of Harold J. Grimm* (Kirksville, MO, 1985), p. 76, citing Emar Barger (ed.), *Malmo Stadsboa 1549–59* (Copenhagen, 1972), pp. 35–36.

39. Sir James D. Marwick, *Extracts from the Records of the Burgh of Edinburgh: AD 1528–1557* (SBRS, 1871), pp. 24, 27, 40, 43–46. For 1546 see p. 124. Houston, "Women in the economy and society", p. 133, cites the instructive case of Marion Alexander in Stirling in 1621 who "confessis she brew eall in ane house be hir self and sell it; quhilk tread she is commanded to leave off seeing she is ane singill woman be hir self, and commanded to entir in honest serveice."

11

Women and the colonial experience in Ireland, c. 1550–1650

Mary O'Dowd

The study of colonisation in Ireland has attracted the attention of some of Ireland's most eminent historians, including the late T. W. Moody, D. B. Quinn, Nicholas Canny, and many others.[1] But despite the volume of literature on Irish colonial projects, almost nothing has been written on the role of gender or women in Irish plantation schemes. There are perhaps understandable reasons for this absence. Much of the research on Irish colonial projects was published before the regeneration of women's history in the 1970s and 1980s and it is not, therefore, surprising that it did not include an assessment of the role of women. More important, however, is the long-term problem of the dearth of source material relating to women in Irish colonial schemes. Very few court records survive for early modern Ireland and only a small number of family papers date to before 1660. In other words, the sort of sources that historians of women have used so profitably in the study of other colonial societies do not exist for Ireland. This chapter attempts to piece together the information which is available and to develop an outline, however shadowy, of the role of women in the Irish colonial experience.

I

Irish colonial projects initially developed out of the need for military defence. In the 1530s the collapse of the power of the earls of Kildare left the Pale area surrounding Dublin vulnerable to attack from neighbouring Irish lords. To deal with this problem, two forts were established in the Laois-Offaly region on the borders of the Pale. These forts became the focus for Ireland's first official colonial project as plans were developed to transform the military garrison into a permanent settlement. The key personnel in the settlement were to be English soldiers who were given the dual responsibility for military defence and civilian settlement. [2]

The military, and therefore exclusively male, basis of the Laois-Offaly settlement was problematic. The soldiers were not committed to the colonial aims of the government and there were many complaints concerning their behaviour in the region. Most seriously for the future of the English settlements which they were supposed to be spearheading, the soldiers mixed freely with the local Irish community and the two forts were regularly reported to have entertained local women. In 1550 Lord Deputy Sir Anthony St Leger suggested that the two forts had as many harlots in them as soldiers.[3] The ultimate failure of the Laois-Offaly plantation, indeed, was attributed by contemporaries to the fact that the soldiers "matched" with local Irish women. The women were alleged to have spied on the garrison and acted as informers to their families. Irish wives of English soldiers, according to one commentator, were directly responsible for much of the depredation in the area. [4]

The Laois-Offaly experience raised two important issues in relation to the role of women in a colony. First, sexual contact between male settlers and local women was perceived to have undermined the colony. Irish women were deemed to have all the worst characteristics traditionally associated with women and none of the redeeming ones: they were lustful, licentious, full of guile and deceit and lacking in personal and domestic hygiene. Consequently, they were incapable of being suitable spouses for civilised men.[5] They represented not only a threat to the male settlers but to the whole civilising influence of English society in Ireland.

Apart from seeming to demonstrate the contaminating effects of contact with Irish women, the failure of the Laois-Offaly colonial project also made clear, as Nicholas Canny has noted, that little could be expected of soldiers as colonisers. In subsequent schemes, recruitment of a wider occupational, social, and gender mix was integrated into the initial plans. In the next wave of colonial projects in the 1560s and 1570s, for example, married English men were identified as an essential element in the colonial community. Thomas Smith also intended to prohibit the tenants on his plantation from marrying Gaelic wives. Smith envisaged a small colony of English who employed the Irish as labourers but did not have sexual or social intercourse with them. [6]

The plans for the Munster plantation in the 1580s developed further the theory of a segregated colonial society. Based firmly on the belief that "intermixture of the Irish with the English" would lead to the overthrow of the colony, the Munster scheme envisaged nucleated settlements "without interruption or intermixture of others". Land was to be leased only to those born of English parents, and female heirs were to marry only those of English birth.[7] The employment of Irish servants was forbidden and no Irish person was to be permitted to reside in any family in the colony. As Michael McCarthy Morrogh noted: "What the authorities wanted were households of English undiluted by Irish nurses, servants, or underlings."[8]

The Ulster plantation project of the early seventeenth century envisaged an even more exclusive colonial society than that planned for Munster. The original intention was to clear the indigenous population totally from certain areas and settle them entirely with British people.[9] Intermarriage between Irish and British was not forbidden by the planners, but implicit in the scheme was the belief that the British settlements would be self-perpetuating. The success of the scheme, as one official noted, depended on a fertility programme. The instructions to the settlers were "to exceed them [the Irish] in multitude if it be possible." [10]

The concern of the planners with the nature of the contact between Englishmen and Irish women is also evident in the final colonial project undertaken in Ireland in the 1650s. This last scheme mirrored the first in that it was dominated by English soldiers; and the attraction of Irish women for lonely English soldiers once more became a problem. But by the 1650s official attitudes had undergone a subtle change. Although relations with Irish women were still viewed with distaste, it was accepted that conversion to Protestantism might have a beneficial effect. Irish women converts were, however, often suspected of conforming "for some corrupt or carnal ends" rather than for religious reasons. Accordingly, inter-marriage between serving soldiers and local women was forbidden unless the woman could pass an oral examination "by a board of military saints" to prove that her conversion was genuine. The artful and deceitful image of Irish women continued to flourish despite the growth in the belief in the redeeming power of Protestantism. [11]

The traditional dual image of the benign and malign powers of women was given a particular formulation in Irish colonial theory. While Irish women were portrayed as guileful and licentious creatures capable of destroying the colonial ideal, English women were hailed as a positive force on whom the future of the colony depended. In 1623, an English commentator on Ireland recommended that the Irish should match their children, but especially their sons, with British or Old English families, because "the child follows more the mother than any in his language and manners".[12] Henry Carey, Lord Falkland, who served as lord deputy in Ireland in the 1620s made a similar point in relation to his proposed plantation in Newfoundland. Mixing of the planters with the local community, Falkland argued, would lead to the "drowneinge of our men". He requested that only educated English women be allowed into his plantation because this would "make a good nation in tyme for those will maintaine the language to ther Children & then it is noe great matter of wha[t] nation the men bee soe the women bee Englishe."[13] The Protestant, English, mother-educator had an essential role to play in early modern colonies. The special tests administered to Irish female converts to Protestantism may, in fact, have been partly motivated by a recognition of the vital contribution of the wife and mother to the evangelical and colonial mission of the commonwealth regime in Ireland.

II

Clearly, therefore, women were considered a central element in the colonial community by the theorists and planners of colonial projects in Ireland. It is, however, difficult to assess the actual number of women who came to live on an Irish plantation. The first scheme was dominated by soldiers but even in the 1560s and 1570s, despite the plans of the sponsors, the majority of recruits appear to have been male. In the Smith and Essex projects in north-eastern Ulster no reference is made to women settlers. In both cases, the plan was to establish a secure settlement with a predominantly soldier population, and then recruit on a wider social and gender basis. As neither scheme got beyond the first stage, it may be presumed that women did not feature in either.[14] Statistical information on the number of women in the two most successful Irish plantation projects in Munster and Ulster is scarce and difficult to interpret. Although population surveys were taken of both at regular intervals in their initial years, none of the surveys provides detailed statistics on gender. The surveyors were concerned to list the main tenants, who were overwhelmingly male, the number of "families" on each estate, and, in the case of the Ulster plantation, the number of adult British men capable of using arms and thus defending the settlement. Only rarely is the composition of the "family" detailed. It is also clear that the government-sponsored surveys seriously over-estimated the number of British families living on the plantation before 1641. Undertakers, concerned to convince the surveyors that they were successfully fulfilling the terms of their land grant, exaggerated the number of freeholders on their estates. Members of the same family, including wives and children, were returned as individual freeholders and, hence, counted as a separate "family".[15]

Some statistics for the Munster plantation provide information on gender. In 1589 the undertakers in the Munster plantation were obliged to certify the number of English tenants on their lands and a small number included a gender breakdown in their reports. On Sir Walter Raleigh's estate one hundred and forty-four men were listed, seventy-four of whom were accompanied by wife and "family". The agent for Sir Christopher Hatton recorded fifteen English men and eight English women on his lands and on another estate it was reported that thirty-two out of thirty-five Englishmen were accompanied by their wives and children.[16] Out of a list of twenty-two tenants on the lands of Sir William Herbert in Castleisland, only one was recorded as not being accompanied by a wife – and he lived with his sister on the estate. The households on the Herbert lands ranged in size from two to ten persons, but the average was four.[17] Other settlers in Munster also recorded households of four or five persons although a small number were much larger.[18] Thus at a rough calculation over half of the men on the Munster plantation were accompanied by their wives and most lived in small households which probably consisted of a man, his wife, children, and one servant or none at all.

In Ulster, an analysis of the government-sponsored surveys, even without taking into consideration their exaggerated nature, indicates that the initial number of British women on the plantation lands was much lower than that in Munster. A survey of 1611 conveys an impression of a small number of undertakers in residence with their wives and "family". The fact that the presence of wives and "family" is recorded in the case of some grantees suggests that this was a positive point to be noted. In the majority of cases where no reference is made to wives or "family" it might be assumed that they were not present. Tenants with wives were also thinly scattered. There are references to promises to bring over more tenants with wives and children and to tenants having returned home allegedly for the purpose of bringing back their families.[19] By the time of the survey of 1618-1619, although the number of undertakers in residence with their wives had risen, it still represented only a small proportion of the total.[20] In 1622 the presence of an undertaker's wife and "family" was still considered to be a point worth emphasising by the surveyor, which might be interpreted as implicitly indicating that men still outnumbered women in many parts of the plantation.[21]

The low female population within the settler community is particularly evident in the records of the London companies which were responsible for the plantation of the new county of Coleraine. As T. W. Moody documented, the city's interest in Ireland was primarily a commercial one. In its agreement with the crown, the city committed itself to fulfilling the building conditions laid down by the government but made little effort to recruit settlers for Ulster. Consequently, the only settlers who came to Ulster directly through the companies' efforts were the workmen employed in building.[22] Some of these workmen brought their wives and children with them, intending to settle in Ireland, but the surviving records convey an impression that the vast majority travelled alone. They came to Ulster to work on a building site and many may have had no long-term plans to stay in the province. In one case, a man arranged for his wife to be given an allowance from his wages while he worked in Ireland; there were probably other men who provided for their families back in England in this way.[23] Others may have come alone in order to assess the situation in Ulster before they committed themselves and their families to permanent settlement.

If the main settlers on the London Company's plantation were the workmen employed as builders, then it follows that the early settlement was a predominantly male one which may have had more of the characteristics of a migrant working community than that of a settled population. One man, a carpenter on the Ironmongers' lands, described how when he and his colleagues began work in Ulster they were lodged "upon rushes in dirty cabins where we lay piled up one upon another",[24] a description which brings to mind the sort of temporary shanty town in which migrant workers live rather than a colonial community with a balanced sex ratio. The mason on the Drapers' Company's lands, George Birkett, was "dieted" in what was described as a "lodging house" where there was "plenty of ale, wine and aquavitae with no want of good fellowship". Birkett was not paid his wages by the company's agent and consequently ran up a huge "score" or debt at the lodging house. He later complained that he was paid his wages in beer and brown bread.[25]

There was a crown garrison near the Drapers' lands in Desertmartin and, against the instructions of the company, land was leased to soldiers serving in the garrison. The company, perhaps recalling previous plantation schemes in Ireland, believed that soldiers did not make good colonists. John Rowley, the company's agent in Ireland, agreed that "honest laborious men out of England" might have conformed more to the colonial ideal but, as he bluntly pointed out, such men were as "rare as black swans" on the company's lands.[26]

The presence of the soldiers added to the male ethos of the society in Draperstown. The lodging house where George Birkett stayed was run by Jane Russell and her husband Roger. Jane was described as a camp follower of the army, having travelled with the soldiers from the Low Countries to Ireland;[27] and the Russells provided hospitality for the soldiers as well as for the workmen on the Drapers' Company's lands. The company's records also indicate that brewing and selling of beer was the most profitable business in the new town. When Birkett's wife eventually joined her husband in Ireland, she decided to start selling beer in her house, partly to pay off her husband's debts but also to "keep him [i.e. her husband] at home".[28] One of the first actions of Robert Russell when he succeeded Rowley as the company's agent was to build a large brewhouse and to try to secure from the company a monopoly of the brewing and sale of alcohol in the town. There were also accusations that Russell only employed workmen who spent their wages in his alehouse.[29] In establishing his brewing business, Russell was in competition not only with Jane Russell and Mrs Birkett but with the many other "cabin brewers" in the town. These shebeens were run by English and Irish men although the brewing appears to have been done mainly by Irish women. Russell maintained that many of the cabin brewers kept Irish servant women to brew beer "whereby much evil and filthiness is committed thereby as one of late murdered her child and such like".[30] Clearly, the existence of a large number of outlets for the sale and drinking of alcohol did not encourage the sort of ideal British society envisaged by the planners of the plantation. Irish men and women mixed freely with the settlers in the shebeens making "rhymes and songs ... and such like behaviour to the raising of quarrels and breaches of the peace."[31]

The lands of the Drapers' Company were situated in one of the remotest part of the city of London's plantation, a fact which made recruitment of suitable settlers particularly difficult, but the records of other companies suggest that life in Draperstown was not that extraordinary. The agent on the Mercers' Company's lands, for example, installed a tap room in the castle for the sale of alcohol,[32] while there were many complaints about the large number of taverns and alehouses in Derry and Coleraine where there was also concern at the troublesome behaviour of the workmen.[33] The government urged the London authorities in charge of the plantation to send men "yt fear God" rather than "common drunkards or disreputable persons".[34]

Historians of the Ulster plantation have argued that a successful settlement of an estate depended not just on a favourable location but also on the willingness and ability of the undertaker to financially assist the relocation of settlers. The London Companies were clearly reluctant to increase their initial investment in their Ulster estates but elsewhere on the plantation, there were undertakers who actively encouraged settlement and may also have succeeded in establishing a more balanced sex ratio in a shorter period than is evident in County Londonderry.[35] In 1622 the composition of the "families" on one English proportion was recorded. The list noted a total of thirty-nine families on the land in the barony of Oneilland in Co. Armagh. The total population was two hundred and seventeen, consisting of sixty-eight men, sixty-two women, and seventy-seven children. Eighteen families had an equal number of men and women while thirteen had more men than women. Only eight families had more women than men. The average household size was five, and in eleven families, the household consisted of a man, a woman, and children. Six families had two men, two women, and children, which may have represented a married couple and grandparents. The average ratio of men to a family was almost 2:1. As in Munster, households were generally small and the nuclear family formed the core of the family unit and in many cases its entirety.[36]

The evidence for the presence of women in the early decades of the Ulster plantation is, therefore, uneven. The surveys suggest a low female presence before 1622, a situation confirmed by the records of the London Companies, particularly those of the Drapers' Company. In some areas, however, the sex ratio was more evenly balanced by the 1620s although it was still in favour of men. It is important to note, however, that a low sex ratio did not have the same wider or long-term implications for society in Ulster as it did in parts of colonial America. The close proximity of the home country, particularly Scotland, meant that a scarcity of women in an Irish colony could be relatively easily eliminated. There is evidence, for example, that Scottish men returned home to look for a wife;[37] Nicholas Canny found that, by 1641, the majority of male British deponents in Munster and in Ulster were married with British wives.[38] This would suggest that, in the course of the 1620s and 1630s, society in the

Ulster plantation underwent a transformation from being a predominantly male society to one in which there was a more even sex ratio. The implication of this change for relations between the settler community and the local indigenous population may also have been significant. In the initial years contact with the Irish-born population was relatively relaxed but as the settlement established itself and began to attract more British women, so too it became more inward looking and contact with the local community may have become more guarded and restricted. In the attacks on the settlers at the beginning of the rebellion in 1641 men and women were subject to violent and humiliating treatment. The clothes of the women seem to have been particularly resented by the attackers, perhaps because they were the most visual reminder of the changed nature of Ulster society.[39]

III

No first-hand accounts by women of their experiences in an Irish colony are known to have survived. The only detailed description that we have of the role of a woman in the early years of a plantation is an eighteenth-century account of a Scottish woman, Elizabeth Montgomery, whose husband was a planter in the Ards peninsula. The account relates how Lady Montgomery had:

> her farms at Greyabbey and Coiner [Cumber], as well as at Newtown, both to supply new-comers and her house; and she easily got men for plough and barn, for many came over who had not stocks to plant and take leases of land, but had brought a cow or two and a few sheep, for which she gave them grass and so much grain per annum, and an house and garden-plot to live on, and some land for flax and potatoes, ...; and this was but part of her good management, for she set up and encouraged linen and woollen manafactory, which soon brought down the prices of ye breakens [i.e. tartans] and narrow cloths of both sorts.[40]

The description suggests that Lady Montgomery was not only fully involved in the economic development of the estate but that she was also an active agent in the encouragement of the plantation settlement.

Lady Montgomery's husband "was by business much and often kept from home".[41] During his absence Lady Montgomery ran the estate and took responsibility for overseeing the building and decorating of the family home.[42] The 1622 survey of the plantation indicates that a number of women were living on the family's Ulster lands without their husbands, a reverse of the situation in 1611 when men were recorded as in residence but not having yet brought over their families. In some cases the women were widows who had taken over their husband's undertaker's responsibilities. In other cases the surveyor noted that the husband was in England or in Scotland.

It is not always clear if this was a temporary or permanent arrangement. In Fermanagh, for example, Lady Worrall was resident on the lands of her husband but he was in England. Sir Robert Hamilton was also in England but his wife, children, and "many servants" were living on his Irish estate.[43] In Cavan William Hamilton's wife with some servants was found on his lands but the survey recorded that Hamilton "resides not upon it".[44] Hugh Mitchell and his wife and family were "usually" resident "but he is now himself in Scotland".[45] Captain Callum was in England but his wife, children, and family were in residence on his lands.[46] Mrs Obbins's husband was recorded as being in prison in England but she was noted as living in the family house in Armagh.[47] Male under-tenants were also noted as being absent while their wife and family remained resident. The small pool of suitable recruits for service in the Irish administration meant that many landlords held official positions which demanded their attendance in Dublin or London. Consequently, the wives of Irish landlords were perhaps more likely to find themselves running estates than their English or colonial counterparts.[48]

It is also possible that in some instances a husband and wife were maintaining two households with the wife being given responsibility for managing and retaining the Irish property. In the 1650s women from Catholic landed families were left to retain an interest in the family's property in Ireland while their husbands, fathers, and brothers went to the continent to secure military employment. A similar situation might have developed among some undertakers' families in Ulster with the men returning to the home county possibly to serve in local government or maintain the family's political interests.[49]

The impression that women played an important role in the economic life of the household is also conveyed by the depositions recorded after the outbreak of the rebellion of 1641. As a consequence of the rebellion a large number of women in the settler community in Ulster were widowed but in the depositions they were able to provide detailed lists of the property and goods which they and their husbands had lost. The lists itemise animal stock, crops, leases, rent arrears, and debts owned. The widows appear to have been very familiar with the business affairs of

their husbands. Most of the widows in Ulster were from farming households and many had a thorough knowledge of the stock on the farm and
could often provide the age of the animals as well as additional details as
to their value. Thus in Co. Cavan, Jane Oliver recorded the loss of fifteen
English and one Irish cow, worth £3 each; six two-year-old English
heifers, worth 25/- (£1.25) each; six one-year-old heifers worth 10/- (50p.)
each; a horse worth £1.10/- (£1.50); as well as grain and household stuff.
Jane Taylor listed among her losses: twenty milch cows and a bull, five
two-year-old heifers and a young bull, one fair breeding mare in foal, as
well as leases and hides and leather in a tanhouse. Christian Stanhope
noted that she and her husband had lost seven travelling geldings and
nags, one standhorse, twenty-four mares, fillies and other horses and
colts (all English breed), twenty English cows, ten fair oxen of English
breed, six Irish fatted beeves, two bulls, twenty-five heads of young cattle
(all English breed), fifty-four English sheep, and wool, and fourteen
swine.[50]
  The details which the women could provide of the animals and stock
lost from their farms suggests that they were all involved in working on
the farm alongside their husbands. As Grey Osterud has pointed out,
pastoral forms of farming depended more on the labour of women to
look after stock than did arable farming[51] and were particularly suited to
the family farm which appears to have been prevalent in the plantation.
There is no sense in the depositions that work on the farm was divided
along gender lines. Dairy or spinning utensils are, for example, rarely
noted. Few of the women deponents list household goods in detail giving
an impression that their loss was of less importance to them than the
farmstock.[52]

IV

In conclusion, this brief survey demonstrates that women were important
in the colonial process in a number of ways. The architects of plantation
recognised the vital role of women in the colony and their potential to
either destroy or nourish the ideal English or British community. After
the fiasco of the Laois-Offaly plantation the sponsors of colonial projects
devised schemes and drew up conditions for planters that were aimed at
keeping British settlers from contact with Irish women. Women were
perceived as the cultural carriers and transmitters of civil behaviour to
the next generation. They were thus central to the cultural and social life
of the colony. While Irish women could lead English men into

"degeneracy" English women could nourish and strengthen the anglicising process.

Asking questions relating to women also adds a useful and refining tool of analysis to the study of the Irish colonial experience. This is particularly the case in examining population statistics and the sex ratio in the colonies. Although the source material has serious limitations, gender analysis helps not only to determine the different types of settlement, particularly in Munster and Ulster, but also points to the way in which the Ulster plantation underwent an important transformation in the 1620s and 1630s as more British women came to live in Ireland.

The examination of the economic role of women in colonial Ireland is still in its initial stages. Much more information can be teased from the surviving sources, particularly the 1641 depositions. But even the brief analysis which this paper provides raises some new questions about the Irish colonial experience. Women appeared to have shared the agricultural work with their male partners; in the undertaker or landlord class a number of women had full responsibility for the management of estates during their husbands' frequent absences. Consequently, it may be worth investigating how many Ulster landlords held official positions or owned land outside Ulster. The deposition material might also be examined to discover how many women were on their own when they were attacked. Re-examining the violence of 1641 from a gendered point of view could also provide a new perspective on the phenomenon of the massacres.

The Irish colonial experience differed from that of other countries in many ways. Ireland's proximity to England meant that contact with the home country was always more frequent than was the case elsewhere. The fact that Irish women were white and Christian also distinguished Ireland from the situation in other colonies where skin colour made a clear distinction between colonisers and colonised. While Irish women were only grudgingly admitted to the commonwealth in Ireland, they were more acceptable as sexual partners in other English colonies. Paradoxically, in the 1650s, English soldiers in Ireland were protected from the evil allures of Irish women by the transportation of Irish women "who were marriageable and not past breeding" to the West Indies.[53] Unlike colonised women in other countries Irish women could, thus, be transformed into the colonisers. An analysis of women and Irish colonies may not therefore provide new insights into women's experiences elsewhere but it undoubtedly adds a fresh perspective from which to study sixteenth- and seventeenth-century Ireland.

NOTES

The author acknowledges the permission of the Deputy Keeper of the Records, Public Record Office of Northern Ireland, and the Drapers' Company, to cite material from the Drapers' Company records.

1. T. W. Moody, *The Londonderry Plantation, 1609–41* (Belfast, 1939); D. B. Quinn, "Sir Thomas Smith and the beginnings of English colonial theory", *Proceedings of the American Philosophical Society*, vol. lxxxix (1945), pp. 543–560; "Ireland and sixteenth century European expansion", *Historical Studies*, vol. i (1958), pp. 20–32; "The Munster Plantation: problems and opportunities", *Journal of Cork Historical and Archaeological Society*, vol. lxxi (1966), pp. 19–41; *Raleigh and the British Empire* (2nd edn, London, 1962); *The Elizabethans and the Irish* (Ithaca, New York, 1966); Nicholas Canny, *The Elizabethan Conquest of Ireland: a pattern established 1565–1576* (Hassocks, Sussex, 1976); *Kingdom and Colony. Ireland in the Atlantic World, 1560–1800* (Baltimore and London, 1988); "The permissive frontier: social control in English settlements in Ireland and Virginia, 1550–1650", K. R. Andrews et al (eds), *The Westward Enterprise* (Liverpool, 1978), pp. 17–44; "Dominant minorities: English settlers in Ireland and Virginia, 1550–1650", A. C. Hepburn (ed.), *Minorities in History* (Belfast, 1978), pp. 17–44; Philip Robinson, *The Plantation of Ulster: British settlement in an Irish landscape, 1600–1670* (Dublin, 1984); Michael Perceval-Maxwell, *The Scottish Migration to Ulster in the Reign of James I* (London, 1973); Michael McCarthy-Morrogh, *The Munster Plantation, 1580–1641* (Oxford, 1985).
2. Robert Dunlop, "Plantation of Leix and Offaly 1556–1622", *English Historical Review*, vol. vi (1891), pp. 61–96.
3. Vincent P. Carey, "Gaelic reaction to plantation: the case of the O'More and O'Connor lordships of Laois and Offaly, 1570–1603" (unpublished MA thesis, St Patrick's College, Maynooth, 1985), p. 217. See also Canny, *The Elizabethan Conquest*, pp. 35–36.
4. Carey, "Gaelic reaction to plantation", pp. 255–256.
5. See, for example, the extracts from Fynes Moryson, *Itinerary* (1607), published in C. L. Falkiner (ed.), *Illustrations in Irish History and Topography* (London, 1904).
6. Canny, *The Elizabethan Conquest of Ireland*, pp. 66–92.
7. Canny, "Dominant minorities", p. 53. The definition of "English" was, after some debate, extended to include members of the Anglo-Irish community.
8. McCarthy-Morrogh, *The Munster Plantation*, p. 36.
9. Philip Robinson, *The Ulster Plantation* is the best introduction to the plan.
10. McCarthy-Morrogh, *The Munster Plantation*, p. 177.
11. J. P. Prendergast, *The Cromwellian Settlement of Ireland* (3rd edn, Dublin, 1922), pp. 231–234.
12. George O'Brien (ed.), *Advertisements for Ireland* (Dublin, 1923), p. 50.

13. Lord Falkland's instructions to his settlers in Gillian T. Cell (ed.), *Newfoundland Discovered: English Attempts at Colonisation 1610-1630* (Hakluyt Society, 2nd series, 160, 1982), pp. 244-245. I am grateful to Dr John Appleby for this reference.

14. Canny, *The Elizabethan Conquest*, pp. 85-92.

15. Nicholas Canny's forthcoming study of the English colonial community in Ireland will provide more detailed analysis of this topic. See, for example, John Rowley's settlement of the Drapers' Company lands before the visit of Sir Josias Bodley (Rowley to the Drapers' Company, 4, 26 October, 22 November 1616, Public Record Office of Northern Ireland (hereafter PRONI), D/3632/A/28, 17-19). Among the freeholders and leaseholders on the Drapers' Company estate were seven members of the Rowley family including three women: see PRONI, D/3623/A/31. "Family" in an early modern sense usually referred to all members of the household.

16. *Calendar of State Papers Ireland, 1588-92*, pp. 168-172; Public Record Office, London, SP 63/144, nos 11a, 28, 68, 73; SP63/145, nos 40, 42.

17. National Library of Ireland, MS. 7861, ff. 177-178.

18. See note 16 above.

19. Lambeth Palace, Carew MS. 30.

20. The survey was printed in George Hill, *An Historical Account of the Plantation in Ulster at the Commencement of the Seventeenth Century 1608-1620* (Belfast, 1877), pp. 445-590.

21. See, for example, Victor Treadwell (ed.), "The survey of Armagh and Tyrone, 1622", *Ulster Journal of Archaeology*, vol. 27 (1964), pp. 143, 144, 145, 148, 149, 151.

22. The only exception being the twelve boys from Christ's Hospital who were sent over by the city to work as apprentices and servants. There is, however, no record of their experiences in Ireland: see Moody, *The Londonderry Plantation*, pp. 168, 173, 278, 322.

23. James Stevens Curls, *The Londonderry Plantation 1609-1914* (Chichester, Sussex, 1986), p. 43.

24. Elias Jerman to the Ironmonger Company, 15 July 1614 in Guildhall Library, London, Ironmonger Records, MS. 17277, p. 37.

25. Robert Russell to Drapers' Company, 2 December 1618 in PRONI, D/3632/A/45, part 2, 209; George Birkett to Drapers' Company, 8 July 1618 in PRONI, D/3632/A/94, 214; Robert Russell to Drapers' Company, 23 February 1618 in PRONI, D/3632/A/45, part 1, ff. 165-166.

26. John Rowley to Drapers' Company, 13 June 1617, in PRONI, D/3632/A/20.

27. Robert Russell to Drapers' Company, 20 November 1618, in PRONI, D/3632/A/45, part 2, 193-195.

28. Same to same, 2 December 1618, in PRONI, D3632/A/45, part 2, 209. There is no evidence that Robert Russell was related to Jane and Roger Russell.

29. Complaints against Robert Russell, 11 December 1618 in PRONI,

D3632/A/105; George Birkett to Drapers' Company, no date (PRONI, D/3632/A/45, part 1, 109).

30. Robert Russell to Drapers' Company, 20 December 1617 in PRONI, D/3632/A/45, part 1, 154–158; same to same, no date, in PRONI, D/3632/A/45, part 1, 109.

31. Ibid.

32. Curl, *The Londonderry Plantation*, p. 126. See also p. 54

33. Moody, *The Londonderry Plantation*, pp. 112, 343.

34. Moody, *The Londonderry Plantation*, p. 168.

35. Perceval-Maxwell, *The Scottish Migration to Ulster*, p. 127. See also Gillespie, *Colonial Ulster*, p. 55. The close proximity of Scotland would have made it easier for Scottish women to travel alone to Ulster to join their husbands. The journey for English women would have been a great deal more arduous.

36. National Library of Ireland, MS. 8014/9. See also Perceval-Maxwell, *The Scottish migration to Ulster*, p. 126.

37. See, for example, T. McCrie (ed.), *The Life of Robert Blair* (Edinburgh, 1848), pp. 116–117.

38. Canny, *Kingdom and Colony*, pp. 96–97.

39. See, for example, the deposition of Elizabeth Crooker of Newry who recorded that the rebels bade her and her companions to "call down their god and see if he would save them and their clothes": see PRONI, Calendar of Co. Down Depositions. In the same source Elizabeth Pierce reported that many of the men and women among the rebels "did confidently averr that ... all the women in Ireland should as formerly go only in smocks, mantles and broughs [i.e. bracks] as well ladies as others and the English fashions to be quite abolished."

40. George Hill (ed.), *The Montgomery Manuscripts (1603–1706)* (Belfast, 1869), pp. 64–65. See also pp. 63, 85–87.

41. Hill, *The Montgomery Manuscripts*, p. 86.

42. Hill, *The Montgomery Manuscripts*, pp. 85–87.

43. P. Ó Gallachair, "A Fermanagh survey", *Clogher Record*, vol. ii (1958), pp. 298, 307.

44. P. Ó Gallachair, "1622 survey of Cavan", *Breifne*, vol. i (1958–61), p. 62.

45. Victor Treadwell, "The survey of Armagh and Tyrone, 1622", *Ulster Journal of Archaeology*, 3rd series, vol. 23 (1960), pp. 129, 146.

46. P. Ó Gallachair, "1622 survey of Cavan", p. 64

47. Treadwell, "The survey of Armagh and Tyrone", p. 129.

48. See also the accounts which Mary McClelland signed during the absence of her husband, in PRONI, T/640/22.

49. Mary O'Dowd, "Women and the war in Ireland in the 1640s", pp 102–108.

50. Trinity College, Dublin, MS. 833, ff. 67, 181; MS. 836, f. 75.

51. I refer here to Grey Osterud's paper delivered at the fifth Mackie conference: see "Introduction", footnote.

52. The research of Nicholas Canny would suggest that the Munster economy was more varied and offered more opportunities to women for diversification than the Ulster economy did. See, for example, his "Migration and opportunity" and "The 1641 depositions as a source for the writing of social history: County Cork as a case study", in Patrick O'Flanagan and Cornelius G. Buttimer (eds), *Cork. History and Society* (Dublin, 1993), pp. 249–308.
53. Prendergast, *Cromwellian Settlement*, pp. 89–90.

12

Motherhood and poverty in eighteenth-century Aberdeen

Lesley Diack

T*he Direction of the Food, Cloaths* and other Necessaries for the Persons of Children falls to the Mother's share during at least their State of Infancy if not during all their Childhood and frequently longer, in which one ought principally to consider their Health and Strength and assistance must be had from those of Skill and Experience.[1]

This was advice on how to be a good mother – dating from the 1740s – given by an educated middle-class doctor to his teenage daughter. In a series of letters, the concerned father discussed not only the merits of good parenting but also a variety of other subjects of concern to an affluent young woman in the eighteenth century.[2] The correspondence constituted a manual of behaviour not unique at this time in Scotland. But this example is striking in its content and scope.

In the late twentieth century advice to mothers comes not only from their parents and from other mothers, but also from government agencies, from health professionals, and – unceasingly it can seem – from the media. There are shops, magazines, and self-help organisations meeting the specific needs of mothers and children. Mothers, moreover, are made virtually into icons of social continuity, and this has its reverse side. It is on the mother that much-publicised critics place much of the responsibility for many social problems: were she to be at home more, it is suggested, there would be less youth vandalism and children would learn better at school and have a better start in life. The list of community problems laid at the feet of mothers can seem endless. In contemporary Britain, furthermore, the perception of single mothers as a financial drain on society is much encouraged. The idea of the intrinsic social worth of mothers thus has an equally powerful negative side to it. In this chapter I shall address the question of how particular forms of such an interpretation of maternity operated – and with what effects for mothers – in eighteenth-century Scotland. I shall focus on the experiences of those mothers whose situation brought them into the orbit of the Poor Law.

I

Eighteenth-century Aberdeen provides a good base for the study of motherhood in poverty. Many of the original records of the period have survived, including some uniquely valuable for the study of poverty. In 1755 the population of the city, according to Webster's analysis, was 16,027;[3] and by the end of the century it had risen dramatically to 24,493.[4] This increase was reflected in the quantity of records produced. The city's administration was growing as well as its physical and geographical size. In the middle of the century two large institutions opened which reflected a growth of concern about the poor of the town – the Infirmary and the Poor's Hospital. Both of these organisations were administered by the town and its male establishment, and both were funded by voluntary means.[5] The records for both institutions have survived, and they help us to construct a reasonably full life of the poor in Aberdeen from the 1740s onwards, especially when used in conjunction with contemporary church, newspaper, and legal records.[6]

One of the main problems with any study of women's history, however, is the lack of available sources written by women themselves. The difficulty is compounded when the object of study is poor women, where analysis must necessarily be based on second-hand reports. Middle-class males, indeed, generated every source consulted for this chapter, and this is reflected in what these sources tell us. For example, in one year in the 1740s, ten times as many detailed records for the male patients as for females survive in the Infirmary records, yet there were only twice as many male patients.[7] Gender, then, was a major factor accounting for the records which were kept, and which have survived. And so too was social status: while there are some detailed records for the fee-paying female patients, very little about poor women has survived – if indeed it ever existed.

Scotland in the eighteenth century was a country in transition. The population structure was changing, new work practices were developing, and there were increasing numbers of poor. The poor relief system which had to cope with this problem was evolving from a church-based one to one which involved a partnership between the church and the civil authorities, but with the church still predominant. Funds for distribution to the poor came from a variety of sources – in the main, fines, bequests, individual donations, investment income, and, of course, church collections. The award of relief to the "deserving poor" was the task of the kirk session,[8] which judged which applicants were worthy and in real need. Institutional care, in the form of workhouses and infirmaries, was becoming a principal means of dealing with the poor. Both the problems and their solutions, then, were becoming increasingly visible.

This was especially true in the towns. The recipients of charity were looked on, essentially, as the weak and the sick of society. In Scotland the able-bodied unemployed had traditionally been excluded from receiving any sort of public help. They could be, and sometimes were, arrested for not having any gainful employment. One *Instruction to the Part-time Constables* of Aberdeen in 1657 urged the arrest of "all idle persons who have no means to live upon and will not betake themselves to some trade".[9] It went on to declare that "all [those] guilty of slaughter, murder and theft" were also to be arrested, making little apparent distinction in the severity of these crimes and "idleness".

How, then, were motherhood and mothers perceived, according to the records of eighteenth-century Aberdeen? The women under examination in this chapter were all involved in the poor relief system to some extent. It is perhaps surprising to note that many of these women were not those who would traditionally be thought of as "the poor". Some were middle-class women who no longer had a male protector and had arrived at a point at which they needed help from the system. It is clear that social class and status were important in determining that they were helped, and the extent of the funds they received. With regard to mothers particularly, the system recognised six main categories. These were: unmarried mothers; widowed mothers; deserted mothers; mothers of abandoned children; mothers-to-be; and foster-mothers. All received help, but in differing degrees. A detailed examination of each group will enable a better understanding of attitudes at the time to mothers and to poverty.

II

The unmarried mother is the category most likely to appear in the archives – especially in the records of the kirk sessions of the Church of Scotland. These church courts were the first official recourse for those in need of relief; they had a fascination with what one might call the juicier details of the lives of parishioners. Their records are often more lurid than the columns of the more sensational tabloid newspapers today: there is scarcely a page without some scandalous story of sexual misdemeanour. But as the century progressed, there were fewer of these cases recorded. It has been suggested that the number of illegitimate pregnancies was declining but there does not appear to be historical evidence for this. The city's population was growing – as we have seen by thirty per cent between the 1750s and the end of the century. It is statistically probable that there were more illegitimate births, yet the number of women brought before the sessions for this reason remained static or even declined.[10] In 1757, for example, there were seventeen cases; in 1797, only two.[11] The decline is difficult to explain. Perhaps there were fewer unplanned pregnancies between unmarried people, or it may have been that the sessions were more involved in other matters and that they were less concerned with the problems of the unmarried mothers of the parish.

Unmarried mothers were likely to appear in the records not just because they required financial help but also because of their moral "fall from grace". About a third of the unmarried mothers who were compeared (or called) before the session in Aberdeen in the middle of the century were also compeared before the Justice Court of the town. The mothers were being punished twice for one and the same "crime" of ante-nuptial fornication. There is no obvious reason why certain of the cases, but not others, were tried before the civil courts as well. A typical entry in the Justice Court book simply states:

> 5th September 1763
> Agnes Strachan servant to Richard Wallace Plumber in Aberdeen was guilty of uncleaness with David Ross son to John Ross Merchant.[12]

This incident had occurred at the end of the previous March, and Agnes

Strachan was now pregnant. The records, incidentally, also note that both the parties involved could write.

The women always suffered more than the men involved in the case. Their crime was more obvious, especially after about six months when their pregnancy began to show. For the session the main problem with these cases was not so much the moral implications, more the financial implications. Who would pay for the upbringing of the child? The session members preferred it to be anyone other than the session itself: they sought to minimise any burden on the church's poor relief fund.

The session records constitute something of a documentary commentary on the sexual and social mores of the time. All the mothers mentioned were from the working classes, but hardly any of the fathers were. Listed as fathers were merchants, lawyers, ship's captains. But the main occupation of the mothers – if any were recorded at all – was that of servant. The occupation of the mother was not always considered relevant: the father's would, if nothing else, give some indication of ability to pay.

Another question that needs to be considered is why no middle-class women were brought before the session? Did no middle-class girls fall pregnant outwith marriage? Was there, within middle-class circles, more of a stigma attached to pregnancy before marriage or was it more that girls from such a background had far less freedom? Or was it simply that they, or their families, were able to maintain the child, and that, therefore, the session did not have to face the financial implications of an unwanted child? Although in many of the cases the session would appear to have been mainly concerned with the financial problems caused by illegitimate children, in certain cases there was more to their interest. What those other points of interest were can be deduced from examining some cases with particularly serious – even sinister – overtones.

The local newspaper of the middle to late eighteenth century was the *Aberdeen Journal*, which started production as a weekly in 1747. Almost from its outset, this paper carried certain advertisements that might be more properly called "wanted notices". These appeared quite regularly throughout the later eighteenth century – inserted by sessions trying to find women who had disappeared from their parish. The session believed that the disappearing woman was pregnant and that she had run away because of her pregnancy. A worthwhile exercise would be the reconstitution of the lives of these hunted women to discover the lengths the church went to find them – although this cannot be systematically done here. A typical example of this type of announcement, however, dated 13 June 1758, reads:

Upon Wednesday last Rachel Anderson of the parish of Tarland
... eloped.[13] Low stature, twenty years of age, pale complexion'd,
brown hair'd, pox pitted, her nose is a little flat, her chin somewhat thin. She wore a blue gown with green manikie cuffs and a
stript petticoat....[14]

The reward for information leading to the apprehension of Rachel
Anderson was one guinea, payable by the minister of the parish from the
session's funds. In effect, sessions put a price on the head of this presumably distraught woman, rather as sheriffs did with outlaws in the American "wild west". It is an indication of how seriously such cases might be
taken. What is not clear is whether a session's decision to advertise was
dictated more by financial or moral considerations. Such pressures on an
already troubled woman must have placed an almost intolerable strain
her. The *Aberdeen Journal* of 12 February 1760 announced that:

last week an unmarried woman was taken ... on suspicion of child
murder ... [and] sent under guard to Forfar ... [A] body was found
in the links buried in a hole in the sand ... [and] she made ample
confession.[15]

It is not surprising to find that women with an ante-nuptial pregnancy
would go to great lengths to hide their condition – and *in extremis* might
resort to infanticide.[16]

The session would not consider the case to be complete until it had discovered the name of the father. This was one of the fundamental facts
that the elders wanted established from the outset of their investigations,
because it was paramount in deciding who would pay for the child's upkeep. In one particularly disturbing case a woman was hounded for four
years, and was compeared before the session seventeen times, in the attempt to get her to state the name of the father. The young woman,
whose elderly husband had recently died, was from the parish of
Newhills on the outskirts of Aberdeen. At first she gave evidence that the
baby was the product of her having been raped on her way home and
that she could not identify the rapist. She was not believed. For years the
saga continued, with the elders eventually excommunicating the woman
for two years until she named the father. Possibly, in this particular case,
the elders knew something not in the records which made them certain
the woman was lying, and was therefore, in their eyes, deserving of the
indignities to which they subjected her. In any event, the woman eventually confessed that the father was her late husband's son – her own step-

son – who was closer in age to her than her husband had been.[17]

The most tragic cases of all are those of unmarried mothers where the child had been found dead. It could have been stillborn, abandoned at birth, or, worst of all, murdered. The newspapers carry many accounts of children thrown down wells, left on hillsides, or even eaten by dogs. For example, in January 1758:

> Last week a new born child had been thrown into the water in the parish of Kildrummy.... [It] was found half-eaten by dogs ... [and] the perpetrators of the crime were being looked for.... [18]

One of the most notorious cases in eighteenth-century Aberdeen, moreover, made it into the *Black Kalendar*.[19] In the early 1750s, in the West-End district of Rubislaw, a young servant girl, Christian Phren, was found guilty of murder and hanged in the Castlegate for her crime. She had burnt her newly delivered baby in the fireplace of her master's house. Her defence was that the baby had been born dead and that she had been cremating its remains. Her crime was compounded because she had concealed her pregnancy, and was therefore held to be guilty of subterfuge, as well as being convicted of murder.[20] Concealment in itself was indeed considered criminal. A report of 8 January 1760 recounts that:

> On Friday se'ennight an unmarried woman ... [was] delivered on the hill of two children ... [She] did not abandon them ... [but] crawled a mile with them to a house ... [and has] since cared for them. The solitary manner of her Delivery ... owing to an Accident rather than design ... [came about because she had] concealed the pregnancy prior to the birth ...[21]

And the crime of hiding a pregnancy was one that the sessions tried to combat by using the midwives of the town to report on pregnancies and births. They also, when an infant was found abandoned, might examine any likely women to see if any of them were producing milk. The fact that women like Christian Phren hid their pregnancy and resorted to murder showed the lengths to which some women felt constrained to go, in order to keep their jobs and to keep out of the poor relief system.

III

The second category of mother in the poor relief records is the widowed mother. The status of these mothers was much higher than that of the unmarried mother, and society apparently felt it owed these women some support. They had conformed to normal life-patterns and were down on their luck through no fault of their own. Therefore, unless they were involved in some moral misdemeanour, their treatment was less harsh than that of the unmarried mother. In many cases widowed mothers appearing in the records were of a higher social status. Poor widowed mothers obtained relief both from the kirk session and as outpensioners of the Poor's Hospital, in much the same way as unmarried mothers. They were always designated "Widow ..."; this indication of marital status remained the form used in poor relief documentation into the twentieth century. Many charities were also established to help better-off widows. In the 1740s, there were over twenty widows in Aberdeen receiving relief from the mortifications of the town. The status of the widow – especially the widowed mother – was attended by an aura of responsibility, and of respectability, which attracted social prestige, with which went recognition of the right to poor relief. In every Poor Law act from the sixteenth century onwards, widows were mentioned as being amongst the worthiest recipients of relief. However. there were still moral overtones to this charity; and moral strictures applied to the recipient women. Many of the mortification and trust funds set up for widows stated that the money was to be given to "those widowes that have beine the wyffes of burgesses of Aberdeine ... of good lyfe and conversations, frie of anie publict scandle, or offence". [22]

The third group of mothers comprised those deserted by their husbands who found it difficult to bring up their children without male support. In the nineteenth century, petitions for divorce to the Court of Session indicate increasing numbers of women being deserted by husbands, who had departed for the Americas or other far-flung regions and had never returned.[23] Some men had perhaps emigrated to create a better life for themselves and their families, but had either died in the attempt or had ignored the fact that they had left a family in Scotland. After seven years the women were able to apply to the Court of Session for a divorce which was usually granted. In the eighteenth century the main types of desertion varied, but most were the result of outside agencies. The majority of deserted wives recorded had husbands who were in the military, with no choice as to where they were posted. The kirk sessions would often allocate money to the wives to go and join their husbands. For example there was the case of

> Isobell Gaull daughter of the deceased James Gaull sometime Wheelwright in Elgin, and now spouse to Robert McAndrew late

Glover in Elgin and one of the Out Chelsea pensioners, presently in ... the Island of Jersey ... [who made] humble application ... for ... a small pittance ... towards Enabling me for Setting out for, and arriveing at the Said Island of Jersey.[24]

To accede to such a request would have been cheaper for the session than continuing to pay for the family *ad infinitum*, and, as we have seen, financial expediency was always a consideration for the sessions. Obviously, the number of deserted wives fluctuated with the political and military situation. Unmarried mothers could also fall into this category. The claim that the father of an illegitimate child was now in the army could be difficult to disprove.

V

The fourth category of mothers to be considered is mothers-to-be. Attitudes towards pregnancy in the eighteenth century were different from those today. There was a midwife for the labour, but no expectation of care before the birth. The more affluent might consult a doctor before the birth for confirmation of the pregnancy, but the poor, for the most part, saw no reason to visit a doctor or midwife until delivery was imminent. For the poor, having a child was an exclusively female experience: the child would be delivered by a midwife, a respected local woman, or a female relative who had some experience of birth. Male doctors were not involved.

In the 1760s, a ward for poor lying-in women was established in Aberdeen as part of an extension to the Infirmary. But the women of Aberdeen scarcely used the facility, and in the short period of its existence only a handful of women were delivered there. The Infirmary also employed a midwife to deliver women in their own homes. This could have been an important period in the history of midwifery in Aberdeen. Not only was a ward for lying-in women established but a training programme for midwives had also been started. Yet all this came to nothing because of the premature death of the pioneering physician, Dr David Skene.[25] Pregnancy was a potentially fatal experience for many women. So much could go wrong and so much did. A vivid example was the epidemic of puerperal fever (popularly known as childbed fever), which occurred in Aberdeen in the 1790s, spread by the lack of hygiene among the midwives and the doctors delivering the women.[26] But poor women were not willing to change the practice of childbirth. Most children were born at home. The new mothers surrounded by other women, a practice they wanted to continue. The poor lying-in ward was not used. And an offer by Skene to pay for the care of the pregnant poor attracted little interest.

Skene's papers have survived. There are no references to cases involving poor women, but there are over ninety sets of case-notes for more affluent ones – the wives and daughters of some of the petty gentry around Aberdeen.[27] One of the most interesting features of these records is the age of the mother at first pregnancy. Most were in their late twenties, and there were no teenage pregnancies. Women in this class would appear to be marrying, and having their children, later. Can this model of family life be applied also to the poor? Was late marriage a method of limiting the size of families? The age of marriage in Scotland has always been regarded as being one of the latest in Europe and as having failed to become earlier in the way it did in England and elsewhere in Europe.[28] Most women would have married by the age of twenty-five. The fertility cycle of women was shorter than now. In the eighteenth century, malnutrition, high rates of death in childbirth, and later marriage ages meant that the fertile period within wedlock was much shorter.[29] Life expectancy then also meant that to be forty was to be considered elderly.

VI

The fifth category identified in the records is the mother who abandoned her child or children. There were two main types in this group: the mother who permanently abandoned her child, and who did not want to be found; and the mother who temporarily abandoned the child but maintained some tenuous contact. Children who were permanently abandoned, the foundlings, were placed in foster care and were provided for from the funds of the Poor's Hospital. An example is reported in the *Aberdeen Journal* in March 1759:

> Thursday night there a female child two or three days old laid down at a door in the Guest raw [row]. Poor infant immediately cared for and put to nurse ... the unnatural mother not yet discovered ...[30]

Mothers of abandoned children were always described as either unnatural or inhuman. Most of the babies were placed in homes on the outskirts of Aberdeen where the rural environment afforded healthier conditions. Attempts were made to trace the mothers but in most of the cases they were unsuccessful. Normally the child was given the surname "Aberdeen", so that this became a distinguishing feature of an abandoned baby. Another was its short life span: very few of these babies survived to adulthood, most died as infants. The child-mortality rate was in any case high, but it was highest amongst the abandoned. As to mothers who abandoned their children later in life, there is more in the records. In these cases the mother's name and her personal circumstances were known, as well as her stated reasons for placing her child, or children, in the workhouse. Usually it was because they could no longer afford to pay for their children's upkeep. In some cases it was because they were now in a second marriage, and the new husband would not maintain the children of the previous family. The town council guaranteed to keep the children until they were of an age either to go out to work or to be apprenticed: twelve for the girls and fourteen for the boys. In most cases the girls would be found a job in domestic service, while the boys were apprenticed to some trade. There was one case in Aberdeen where the mother did not return for her child when she came of age. The town council repeatedly wrote to her. This correspondence continued for a year, until the town threatened the recalcitrant mother with legal proceedings.[31] Their legal case, however, was not that she refused to take her child out of the house, but rather that she had abandoned her eleven years earlier.

The final type of mother recovered from the records was the foster mother – those who cared for some of the abandoned children of the Aberdeen. These foster parents were paid for by the town council from private charity. They appear regularly in the records of the Poor's Hospital. Most of the foster mothers lived on the outskirts of the city. The money for the care of the child was paid, not to the mother herself, but to the couple. Specific monies were allocated for the infant's clothing and shoes. Often the wife would also act as wet nurse.[32]

VII

In the sixteenth century, John Knox, in his *History of the Reformation*, listed those that he thought should be helped by the church as "the widow and the fatherless, the aged, impotent or lamed.... And ... also ... all persons of honesty fallen into decay and penury."[33] By the eighteenth century, these worthy sentiments had been replaced by more pragmatic considerations. Mothers were a focus of attention for a number of practical reasons. They had difficulty working because of childcare problems. Without the support of a man, they had little chance of earning enough to live on and fulfil their maternal responsibilities. Even if earning, they usually received one-third to one-half of a male breadwinner's wage, and so were much less able to support a family. Force of such circumstances demanded of the authorities that they pay attention to the plight of poor mothers.

But it is not true – and this is a preconception which has persisted right up to the present in the ideas about social security referred to at the beginning of this chapter – that women were the main recipients of poor relief. Commentators continuously make this assumption, and it informs the theory behind all the relevant parliamentary acts. Yet when gender-differentiated calculations are made, it becomes clear that more men were in receipt of relief than women and that the men received proportionately larger amounts of relief. Women most often were helped only when they were also responsible for children, and they were also frequently subjected to moral stipulations. For eighteenth-century Scottish women, motherhood at least meant that, if they fell into poverty, they had a greater chance of being eligible for relief than other women. But they still got less in relief than a man in a comparable position. Only a much more consistent attitude by Scottish historians to the gendering of the story of their country's past will allow the full implications of such facts to emerge. And only then will it be possible to give its proper weight to the history of motherhood – which plays such a key role in social ideology (and mythology) – and to place that history firmly in its broader historical context.

NOTES

1. Alexander Monro (Primus), "The professor's daughter: an essay on female conduct", in *Proceedings of the Royal College of Physicians of Edinburgh*, January 1996, vol. 26, no. 1, supplement 2. This edition was transcribed with an introduction and notes by P. A. G. Monro, a descendant of the author. The letters that the Essay are based on were written from 1739–1746, when the daughter was twelve till she was nineteen. As part of her education Monro (primus) made Margaret, his daughter copy the text out twice and he corrected any mistakes.
2. Subjects covered include – the Education of Girls, general Conduct of Life, Commerce with Men, Government of servants, the management of Children, a Summary of religion, and the Origins of Government. The text of Monro's essay fills over 170 pages.
3. J. G. Kyd (ed.), *Scottish Population Statistics including Webster's analysis of*

population 1755 (Edinburgh, 1952), p. 51.

4. D. J. Withrington and I. R. Grant (eds), *The Statistical Account of Scotland*, vol. XIV (Wakefield, 1982), p. 293.

5. Both of these organisations opened to the public in the early 1740s. Further information can be found in A. Walker, *The History of the Workhouse or Poor's Hospital of Aberdeen from 1739–1818* (Aberdeen, 1885); I. Levack and H. Dudley, *Aberdeen Royal Infirmary: the People's Hospital in the North East* (Aberdeen, 1992); Lesley Diack, "A woman's greatest adventure: the development of maternity care in Aberdeen since the eighteenth century", in T. Brotherstone and D. J. Withrington (eds), *The City and its Worlds* (Glasgow, 1996).

6. The records of the Church and of the Poor's Hospital are held in Aberdeen District Archive (ADA) and the records of the Infirmary are held by Northern Health Services Archive (NHSA). The *Aberdeen Journal* was first published in 1747.

7. NHSA, GRHB 1/1/2, Minute Book of the Infirmary 1742–1751.

8. The kirk session was the lowest level of the church court in Scotland it was based at a parish level and constituted the minister as moderator with the rest of the elders as the members. Their remit was to deal with discipline, poor relief, and other less important business.

9. ADA, Justice Court Book vol. 1, 1657–1688.

10. ADA, CH2/448/35, CH2/448/42, The Kirk Session records of St Nicholas.

11. In 1757 six of the cases were brought before the Justice Court for discipline as well.

12. ADA, Justice Court Book, vol. IV, 1690–1783.

13. "Eloped" meant simply "ran away".

14. *Aberdeen Journal*. It later transpired that Rachel had been accused of child murder and that was probably why she disappeared.

15. *Aberdeen Journal*. This case comes from the parish of Montrose some forty miles to the south of Aberdeen. These types of cases always appeared in the Domestick Occurrences columns of the newspaper. These columns now roughly equate to the Births, Deaths and Marriages in the newspapers of today.

16. In Scotland, from 1690, there was a legal presumption that a woman concealing an unmarried pregnancy was guilty of murder if the infant should die. The last execution under this statute was in 1776, whereafter the sentence was more likely to be banishment. The law was not changed until 1809, when the penalty was changed from death to two years imprisonment. See R. Mitchison and L. Leneman, *Sexuality and Social Control: Scotland 1660–1780* (Oxford, 1989), pp. 200–230; and John Burnett, *A Treatise on Various Branches of the Criminal Law in Scotland* (Edinburgh, 1811), pp. 571–575.

17. Scottish Record Office (SRO), CH2/280/1, The Kirk Session records of Newhills. The first reference to this case is on the 16th September 1711. Mar-

garet Tait, widow of William Walker was excommunicated from 26th October to 3rd October 1714. The last reference to Margaret Tait and her stepson, James Walker was on the 1st May 1715.

18. *Aberdeen Journal.*
19. James Bruce, *The Black Kalendar of Aberdeen* (Aberdeen, 1840).
20. SRO, JC 11/17 Northern Circuit Book of the High Court of Justiciary Minutes, 7 October 1752. Christian Phren was accused of parricide and child murder and convicted on five counts: that she had brought forth a child; that she had concealed a pregnancy; that she had no assistance at the birth; that the child was found dead; and that she had placed the child in the fire.
21. *Aberdeen Journal.*
22. *Mortification Accounts.* The reference to "good ... conversations" meant that they should not be guilty of scandal mongering or gossiping.
23. SRO, CS
24. Moray District Archives (MDA), CH2/145/10, The Kirk Session records of Elgin, 1733–1770. In the period 1741–1751 only five mothers were given money to join their husbands in the records of St Nicholas in Aberdeen (CH2/448/35).
25. Dr David Skene (1730–1771) was instrumental in the allocating of space for poor lying-in women in the extension to the Infirmary in 1758. Further information on Skene can be found in H. Lesley Diack, "Dr David Skene and his contribution to women's health", in A. Adam, D. Smith & F. Watson (eds), *To the greit support and advancement of helth* (Aberdeen, 1996).
26. Further information can be found in Diack, "A woman's greatest adventure".
27. AULSC, MS 476.
28. The information on population and marriage ages was supplied by Mr R. E. Tyson of the Department of History at the University of Aberdeen. It is as yet unpublished.
29. Recent research on anorexia has shown that women have to be of a certain weight before they will have periods and therefore healthy enough to be producing eggs. This has been applied to the "historical period" by E. Le Roy Ladurie, "Famine amenorrhoea, seventeenth to twentieth centuries", in R. Forster and O. Ranum (eds), *Biology of Man in History* (Baltimore, 1975).
30. *Aberdeen Journal.*
31. ADA, Town Council Records.
32. ADA, Poor's Hospital Ledger Books.
33. John Knox, *History of the Reformation*, vol. II (Edinburgh, 1949) pp. 290–291.

13

*F*eminists – citizens – mothers: debates about citizenship, national identity and motherhood in nineteenth-century Germany

Lynn Abrams

*T*hroughout *Europe*, the period following the French Revolution was characterised by the circulation of discourses on nationalism and citizenship and by attempts to forge and consolidate the nation state. It has been noticeable, however, in the outpouring of historical writing on nationalism in recent years, that the gendered nature of this process has been largely ignored. Yet, as Joan Scott has reminded us, "gender is one of the recurrent references by which political power has been conceived, legitimised, and criticised."[1] The absence of women from the narrative, their positioning as objects outside the national project or as passive objects (usually mothers) to be utilised by promoters of the nation state, perpetuates a separate-spheres model. This confines women to the private sphere and delegitimises, or silences, their political involvement.[2] Despite the massive contribution of women's history to the historical narrative, politics and nation forming are still, to some extent, portrayed as gender-free or gender-neutral.[3] We have little insight into the meaning of a national identity for women and the ways in which women intersected with the discourses on nationalism and nation-state formation.

In Scottish historical writing on national identity and culture there has been virtually no acknowledgement of the notion of gendered identities.[4] Women are almost entirely missing from the analysis despite the fact that citizenship was implicitly defined as the domain of men.[5] Moreover, much Scottish women's history, whilst seeking to identify a distinctly Scottish experience, has provided few insights into the relationship between Scottish women's experience and their political identity as members of the Scottish nation.[6]

In this chapter, I discuss German feminists' intervention in a political and legal discourse in the late nineteenth century – a period in modern German history which might be described as one of nation formation and consolidation. I propose that women in Germany *did* perceive their position within, and against, the state as different from – yet as legitimate as – that of men. And I provide evidence of this based on the ways women talked about citizenship and their position in the new nation state.

The period between 1871 and World War I saw German identity being shaped in a number of arenas, one of which was the legal sphere. Following unification, reform of civil law was arguably one of the defining processes in the creation of the German nation state and a national identity. The decision, in particular, to unify the civil code (*Bürgerliches Gesetzbuch*, BGB) – a process only completed in 1900 – presented feminists with a golden opportunity to influence the laws on marriage, divorce, property, and the guardianship of children. Moreover, it offered a space for the assertion of women's rights and identity in the new nation state at a time when women did not have the vote.[7] By the 1890s the dominant strand of the moderate German feminist movement saw no contradiction in defining women's legal and political and thus national identity both as citizens *and* mothers (indeed the two were mutually enforcing). They thereby abandoned what might be described as the liberal, individualist, equal-rights standpoint which had been advocated by leading German feminist writers just a few decades earlier, in favour of an advocacy of a distinctive female sphere. However, it was precisely this belief in the value of domesticity, and the promotion of women (and especially mothers) as guardians of morality, that legitimised women's claim to equal citizenship and political engagement.[8] In an atmosphere where the politics of elections and debate was dominated by men, women had to infiltrate or permeate political culture using their own language of responsibilities and duties towards the nation state.[9]

[187]

The most radical early analyses of marriage and family law were formulated by writers of the *Vormärz* (pre-revolution), and immediate post-1848, era who had been influenced by liberalism and Enlightenment thought. Many of these women belonged to religious dissenting groups such as the German Catholics and the Protestant Friends of Light. Drawing heavily on their own experiences the dissenters were amongst the first to criticise the legal institution of marriage and demand legal reform in order to improve the position of married women. Although the dissenters did not reject the concept of marriage itself – indeed marriage was held to be at the centre of the family and the state – they did reject arranged marriages; marriages made for financial or property reasons; and, indeed, all marriages which by their nature incorporated the subordination of the wife.[10] For these writers, love was the key to a happy and equal marriage. Such a *Liebesehe* (marriage for love) required not just equality of the spouses within marriage but also equality before the law. Thus, women's legal and political emancipation was a prerequisite for a successful marriage. Louise Dittmar (1807–84), a Protestant religious dissenter who published numerous works during the tumultuous revolutionary years of the 1840s on a range of social issues including the condition of women, articulated similar ideas in her work entitled *Das Wesen der Ehe* (The Essence of Marriage) published in 1849.[11] For Dittmar, who has been described as "the most articulate representative of the radical liberal position on gender in the *Vormärz*",[12] the economic and political dependence of the wife upon her husband was the main cause of unhappy marriages.[13] It followed from this that:

> Marriage, as a free community of individuals, can only function if both partners possess the same rights to liberty and freedom in the political realm without a sexual hierarchy.[14]

Dittmar's analysis was based on the notion of fundamental human rights and a rejection of the traditional liberal position which qualified the demand for equality for all individuals by an insistence on natural gender difference.[15] In this respect, Dittmar differed not only from leading male liberal thinkers but also from other female advocates of women's rights like Louise Otto and Fanny Lewald. They based their demands for women's equality on the belief in women's (feminine) difference.

The period of reaction following the 1848 revolution meant that the woman question was pushed to the sidelines, and the articulate and radical arguments of women like Dittmar were momentarily forgotten. It was only the announcement in 1874 – just three years after unification –

that a commission was being set up to draft a new civil code for a unified Germany that prompted feminists to raise their voices again in favour of an improvement in the legal status of women. Yet, with a few exceptions, these voices rejected the radical standpoint advocated by Louise Dittmar. One of the more notable exceptions was Hedwig Dohm (1831–1919). She, in some respects, was the remaining torch-bearer of the radical tradition established by the feminists of the *Vormärz*, but she was positioned outside the organised women's movement.[16] Heavily influenced by the translation of John Stuart Mill's *The Subjection of Women*, Dohm demanded nothing less than full legal equality for women, including the vote. For Dohm women's position would only undergo a fundamental change when women had access to the decision-making process, a prophecy that was to be quite telling later on in the campaign to influence the civil code.

Hedwig Dohm explicitly acknowledged her debt to Mill in *Der Frauen Natur und Recht* (Women's Nature and Privilege), published in 1876. Here she argued that women's subordinate position within marriage could only be reversed if women were granted the vote. "Marriage", she wrote, "is an almost absolute form of the mastery of men, guaranteed by law."[17] The solution to this legally sanctioned patriarchy, according to Dohm, was to grant women the vote:

> Women require the vote because every class which does not participate in political life is suppressed; the participation in political life necessitates that in the course of time equality before the law will be the result. The classes who are not permitted the vote are in the power of the other classes who do have it. Laws such as those on women's property, their rights over their children, marriage, divorce, etc. are impossible in a country where women have the suffrage. Men, they say, represent women. When did women ever give men the right to represent them? [18]

Hedwig Dohm was not alone in expressing fury at the subordinate status of women in civil law, but she was one of relatively few in the women's movement to present her arguments in such a direct and uncompromising way. For Dohm and her like-minded predecessor, Louise Dittmar, it was necessary to attack the very foundations of liberal ideology, while, at the same time, utilising key liberal tenets such as freedom and equality of the individual in their arguments for women's emancipation. Woman's equality under the law was regarded by Dohm – and others before her – as a fundamental right which preceded all other improvements in women's position. From the 1880s, however, the moderate women's movement appeared to prioritise women's legal status as wives and mothers over their status as individuals or citizens.[19] This was part of a broader approach adopted by the General German Women's Association (*Allgemeine deutsche Frauenverein*, ADF) for the last third of the century, which was characterised by an advocacy of changes in the position and status of women based on the concept of difference. The campaign for reform of family law was very much part of this approach so that the radicalism of writers like Dohm and Dittmar was abandoned in favour of a campaign that aimed to raise the status of women primarily within the family with respect to husbands and children. Hedwig Dohm rejected tinkering with the legal provisions with regard to marriage. This, in her view, would only gain short-term advantages and would not address the fundamental problem of inequality and patriarchal power.

Common to the writings of Dittmar and Dohm was a critical engagement with the ideology of the polarisation of the sexes and the predominant bourgeois liberal belief in natural sexual difference and separate spheres. In their writings both argued that any differences that did appear to exist were the consequence of social conditioning. Dittmar rejected the liberal conception of gender relations as determined by character traits based on sexual difference. It was social conditioning and denial of equal opportunity, particularly in the realm of education that "*predestined*" a woman for domesticity.[20] Given equality of opportunity women would gain access to all spheres of economic and cultural activity. Hedwig Dohm continued this line of argument almost two decades later.

> Women are as different from each other in certain traits of character as men, according to their status in life, their class and their upbringing; but peculiarities which arise from special causes can never form the characteristics of the sex ... [21]

And later she criticised discrimination based on biological difference in her characteristic, forthright style:

> Because women bear children they are to have no political rights, and if I say, because men do *not* bear children they shall have no political rights, I see no reason why the one remark should not be considered as profound as the other.[22]

By the 1880s, the mainstream women's movement had abandoned the language of equal rights and increasingly adopted difference as a bargaining counter in its campaign to influence the drafting of the civil code. In this respect the ambiguous legacy of Rousseau and his prescriptive ideas on woman's role as the moral foundation of the (male) political sphere is evident. While the feminist campaigners concentrated their efforts on the amelioration of the status of women as wives and mothers – at the expense of more fundamental individual rights – their claim to citizenship based on the rights of mothers as moral guardians permitted their entry into the public sphere.[23] In this respect German women were in good company. Elsewhere in Europe – including Scotland – earlier in the century, women had set up reform associations and had campaigned against slavery, for prison reform, and for political rights on the basis of women's superior morality and their patriotic duty as wives and mothers.[24]

In Germany, the issue of civil law reform probably galvanised more grass-roots support for the women's movement than the better-documented campaigns around education and employment. This was because the law affected all women of all social classes. And the ways in which the campaigners articulated their response to the reform of the civil code – that is, the way in which they talked about their conception of women's position in the unified German state – can tell us something about their notion of the female citizen, her duties, her responsibilities, and her rights.

The drafting of a new law which would supersede not just the Prussian civil code (often regarded as relatively woman friendly) but also those codes recognised as being less friendly to women – such as the Napoleonic *Code Civil* – offered a unique opportunity to influence the future legal status of women in the entire realm of civil law. Hitherto, the diversity of law codes and women's ignorance of the laws affecting them had hindered a concerted campaign by women's organisations in favour of improved legal status for women. Moreover, in the early 1870s when the women's movement was called upon to react to the government's law codification, the movement was still in its infancy and ill prepared for such a task. During the 1870s and 1880s, feminists found they needed to embark on a massive education campaign, both to find out for themselves the reality of women's legal position and to inform women of their status as a pre-condition for mobilising them to demand reform. The process of collecting information had simultaneously raised the profile of women's subordination within marriage. In 1876, the General German Women's Association, with the support of its branch associations, petitioned the Reichstag, requesting that the position of women be taken into account in the framing of the family law of the new civil code.[25] Immediately, then, the women's movement had signalled its primary concern with the more restricted female sphere of the family, as opposed to the issue of individual rights advocated by the early liberal feminists. The Reichstag disregarded the petition, and clearly its message was not absorbed by those drafting the family law. Gottlieb Planck, the National Liberal largely responsible for these statutes, stated that:

> in marriage law, the principle of individual freedom should not prevail, but marriage is to be seen as an independent moral and legal order by the will of the spouses.[26]

In 1888, the women's movement was profoundly disappointed by the first published draft of the new civil code. Although some concessions had been made in the realm of women's ability to pursue a trade or a court case, these rights were severely restricted by those of the husband in respect of his wife's property and her person, so that the legal status of the married woman was largely unaltered. It was this rebuttal that prompted women to organise and to campaign more assertively against the proposed laws affecting women's position as wives and mothers. A second petition, similarly worded to the first, was, however, in the words of the association's leader Marie Stritt, "as good as ignored".[27]

Although the women's movement has been criticised for failing to press its demands, this early campaign for improvements in women's legal status was simply the opening salvo presaging future campaigns. These were to adopt a more radical, or at least more vocal, stance. In particular a group of female-rights activists used this political engagement with the Reichstag to formulate their conception of a woman's position vis-à-vis the state. They regarded a woman's legal status in relation to the family as central to her emancipation. They thus tried to foster what might be termed a double-vision of women as wives and mothers and as citizens. Indeed, for them, a woman's right to citizenship was based on her role as a wife and mother. In particular the women's movement criticised the continued subordination of the wife to the husband and the maintenance of the husband's right of decision in all domestic matters; the provisions relating to married woman's property; the proposal to give a married woman no rights to property brought to a marriage; the failure to grant a woman power in matters relating to her children, and the lack of legal recognition of illegitimate children; and, finally, the restrictions proposed to the divorce law, which reduced the number of grounds for divorce and insisted upon the apportionment of guilt.

By the 1890s, when it was clear that, far from improving women's legal status, the new civil code threatened to lead to a deterioration, the feminist legal activists organised a massive campaign. Twenty-five thousand signatures were collected within the space of a few weeks following the second reading of the civil code in the Reichstag in 1892. Campaigners used the journal *Frauenbewegung* for publicity. They organised lectures and courses on the law. And they motivated what was known as a *Frauenlandsturm* (women's reserve) against the revised code.[28] This campaign served to crystallise debates within the women's movement on issues concerning women's legal status. The formation of the Federation of German Women's Associations (*Bund Deutsche Frauenvereine* – or BDF) in 1894, and the first general meeting held in Munich, galvanised the campaign once more. At this meeting, the sixty-five delegates were agreed that the legal question was the most important issue for the BDF. Another petition, this time containing around fifty thousand signatures, was presented to the Reichstag; and two pamphlets produced by local organisations were distributed across the whole country.[29] Leading activists undertook propaganda tours to enlighten and educate women. In 1895, a pamphlet entitled *Woman in the new Civil Code* spelled out the limitations and contradictions of the proposals contained in the draft law:

> The position of the married woman is now, as before, in tutelage to the husband. He has the decisive voice in all domestic affairs, can limit the rights of the wife in the home and in her ability to pursue a trade, he can limit her ongoing duties *vis-à-vis* a third party [i.e. a child] and she may only have recourse to the guardianship court if he misuses this power ... the law maker assumes ... that the inexperienced woman requires protection and thus she must be placed under guardianship ...[30]

The first reading of the draft code in a plenary session of the Reichstag in February 1896 brought the hope that the women's concerns had been heard, but, in the event, only the Social Democrat deputies supported the women's movement on all points. At this point – we should remember here Hedwig Dohm's advocacy of the franchise as a prerequisite for all other reforms – it became clear that the women's movement would never be able to influence political decision-making without the vote. At its 1896 Kassel general meeting, the BDF decided on renewed agitation and established a legal commission with nine members. But evidence that the BDF's campaign had had virtually no impact on the law makers was presented at the second reading at the end of June 1896. The new Civil Code did recognise women as independent legal persons, but in matters relating to marriage the subordination of the wife was retained. Paragraph 1354 of the code stated:

> The husband holds the power of decision in all matters of married life; he decides in particular the place and style of residence, the way of life, the furnishing of living rooms, the domestic budget, the mealtimes, holidays, etc.[31]

Moreover, married women's property law was not reformed to the benefit of women, although a married woman was permitted to retain her independent earnings. In respect of children, what appeared to be a positive reform for women was soon interpreted as a superficial change of wording. In place of "paternal" power over children, the code recognised "parental" power, but, as many critical commentators pointed out, in practice this would mean paternal guardianship as long as the father was alive. And in the case of disagreements over the care of children the father's decision took precedence in law. Finally, divorce law was made far more restrictive than the Prussian law had been. It was no longer possible to obtain a divorce on the grounds of insurmountable aversion or by mutual consent. The divorce process was imbued with the guilt principle which meant divorces became far more adversarial. Moreover, the grounds were restricted to four absolute reasons – adultery, bigamy, desertion, and unnatural intercourse; and to other so-called relative reasons which included serious mistreatment and neglect of marital duties.

On 29 June 1896 one last big demonstration was held in the Berlin Concert Hall, with BDF representatives from all over the country present. The legal status of women continued to be discussed at general meetings of the BDF, and a final mass petition contained the following demands: the abandonment of the husband's exclusive right over the wife's property in respect of the usufruct and the management of it; the granting of parental power to the mother on an equal basis with the father; the granting of parental power also to illegitimate mothers and the establishment of the duty of fathers of illegitimate children to the maintenance of their children.

Throughout the course of the legal campaign, these feminists had refrained from demanding equal rights for women as individuals. They appealed, rather, to traditional bourgeois liberal ideology. This emphasised sexual difference and stressed the need to campaign for women's rights as wives and mothers – a language legitimised by the separate-spheres ideology which was recognised by the majority of law makers. But even this was too radical for the majority of Reichstag delegates. They supported the emphasis on the family as a moral and spiritual unit in the Family Law of the BGB (the civil code). The feminists did at least recognise the changing socio-economic realities of women's lives, and wanted to see changes in the law to reflect this.

Having failed to achieve its aims to reform the legal status of women, the feminist movement, after 1900, was forced to try to ameliorate women's legal position by recourse to alternative subversive strategies. Having built up considerable support during its legal campaign it was reluctant to squander it. It therefore resolved, even before the implementation of the BGB, to continue educational work to make women aware of their legal position under the new law code and to encourage them to seek legal advice. In particular women were encouraged to insist on drawing up a marriage contract in order to protect their property; to this purpose a pamphlet containing four alternative contracts was distributed through local affiliated organisations, and through the Legal Advice Centres (*Rechtsschutzvereine*). This constituted one of the most practical and effective strategies undertaken by feminist organisations. The centres, staffed by volunteers, were established in many of the major towns and cities. They existed to provide free legal advice to all classes of women, and, if the example of Hamburg is typical, they dealt primarily with issues concerning marriage, property, and divorce.[32] So, although the opportunity to achieve wholesale legal reform had been lost, one can talk of the legal campaign continuing by other means.

It is tempting to be very critical of the German women's movement which, it seems, passed up the opportunity of staking women's claim to equal membership of the nation state by basing its legal campaign on a kind of double vision of women – as wives and mothers and as citizens. It might be argued that the price paid by ordinary women for the tardiness of the moderate feminists was quite high. The BGB contained few improvements to women's legal status, and actually worsened it in some respects. Female victims of domestic violence were virtually ignored by the women's movement. Criticism of the new, more restrictive divorce laws in the BGB was muted. And the movement's emphasis on motherhood as a source of strength played into the hands of conservatives who continued in their belief in women's subordination, basing themselves on the idea of difference. Many provisions contained in the 1900 Civil Code remained in force until the 1950s; even the passing of the Equal Rights Act in 1957 did not entirely mean the end of women's subordination within marriage, since the 1957 Constitution contained a clause which read:

> The wife runs the household on her own responsibility. She is entitled to go out to work insofar as this is reconcilable with her duties in marriage and the family.[33]

Since the French Revolution, European women who had claimed equal rights and engaged in political activities alongside men had been ridiculed and vilified. Edmund Burke's description of the Parisian women who marched to Versailles as "the abused shape of the vilest of women" and the denunciation of the revolutionary women's clubs as "a plague to the mothers of good families" were followed by similar examples of intolerance of women apparently transgressing the boundaries of nature during the 1871 Paris Commune.[34]

In Scotland the situation was not dissimilar. In 1819, in Glasgow, the presence of women alongside men in agitating for political reform was lamented by the local newspaper. "We were truly grieved to see females in the procession", it commented. "Their character and dispositions being naturally so averse to any such public exhibition of their persons."[35] Women workers in the Dundee jute industry were portrayed as "unreasoning" and "foolish" when they publicly paraded their grievances against their employers on the streets.[36] Suffrage campaigners who adopted militant tactics in England and Scotland were treated like criminals and lunatics and denied basic human rights in prison as a consequence of their transgressing traditional feminine roles.

It is perhaps not surprising, then, that German women adopted a more cautious approach, utilising both the acceptable tactics of political campaigners and a language which did not alienate their opponents. And German feminists were not unique in Europe – as other chapters in this book indicate – in staking a claim to citizenship within the new nation state as wives and mothers; nor were they unusual in using this position as a source of strength. Marriage and motherhood were, in the eyes of most men, the prime constituents of female citizenship, and therefore the feminist campaign to stake a claim to equal citizenship on the grounds of improved rights within the private sphere legitimised a political engagement on the basis of a duty to the nation state.

NOTES

1. J. W. Scott, *Gender and the Politics of History* (Cambridge, 1988), p. 48.

2. On motherhood as a prime duty of citizenship see G. Bock and P. Thane (eds), *Maternity and Gender Policies: women and the rise of European welfare states, 1880s-1950s* (London, 1991); S. Koven and S. Michel (eds), *Mothers of a New World: maternalist politics and the origins of welfare states* (London, 1993).

3. See S. Reynolds, *France between the Wars: gender and politics* (London, 1996), especially the introduction. An exception to this rule is L. Colley, *Britons: forging the nation 1707-1837* (London, 1996).

4. D. McCrone in *Understanding Scotland: the sociology of a stateless nation* (London, 1992), only acknowledges in passing that the archetypal Scottish identity is based on a masculine identity associated with the military and manual work: see p. 190.

5. "We allow a woman to sway our sceptre, but by law and custom we debar her from every other government but that of her own family ...", W. Alexander, *The History of Women from the Earliest Antiquity to the Present Time* (1779) cited in L. Colley, *Britons*, p. 253.

6. See E. Gordon, *Women and the Labour Movement in Scotland 1850-1914* (Oxford, 1991); E. King, "The Scottish women's suffrage movement", in E. Breitenbach and E. Gordon (eds), *Out of Bounds: women in Scottish society 1800-1945* (Edinburgh, 1992), pp. 121-150; J. Smyth, "Rents, peace, votes: working-class women and political activity in the First World War", in Breitenbach and Gordon, pp. 174-196.

7. Until 1900 civil law in Germany resembled a patchwork with each state possessing its own civil code.

8. See Colley, *Britons*, pp. 286-296.

9. The language of infiltration and permeability is borrowed from S. Reynolds, "The permeability of public life", in her *France between the Wars*, pp. 156-180.

10. Sylvia Paletschek, *Frauen und Dissens: Frauen im Deutschkatholizismus und in den freien Gemeinden 1841-1852* (Göttingen, 1990), pp. 166-167.

11. On Dittmar's life and works see Dagmar Herzog, "Liberalism, religious dissent, and women's rights: Louise Dittmar's writings from the 1840s", in K. Jarausch and L. E. Jones (eds), *In Search of a Liberal Germany* (Berg, 1990), pp. 55-85.

12. Herzog, "Liberalism", p. 58.

13. L. Dittmar, *Das Wesen der Ehe*, (Leipzig, 1849), p. 126.

14. Dittmar, *Das Wesen der Ehe*, p. 94.

15. On male liberal writings on sexual difference see K. Hausen, "Family and role-division: the polarisation of sexual stereotypes in the nineteenth century: an aspect of the dissociation of work and family life", in R. J. Evans and W. R. Lee (eds), *The German Family* (London, 1981), pp. 51-83.

16. On the writings of Hedwig Dohm see C. Weedon, "The struggle for women's emancipation in the work of Hedwig Dohm", *German Life and Letters*, no. 47 (1994), pp. 182-192.

17. Hedwig Dohm, *Woman's Nature and Privilege* (tr. C. Campbell, Westport,

Conn., 1976), p. 112.

18. H. Dohm, *Der Frauen Natur und Recht* (Berlin, 1876), p. 165.

19. This is in contrast with the position of English feminists who challenged liberal idealisation of the family and support for the concept of separate spheres quite consistently. See M. Lyndon Shanley, *Feminism, Marriage and the Law in Victorian England, 1850–1895* (Princeton, NJ, 1989).

20. Dittmar, *Das Wesen der Ehe*, pp. 55–56.

21. Dohm, *Woman's Nature*, p. 13.

22. Dohm, *Woman's Nature*, p. 125.

23. See Colley, *Britons*, pp. 290–296.

24. See E. King, "The Scottish women's suffrage movement", pp. 124–130.

25. M. Twellmann, *Die deutsche Frauenbewegung*, vol. 1 (1972), p. 195.

26. M. John, *Politics and the Law in Late Nineteenth Century Germany* (Oxford, 1989), p. 217.

27. Marie Stritt, "Rechtskämpfe", in H. Lange and G. Bäumer (eds), *Handbuch der Frauenbewegung*, vol. II (Berlin, 1901), p. 136.

28. On the activities of the Frauenrechtlerinnen see T. Wobbe, *Gleichheit und Differenz: politische Strategien von Frauenrechtlerinnen um die Jahrhundertwende* (Frankfurt, 1989), pp. 46–47.

29. M. Stritt, "Rechtskämpfe", p. 142.

30. S. Proelss and M. Raschke, *Die Frau im neuen bürgerlichen Gesetzbuch: eine Beleuchtung und Gegenüberstellung der Paragraphen des Entwurfs eines bürgerlichen Gesetzbuchs für das Deutsche Reich* (2 Lesung) (Berlin, 1895), p. 1.

31. T. Kipp and M. Wolff, *Lehrbuch des Bürgerlichen Rechts* (1931), p. 107.

32. On the *Rechtsschutzvereine*, see Marie Stritt, "Rechtsschutz für Frauen", in Lange und Bäumer (eds), *Handbuch der Frauenbewegung* vol. II (Berlin 1901), pp. 123–133.

33. U. Gerhard, "Women's rights and the law since the nineteenth century", in I. Drewitz (ed.), *The German Women's Movement* (Bonn, 1983), pp. 130–131.

34. See L. Hunt, *The Family Romance of the French Revolution* (London, 1992); D. Shafer, "Plus que des ambulancieres: women in articulation and defence of their ideals during the Paris Commune", *French History*, vol. 7 (1993).

35. Cited in E. King, "The Scottish women's suffrage movement", p. 125.

36. See E. Gordon, *Women and the Labour Movement in Scotland*, pp. 177–178.

14

Gendering the asylums: Ireland and Scotland, 1847–1877

Oonagh Walsh

The nineteenth century could be described as the century of the asylum. In Ireland, as elsewhere across Europe, the period between 1800 and 1860 marked the construction of many county and regional asylums. The Connaught District Lunatic Asylum (CDLA) was opened at Ballinasloe, Co. Galway in 1833. Intended primarily for the care of the so-called "lunatic poor", it also made available some accommodation for paying patients. In this chapter, I examine the experiences of male and female patients within the CDLA and make brief comparisons, where appropriate, with the Scottish system. The two countries operated very different schemes for the care of the insane, with the Scots relying far more upon a policy of boarding out lunatics in private homes or placing them in small-scale asylums run by private individuals. There were seven public asylums[1] – known in Scotland as "chartered asylums".[2] The distinction made between public and private institutions was "that the first [the public asylums] are under the superintendence of persons having no immediate pecuniary interest in their management; and the second [the private institutions] are conducted by individuals whose pecuniary advantage is directly concerned."[3] This emphasis upon the primacy of finance in the care of the insane had important repercussions as far as the treatment and recovery of patients was concerned. Ironically, lunatics fared better in institutions where they had no financial obligations towards their carers. It was not merely the case that unscrupulous individuals detained patients once they had recovered, in order to ensure a continuation of income, but they treated their inmates, on the whole, far worse than their counterparts in the public asylums. The private system, although theoretically subject to biannual inspection by the county sheriff, was more difficult to regulate than the large-scale government-funded asylums. The latter became prevalent in Ireland from the early nineteenth century.

The CDLA opened in a generally optimistic atmosphere as far as lunacy reform was concerned: the construction of the building, and the aspirations of the asylum board of governors, reflected this optimism. Since the end of the eighteenth century, there had been a new development in asylum care, based on the belief that lunatics could be cured through a process of humane treatment. Restraint and coercion of patients was discouraged, and therapy ranging from manual work through to painting and reading (regimes were tailored to the individual, and were imbued with class concerns) was advocated. This period in the treatment of the insane is often referred to as the "moral phase", with its emphasis on recognising lunatics as reasonable beings.[4] Thus asylum buildings were supposed to echo a patient's normal surroundings, with the maximum possible freedom allowed to the individual. Of course, most asylums fell far short of this ideal, both through financial restraints and because of a reluctance to embrace such a radical concept, but the influence of this thinking may be seen in the construction of the original buildings at the Ballinasloe asylum. There were no bars on the windows, the individual cells and dormitories were generously proportioned, fires were open, and the floors were made of wood rather than stone or slate – indicating that the governors believed the patients would be what they euphemistically described as "clean and tidy in their habits". Shortly after the asylum opened and received largely incurable patients from the "insane wings" of the county gaols and workhouses, there came the realisation that a considerable proportion of the patients were not amenable to moral treatment. Thus within a relatively brief period, the Ballinasloe asylum moved from a vision of itself as a rehabilitative institution to one of itself as catering largely for the long-term insane. In the 1850s, one third, on average, of the patients were discharged recovered.[5] The fact that a considerable proportion of the asylum population was deemed incurable had an impact upon the experiences of all those connected with the asylum. In Scotland, it is more difficult to present a clear picture of rates of release. Recovery rates in Aberdeen asylum, in comparison with Ballinasloe, were higher at forty-seven per cent of admissions between 1850 and 1854.[6] However, they dropped as low as twenty-one per cent in some private asylums. The recovery rate for public asylums was on average four per cent higher than for private, a figure which is more significant when one considers that the public asylums took in the most violent and notorious cases, which the private asylums had the freedom to reject. [7]

I

The patient body at Ballinasloe had limited contact with the hospital administrators, and in particular with the Board of Governors, whose decisions had a direct impact upon their lives within the institution. Like many such Victorian bodies, the CDLA was organised hierarchically, with the chain of command descending from the Lord Lieutenant, through the Board of Governors, to the asylum manager, to the nursing staff, and finally to the patients. Thus the key contacts for the inmates were the nurses, known in the nineteenth century rather ominously as "keepers". The patients obviously encountered the asylum physician at intervals, both at times of physical illness and also on an annual basis when their case histories were updated, but it was the nurses with whom they came into daily contact. In the Ballinasloe asylum, women accounted for three-quarters of the total nursing staff, and cared for male as well as female patients. Male keepers, on the other hand, were confined to the care of male patients only – apart from the occasional incursion into the female wards to subdue women who were deemed unruly. To a significant extent, then, the eventual recovery and release of the patients depended upon the nurses. so that, although they were placed in a lowly category within the hierarchy outlined above, they wielded a good deal of power in a practical sense – a somewhat unusual situation for women in the nineteenth century. In Scotland too, female nurses wielded considerable power in the royal asylums, but in the private institutions, the manager or medical superintendent had a greater degree of direct control. However, given that the care of male and female patients was segregated, nurses in Scotland came into contact with a greater range of patients than did the male attendants. There too, women were expected to nurse both sexes, while men were largely confined to the male wards:

> It is obvious that a night-watchman cannot, with propriety, be intrusted with these duties [night-nursing] on the female side of the house ... it appears to us a preferable plan to appoint a woman to visit both sides of the house. [8]

The calibre of nursing staff was a constant preoccupation for the asylum administrators throughout the nineteenth century. Concerns regarding qualifications and training were continually expressed by the governors and by the government inspectors. This reflected an anxiety common in other such institutions from the beginning of the century. In general, nursing staff in hospitals, workhouses, asylums, and poor houses had an appalling reputation. The concept of professionally trained nurses did not evolve until the 1860s. This was for several reasons, perhaps the most important of which was the belief that nursing was merely an extension of the supposedly innate feminine tendency to nurture and protect. Thus, the job was undervalued and neglected until it was proven that hospital-trained nurses could make a significant difference to patient survival rates. Another contributing factor to the lowly status of nursing was the fact that in many public institutions former inmates and patients frequently stayed on in the roles of nurses. Able-bodied female workhouse inhabitants commonly worked for their keep in the institution, supplying an often inadequate level of care for their fellow inmates. Although such cases were far from the majority, there existed a perception that many nurses were former prostitutes, stemming from the not uncommon practice of employing cured women, as wardsmaids and kitchen workers, in the lock hospitals (hospitals for the treatment of venereal diseases).[9] In 1854, for example, the head nurse of a London hospital told Florence Nightingale that

> in the course of her large experience she had never known a nurse who was not drunken, and there was immoral conduct practised in the very wards, of which she gave me some awful examples.[10]

The necessary exposure of nursing staff to male as well as female nudity and disease strengthened the perception that only "fallen women" could undertake such work. This factor ensured that the entry of middle-class women to the nursing profession occurred at a relatively late stage. Finally, in Ireland in the nineteenth century, nursing in public institutions was increasingly dominated by religious orders of nuns, whose work, like their lives, was vocational and therefore frequently unpaid. This strengthened the perception that nursing was a low-status occupation.

In the Ballinasloe asylum, former patients were never recruited as nursing staff, although several inmates worked their lifetimes in menial roles within the institution. Female nurses were drawn from a wide geographical area, with many of the original staff moving from Dublin, where they had gained experience in established asylums such as St Patricks. Nurses were believed by the board of governors to have a key role to play in the rehabilitation of patients, and this view was shared by the asylum inspectors. However, in the latter part of the nineteenth century, it would appear that there was considerable difficulty in recruiting staff. The 1857 inspector's report recommended that:

> A higher class of servant ... should be sought, and care should be taken, in their selection, not alone that they are possessed of the qualities ... of intelligence, temper and kindness ... but that they are sufficiently educated to be enabled to contribute to the recreation of the patients by reading for their amusement. Such occupations will beguile the wearisomeness of their watching in the wards, and, helping to cheer and tranquilize the patients, will render their attendance a more grateful task. [11]

Behind the inspector's recommendation was a double concern for the patients and their treatment at the hands of the nurses. The asylum staff were dealing not with physical but with mental illness and with patients who were often quite active and difficult to control, and who might spend the remainder of their lives within the asylum. They were, therefore, a rather different nursing prospect than physically ill patients in the county hospitals. In addition, many of the patients, by virtue of the fact of their residence within the asylum, were somewhat marginalised in society. They often lacked familial support, thereby increasing their vulnerability. As pauper inmates of a lunatic asylum, the patients depended heavily upon the goodwill of the nursing staff for reasonable treatment. It would appear that the asylum administrators feared they did not receive it. In 1847, the manager commented:

> They [the nurses] are in general of an inferior class, and not sufficiently intelligent for their situations, particularly the females. No suitable persons offer, nor can be heard of about the country, with recommendations when vacancies occur.

And the inspector went on to add:

I minutely examined several, whom I found, with some few exceptions, very ignorant, and badly calculated to contribute to that system of moral government, upon which the value of the asylum depends.[12]

Levels of education amongst the nursing staff were low; indeed in mid-century, the board of governors discovered to their dismay that there was a higher level of literacy amongst the patients than the nurses.

The low standards of education and training which were found in the nursing staff, would seem to suggest that the asylum recruited from an especially disadvantaged sector of the population. However, the wages and working conditions were a good deal more attractive than in comparable, unskilled employment. When the CDLA opened in 1833, a male keeper was paid £12 12/- per annum, with an additional £4 4/- for clothing, and a female keeper received £4 4/- per annum, with £2 2/- for clothing.[13] The large wage gap reflects the general contemporary practice of low female wages. The discrepancy, moreover, looks more acute when one considers that female staff were expected to provide nursing care for male patients in addition to female ones. Both male and female keepers received bed and board as part of their remuneration, which added considerably to its overall value. By comparison with asylum wages in England, Irish employees were poorly paid. At Colney Hatch, for example, male keepers were paid £25 per annum plus board, lodgings, and laundry, with females receiving £15 per annum with the same benefits.[14] But in terms of contemporary Irish wages, particularly for women, the asylum offered well-paid, secure work. In 1863, wage levels had risen in Ballinasloe, to £20 per annum for a head male attendant, and £17 15/- for a head female nurse, with the usual benefits; but the quality of recruits had not particularly improved. Discipline amongst staff appeared difficult to maintain, and the matron, who was in charge of nursing staff, repeatedly made complaints to the boards of governors regarding the wayward behaviour of the nurses. Female nurses were most often reprimanded for theft, insubordination, and lapses into drunkenness, and males for ill treatment of patients. The board was very reluctant to actually dismiss staff, because replacement proved so difficult; so a nurse frequently received several warnings before being sacked. One woman, finally dismissed in 1848, had a long career of transgression behind her:

The Matron reported Nurse ____ for drunkenness and insubordination, and the governors having frequently fined and cau-

tioned her – *Resolved* that it appears she is not a fit person to have
any charge over lunatics, and that she will be therefore dismissed,
and as she was brought here originally from Dublin, *Resolved* that
she be allowed 15/- for travelling expenses to Dublin, and also
10/6 being for her proportion of clothing since November last, as
she was originally employed at that period of the year 1833. [15]

As the nurses took charge of the distribution of food to the infirm and
confined patients, opportunities arose both for embezzlement and
favouritism.[16] In May 1848, another female nurse was brought before the
board to answer charges from the matron of "having given
dissatisfaction to her in the discharge of her duties particularly in the
distribution of milk, and having been disrespectful when spoken to". In
this case the nurse was merely "warned to be more attentive, and
demean herself with due propriety in future".[17] Male keepers were in the
earlier nineteenth century primarily hired for their ability to restrain
violent patients; in 1853, this policy had its most extreme effect, when a
patient died as a result of excessive force in restraint. The case was
serious enough to warrant a government investigation, which resulted in
the dismissal of the keeper concerned.

Although it could not be proved that the attendant had caused
the patient's death by ill-treatment, the board felt satisfied that
unnecessary violence had been exercised in restraining him. It
appeared also that mechanical coercion was used without the
knowledge of the manager or visiting physician. Altogether the
circumstances were such as warranted the board in ordering the
attendant to be dismissed, as well as another, who grossly pre-
varicated in his statements, from a manifest desire to shield his
fellow servant.[18]

The issue of the extent of actual control which nurses exercised over
the patients was an important one. The keepers came into the closest and
most regular contact with the patients and observed any significant
changes in an inmate's behaviour before it generally came to the attention
of the matron or physician. Indeed, these two depended heavily upon the
comments of the nurses when updating patient records. Thus the attitude
of the staff towards the patients constituted a significant part of the institutional process. The records periodically suggest that there was some
concern over the treatment of patients by keepers. In 1847 for example,
the inspector raised the issue of the prolonged use of mechanical restraint

by the keepers at Ballinasloe on patients kept in the basement cells, who were regarded as the most difficult cases:

> It behoves the superior officers to be most vigilant in their superintendence upon the classes confined to the basement story, as the apartments are detached from the other wards, and, consequently, out of the range of ordinary inspection. [19]

These muted appeals to the "superior officers" notwithstanding, it was nevertheless the case that nurses exercised a good deal of independent authority. One of the areas of contention between nurses and the board of governors was the use of mechanical restraint. The board sought its almost total abolition on liberal humanist grounds, while the nurses argued for its retention on the pragmatic grounds of experience. From the middle of the century, those concerned with the management of Irish asylums directed a good deal of attention towards the question of restraint, with the government even commissioning a survey in 1857 of all public asylums to determine the extent of its use. The reply from Ballinasloe by the asylum manager indicated that restraint was used, "but very seldom, and in violent cases, to prevent the patients injuring themselves, or taking off blisters or surgical dressings." In answer to the question as to who issued instructions to use restraint, the manager replied that:

> the physician, sometimes in the prescription book, at other times by his directions – in my presence, and given out by myself to the attendant, also by myself for violent cases at night; all these occur very rarely. [20]

It would appear, however, that not only was mechanical restraint being employed more frequently than the manager suggested, but that it was also being sanctioned by the nurses on their own judgement. In 1847, the inspector reported that:

> I found one very unfortunate patient who was represented as being a very dangerous and violent woman: she had a strong leather muff strapped round her arms, which bound the parts so tight as to cause considerable marks of pressure, and which appeared to have been continued for some length of time. This practice cannot be too strongly condemned, as being most cruel, and fraught with great evil to the unfortunate sufferers. [21]

On investigation, it was found that the female keeper had sanctioned the use of restraint in this case, without the approval of the manager,

[206]

physician, or matron. In the case of the patient death mentioned above, the government inquiry concluded that "he (the manager) had not been sufficiently strict in his supervision of the attendants, for which negligence he received a strong official reprimand." [22]

Unauthorised use of restraint was a problem in Scotland also. The private asylums were most guilty with regard to the use of coercion to maintain order:

> personal restraint is habitually had recourse to in almost all the houses. The strait-waistcoat and leather muffs are generally left in the keeping of the attendants, to be applied at their discretion. [23]

Following complaints by inspectors regarding the over-use of restraint, one of the private licensed houses simply attempted to conceal its prevalence.

> Instruments of restraint were kept by the attendants, who removed and attempted to conceal them on the approach of visitors; that the patients were restrained by means of manacles, fastening the arms behind the back, and also to rings fixed in the wall.[24]

Given the concern which existed amongst private asylum managers to keep costs to a minimum, as well as a reluctance on the part of the nurses, whose duty it frequently was to wash linen, patients were often stripped at night, to prevent them soiling their clothing.

> A certain number of the patients, males as well as females, were stripped naked at night, and that in some cases two, and in one case even three, of them were placed to sleep in the same bed-frame, on loose straw, in a state of perfect nudity. [25]

Several of the patients mentioned in this report were actually paying sums of between £35 and £53 per annum for their keep – a considerable amount of money in the 1850s. A major problem for the authorities was the fact that the use of restraint was often unrecorded. A private asylum in Musselburgh for example, claimed that restraint was rarely used and that its use was always noted in the register; but it was found on an unannounced visit that

> [a] female patient ... was in the airing court, in a strait-jacket, and fastened to a paling by a strap. Still there was no entry of restraint in the register.[26]

As the nineteenth century progressed, nursing standards rose steadily. In the Irish case the board of governors moved from a position where practically any candidate was accepted, to one in which nurses were required to have a certain standard of education – and to prove to the board that they were fit persons to have charge of the insane. By the turn of the century, nurses were required to provide the names of three referees, to be educated to at least national school level, and to "pass a medical examination as to physical and mental fitness." They further had to sign a declaration which bound them

> to obey the rules of the Asylum, to avoid gossiping about its inmates or affairs, to be careful of its property, to promote, as far as I am able, its objects, and to endeavour generally by my own good conduct and demeanour to sustain its respectability.... I am liable to dismissal without warning for acts of unkindness to the inmates, intemperance, disobedience of orders, or any transgression of the Rules.

The sense that nurses had more of an obligation towards their patients than mere custodial care made a significant difference to the profession.

II

Comparisons of the experience of male and female patients within the Connaught District Lunatic Asylum provide some interesting hints as to the relative importance of particular strata of nineteenth-century Irish society. Rates of admission, ascribed causes of insanity, length of stay in the asylum, and the efforts of relatives to either admit or have released patients all suggest a complex series of engagements. Perhaps the most striking, and also the least surprising similarity which male and female patients share, is the marital status of the majority. Unmarried persons were most likely to be admitted to the asylum and were least likely to leave.[27] The proportion of single persons in any one year varied, from approximately 80% of males and 55% of females in 1852 to 58% of males and 52% of females in 1857. This high proportion of unmarried patients was not unique to Ballinasloe, but reflected patterns in other Irish asylums and indeed in Britain. The reasons are varied, but the principal one may be the perceived importance of parental ties. A father, nominal head of a household and main breadwinner, was least likely to be admitted to the CDLA. An unmarried son or brother, on the other hand, was less significant in terms of dependants, particularly in those families where remaining siblings were capable of assuming the patients' workload. Similarly, a mother would be seen as central to the organisation of a household, especially one with children. Thus married patients, particularly those with dependent offspring, tended to be released from the asylum with the greatest frequency, either by the asylum authorities themselves or on the request of relatives. General familial structures must have played a part in terms of readiness to commit a spouse to an asylum, with perhaps a reluctance on the part of wives to have their husbands admitted, on economic grounds as well as those of perceived authority.

A factor which tends to support this thesis that the least "expendable" proportion of the general population stood the greatest chance of being released from the asylum relates to the fate of widows and widowers admitted to the CDLA. Of the 20 widows admitted to the asylum between 1850 and 1860, 13 died there. Four out of the six widowers admitted in the same period also died in the asylum. Although the majority of these patients had grown children, it tended to be those parents who lived with unmarried offspring that were most likely to be taken home again. This is not to suggest that Irish society strictly categorised persons in terms of their usefulness or otherwise, but that family circumstances appear to have had a significant impact upon the likelihood of an individual's release, apparently independently of that individual's actual state of mental health. There does not seem to be a significant gender difference in terms of widow(er) release rates.

One area in which differing patterns of male and female admission and release emerge, however, is amongst married patients. A higher proportion of married women were admitted to the CDLA than men; in some years, married women accounted for almost half of the female admissions (1857), as opposed to less than 30% of the single highest male rate in any one year. Although many of the married women were admitted for reasons associated with childbirth, in many cases the supposed cause of their insanity was not noted. In psychiatric history there is a (perhaps understandable) perception that institutions such as the Connaught District Lunatic Asylum had its most negative impact on women. Given the general societal context of limited opportunity for women in educational and economic terms in rural Ireland, it is often presumed that they were more subject to the controls of their male relations, be they fathers, husbands, or brothers. In the post-famine period in particular, women were believed to have fewer choices, and to be bound more closely by patriarchal structures. While this picture may indeed apply to a proportion of the female population, one finds that it is not reflected clearly in the experiences of the patients at the Ballinasloe asylum. One might expect, for example, that women patients would be committed in the main by the male heads of households. However, if we examine one year, 1871 (by which time post-famine social changes should have been well established), we find that the picture is far from clear.

In seeking the committal of any individual to an Irish asylum in the 1870s, a statement alleging insane behaviour had to be sworn before two justices of the peace, and the patient had to be examined by a medical officer. Thus in effect a charge of insanity had to be levelled at the potential patient, and the justices, along with the medical officer, supported or rejected the claim. Any person could bring the charge, although in the majority of cases the individual was a relative. The results for the admission of women, married and single, are interesting. In 1871, eighteen married and twenty-one single women were admitted to the CDLA. Of the single women, twelve of the total were committed by other women: in eight cases by their mothers, in three by their sisters. Committals by fathers occurred in only three cases; indeed, in terms of masculine authority, brothers were in this year more significant, being responsible for seeking admission in four cases. The mothers were furthermore acting upon their own authority in committing their daughters – in six out of the eight cases the father was alive at the time of committal. While it is not an especially cheering example of nineteenth-century female authority, it is nevertheless interesting that women played an active part in the process of admission, and did not merely transfer such a pro-active role to their male partners. In some of these cases, the mothers and sisters were not the principal focus of the patient's insane actions, but they were the ones who provided the testimony. With regard to married women, only one was admitted on the word of another woman. However, less than half of the total were actually committed by their husbands, despite the fact that the husbands were all alive at the time of committal, bar one. Two fathers and two sons sought the admission of married women, even though the husbands were in these cases alive.

In Scotland, the boarding-out system meant that the role of relatives in the admission of patients was significantly reduced. However, there are some specifically gendered issues implicit in the Scottish system. One is the greater willingness amongst managers of licensed houses to take female patients, as they were generally easier to control than men. Another which comes into particularly sharp focus when compared with Ireland is the rate of illegitimate births amongst female lunatics who resided outside asylums. At Ballinasloe, for example, there is an extremely low rate of illegitimate births recorded for female patients, before or after admission, throughout the nineteenth century. In Scotland, by contrast, seventeen per cent of female lunatics of childbearing age living outside the chartered asylums had had illegitimate children, and some had more than one child.[28] The Commissioners for Scotland believed that this figure was in fact higher, as not all of the births were recorded:

> It is not surprising that in a number of parishes idiot and imbecile females have become mothers, and, in general, to unknown fathers. Such cases are by no means exceptional, for they were admitted of and spoken of as common occurrences.[29]

The conditions under which many lunatics were boarded, with little check kept by the authorities, left at least some women in a vulnerable position. However, the concern which the inspectors expressed over the plight of these women was intensified for another reason. In the late nineteenth century, so-called "mad-doctors" were becoming increasingly convinced of the significance of hereditary insanity, and detailed case notes were compiled within institutions regarding familial histories of insanity. One solution to stem the rise in lunatics was admission to asylums, where the female lunatics were far less likely to become pregnant. This strategy can also be read more positively, as a means whereby women received a degree of protection from sexual exploitation. Either way, the asylum became an increasingly popular means of dealing with the mentally ill in the nineteenth century.

The admissions procedure to Irish asylums required, as indicated above, that the patient be deemed dangerous or violent. These two terms applied not merely to those individuals who presented a threat to others but also to those who were suicidal, self-destructive tendencies being viewed as seriously as violence directed outwards. There is an interesting division in gender terms between the reasons for committal for men and women. If we use again the data for 1871, a picture of greater violence from men towards others appears to emerge. The sworn statements fall into two main camps, with a far greater tendency towards suicide or self-harm ascribed to women, and more violence towards others attributed to men. Out of thirty-nine female patients, twelve were admitted because they were suicidal, and a further six through threatening to kill both themselves as well as others. Of the fifty-four male patients, eight were designated solely suicidal, and two as dangerous to self and others. Thus four-fifths of male patients were deemed a serious threat to others, while just over half of the women were. Does this indicate a genuinely gendered division of mental illness, or does it reflect nineteenth-century assumptions regarding appropriate behaviour of men and women?

This is, of course, a difficult question to answer. Cultural determinism is highly pervasive and largely unconscious. Because women were deemed more passive and less violent than men generally, this may have had an impact upon designation. In one of the best known literary representations of madness, Shakespeare's *Hamlet*, the male protagonist directs his insane violence towards others, while Ophelia commits suicide. Even when insane, then, women might be presumed to be less likely to injure others, while men, with rational control effectively suspended, could be expected to give vent to greater aggression. The sworn statements given in support of an application for admission were by their nature highly subjective, and in the absence of an actual physical assault on a third party, the evidence was largely interpretative. Statements such as "from her conduct and demeanour [she is believed] to be a dangerous lunatic" were common.[30] A "fierce expression" was also frequently cited as evidence of insanity.[31] The sense that men were more likely to constitute a greater threat to the broader social order was strengthened by the fact that female violence was largely contained within the familial unit. This partly reflects the more constrained lives led by women in the nineteenth century. When they became ill, their immediate relations bore the brunt of the attacks. Men, on the other hand, were far more likely than women to assault strangers, often at considerable distances from home. In addition, there was a sense that men represented a greater sexual threat than women. Insanity removed the reserve which normally regulated appropriate sexual behaviour, but – as the quotations which follow illustrate – while women were inclined towards immodest displays and extreme exhibitionism, men were more likely to attempt sexual assault:

she slipped off her clothes publicly ... many times [she] raised her clothes, and stripped herself, and used to go through the village singing, dancing and crying and making a disturbance ... she is outrageous and committed several acts from which it appears that [she] was discovered and apprehended under circumstances denoting a derangement of mind.[32]

[He] left his home and wandered at large without fixed purpose, tearing his clothes, entering stranger's houses forcibly ... and conducting himself in a noisy and riotous manner to the terror and annoyance of those in his company, partially dressed and bareheaded.[33]

He was seized with an Epileptic fit after which his manner became violent and he tore off his clothes and ran among the fields naked and attempted to assault the woman who was bringing him back and he has since continued in the same violent condition.[34]

The subject of mental illness and incarceration is one weighted with difficulties. In comparing male and female experiences of the process, whether from within or without the institution, one is implicitly beginning from a position in which both sexes share certain disadvantages. However, it would appear that patterns of power and advantage did not necessarily reproduce the patriarchal structures operating in the wider world.

NOTES

1. The term "public", although commonly used by the Inspectors, is somewhat deceptive, as the chartered asylums were largely opened and maintained through private subscriptions.
2. At Aberdeen, Dumfries, Dundee, Edinburgh, Glasgow, Montrose and Perth.
3. *Report of the Royal Commissioners on Lunatic Asylums and the Laws relating to them in Scotland with Appendix and an Index* (PP., 1857), p. 49 (hereafter *Royal Commissioners, Scotland*).
4. The best known exponent of moral treatment was William Tuke, whose establishment of the York Retreat marked the beginning of moral treatment in Britain. Despite the initially encouraging results, moral treatment proved disappointing in terms of recovery rates, and by the end of the nineteenth century even the staunchest of advocates admitted there was little which could be done for many lunatics.
5. This rate was somewhat less than the average calculated across a range of asylums by William Browne in 1837, although Browne's figures may not be entirely reliable, based as they were on wildly differing institutions over varying periods of time. Salpetrière and Bicêtre in France for example had rates of thirty-four recoveries per hundred patients, while Senavra in Milan returned rates of fifty-eight per hundred. W. A. F. Browne, *What Asylums Were, Are and Ought to Be* (Edinburgh, 1837; edited with an introduction by Andrew Scull, London, 1991), p. 71.
6. *Royal Commissioners, Scotland*, p. 93.
7. "The proprietor of a private asylum has the power of refusing admission, or of discharging his patients at pleasure; and this power is more freely exercised than is the similar one possessed by the chartered asylums ... troublesome patients are frequently avowedly rejected." Ibid., p. 14.

8. *Royal Commissioners, Scotland*, p. 93.
9. Maria Luddy, *Women and Philanthropy in Nineteenth Century Ireland* (Cambridge, 1995), p. 107.
10. Cecil Woodham Smith, *Florence Nightingale* (Suffolk, 1952 edn), p. 47.
11. *Report of the commissioners of Inquiry into the state of the lunatic asylums and other institutions for the custody and treatment of the insane in Ireland; with minutes of evidence and appendices*, vol. XXVII, p. 34 (hereafter *Report of the Commissioners*).
12. *Report on the district, local and private lunatic asylums in Ireland, 1847* (1848), vol. XVII, p. 355 (hereafter *Report on the district, 1847*).
13. Board Minutes, CDLA, August 29, 1833.
14. Elaine Showalter, *The Female Malady: women, madness and English culture 1830–1980* (London 1987), p. 259.
15. Board Minutes, CDLA, 21 February, 1848.
16. This had serious repercussions during the Great Famine, when the death rate in the asylum rose sharply. Patients were dying in some cases as a result of malnutrition, despite their regulated food allowance, and it would appear that some of the nurses were stealing and selling the patient's food. See Oonagh Walsh, "'A lightness of mind': gender and insanity in nineteenth-century Ireland", in M. Kelleher and J. Kelly (eds), *Gender Perspectives in 19th century Ireland: public and private spheres* (Dublin, 1997).
17. CDLA Board minutes, May 1, 1848.
18. *Report on the district, criminal and private lunatic asylums in Ireland for 1853* (PP., 1854–55), p. 11 (hereafter, *Report on the district 1853*).
19. *Report on the district, 1847*, p. 355.
20. *Report of the commissioners*, Appendix G.
21. *Report on the district, 1847*, p. 356.
22. *Report on the district, 1853*, p. 12.
23. *Royal Commissioners, Scotland*, p. 143.
24. *Royal Commissioners, Scotland*, p. 121.
25. *Royal Commissioners, Scotland*, p. 114.
26. *Royal Commissioners, Scotland*, p. 114.
27. Scottish release and recovery rates are more difficult to calculate, given the dual public/private system. In licensed Scottish asylums, there was no legal requirement that a patient be discharged, once cured. If one examines the returns from the Aberdeen Royal Asylum, however, one finds a broadly similar picture to Ireland. Female admissions outnumber male at two hundred and thirty-four to one hundred and eighty-seven in the five years between 1850 and 1854, but female recovery rates are also higher, at one hundred and twenty to seventy-nine. This pattern is echoed in those licensed asylums for which records exist. See Commissioners Report, p. 203.
28. Compiled from the returns by the Commissioners for Scotland, Appendix K, pp. 244–263.

29. *Royal Commissioners, Scotland*, p. 185.
30. Committal no. 5, 1871. CDLA archive.
31. See for example committal no. 7, 1871.
32. Committals nos 63, 69 and 77, 1877.
33. Committal no. 2, 1871.
34. Committal no. 46, 1877.

15

Women and the creation of the Chicago Juvenile Court in the 1890s

Elizabeth J. Clapp

LADIES – *We the undersigned,* are moved to issue this circular because our experience has proved to us that the increasing complexities of social life, and the growing interdependence of human relations, while augmenting woman's knowledge and enlarging her interests, are also adding to her duties. Prominent among these duties are the care and protection of our social dependents, the aged poor, the sick and insane and the children. While neglect of the first classes is cruel, neglect of the children is in addition, social suicide.[1]

This appeal addressed to the "Women and Women's Clubs of Illinois" in February 1896 expressed a growing belief among middle-class white women that it was their duty to become involved in social welfare reform on behalf of society's dependents – women and children. At a time when women were not expected to play a part in public life, nor were they able to vote, increasing numbers of middle-class women became involved in campaigns for social welfare reform which often propelled them into public life and, ultimately, politics. Like the framers of this appeal, other female reformers demanded that women should take a central part in campaigning for reform, and they articulated it in terms of women's maternal duty. Thus, many women voicing similar beliefs played a key role in campaigning for social welfare reforms during the Progressive Era (c. 1890–1920), especially those which focused upon children.

One of the earliest social welfare reforms of the American Progressive Era was the establishment of juvenile courts in cities across the United States. Juvenile courts represented a major change in the way in which the law dealt with wayward children, and the passing of juvenile court laws by the vast majority of state legislatures between 1899 and 1920 marked the recognition by those states of their duty towards dependent and delinquent children. The first and probably most influential juvenile court was that in Chicago – legally constituted by the Illinois Juvenile Court Law of 1899. Women were the dominant influence in pushing for this reform in Chicago and they did so in the name of their duty as mothers. Women's involvement in the juvenile court movement has not been widely recognised by historians, however.

Traditionally, historians have associated the juvenile court movement with Judge Ben Lindsey and his Denver Juvenile Court, and have sidelined the role of women in it. Even those who have acknowledged the role of women in the movement have been little influenced by developments in women's history.[2] Nonetheless, the juvenile court movement raises a number of issues of concern to historians of gender and provides a useful illustration of many of the matters currently being debated in the field of gender and the rise of welfare states.

Women played a central role in the movement which created the juvenile courts, sometimes as individuals but more often as members of women's clubs, settlement houses, and national organisations. The extent of their involvement varied, but it was rare for a state to pass juvenile court legislation without, at least, the active support of local women. Clearly male reformers were also involved, but by placing the juvenile court movement within the context of recent scholarship by historians of women, it has become necessary to challenge previously held assumptions that men were the central and dominating force behind it. By examining closely the pioneer juvenile court in Chicago, it becomes clear to what extent women, acting in accordance with culturally determined female values, shaped the juvenile court movement. This study, though, goes beyond the simple task of writing women back into the history of the juvenile court movement to reveal a more complex picture of women's social welfare reform in the Progressive Era. It seeks to examine the interaction between gender consciousness and the shaping of social welfare reform.

The kind of gender consciousness which prompted women to become involved in social welfare reform during the Progressive Era has recently been labelled "maternalism".[3] Historians of women argue that maternalism was a political concept which accepted the principle of gender difference, particularly women's identity as mothers, but which maintained that women had a duty to extend their domestic and familial values beyond their own homes to society at large.[4] By emphasising woman's role as universal mother and her unique expertise in child welfare, the discourse of maternalism enabled female reformers to demand legislative reform to protect children. "Maternalism" has, however, been used too indiscriminately by historians.[5] By focusing more closely upon the Chicago juvenile court movement, it becomes apparent that not all women reformers were the same and that they used maternalist discourses for different purposes. There were, in fact, different versions of maternalism. Gender consciousness, though a highly significant factor, was not the only one in prompting women to pursue reform in the treatment of dependent and delinquent children in Chicago.

The Chicago Juvenile Court represented a departure from earlier methods of dealing with dependent and delinquent children, not only in Chicago but in the rest of the United States.[6] For, not only did it mark a final recognition by the State of Illinois of its duty towards children, it also symbolised a new attitude towards young people in the justice system, seeing them as children in need of help rather than as criminals to be punished. It was not, however, a sudden invention by a single reformer, but was the result of agitation during the 1890s by two groups of women reformers. The two groups – the Chicago Woman's Club and the Hull House community – worked together but their concerns were not identical.

The Chicago Woman's Club was founded in February 1876, by Mrs Caroline Brown, a Bostonian, and several of her friends. Its stated aims were:

> a desire to enlarge our vision, to enable us to share in the wider interests of the community, to do our share of the world's work; we wished to prevent wrong and harm to those unable to help themselves, to bind up wounds, to create that which was lovely, to take the place of the unsightly.[7]

The club was part of a wider trend among middle-class women in the late nineteenth century to organise themselves into voluntary associations.[8] Like these other agencies it was neither a political nor a suffrage organisation but sought to better the world and its members through charity, philanthropy, and culture. Typically the leaders of the Chicago Woman's Club in the late 1880s and 1890s were white, middle-class, and Protestant. The majority of them were married and were mothers, but their children were usually beyond the earliest years of childhood. The exceptions to this profile were the increasing numbers of professional women who joined the club from the 1880s onwards. Many club members were socially prominent, either in their own right or as the wives of prominent Chicago men.[9]

Though the club was in part a cultural organisation concerned with self-improvement, involvement in the Chicago Woman's Club gave its members the emotional support and sense of sisterhood necessary to allow them to play a greater part in the community outside their homes and to involve them in reform activity in the public sphere within a maternalist framework.[10] Consequently, members of the club quickly became involved with questions of reform and philanthropy. In entering into such work members of the Chicago Woman's Club were prompted by their own identification as mothers and the perceptions of family life and childhood which this produced. In so doing they were working within the bounds of women's accepted role in society. The historian Molly Ladd-Taylor has labelled such women, "sentimental maternalists".[11] They were clearly committed to the ideals of motherhood and domesticity which late-nineteenth-century society dictated for middle-class women, while at the same time they believed that these ideals required them to extend their maternal instincts beyond their own homes and to apply their domestic values to society at large.[12] As the club's historians noted:

> It has broadened the views of women and has tended to make them more impersonal and has widened their sympathies. They have learned to assume responsibility outside of home interests, and to consider the study of conditions in city and state as an extension of their concern – constituting as they do the larger home. The idea of practical work for the community was fundamental in the minds of the founders.[13]

The kind of "sentimental maternalism" that the club women represented was conservative, both in its views of women's role in society and in its wider social ideas. In their social ideas the club women reflected the concerns of their social class. As members of the social élite they were anxious to preserve the existing structures of society, but they were also increasingly aware that the problems created by rapid industrialisation and urbanisation could not be ignored. As their charitable work carried them into Chicago's slums, they began to realise that if something was not done to alleviate the poverty and distress they found there, there would be social unrest.[14] However, while their fears for social stability may well have prompted them to seek means of improving social conditions, it was their gender consciousness which shaped the kind of reform they pursued.

From the beginning, the Chicago Woman's Club was concerned with matters affecting women and children, especially those of the poorer and criminal classes. Their concern with child welfare was a reflection of the increased emphasis placed upon childhood within the wider society. Childhood was to be cherished and carefully regulated as a preparation for adulthood. Intellectual currents and the child study movement of the late-nineteenth century placed the responsibility for the proper rearing of children upon educated mothers.[15] It is therefore unsurprising that the women of the Chicago Woman's Club, imbued as they were with a gender consciousness which emphasised the importance of motherhood, should consider it their responsibility to ensure that these children should be reared properly.

Working within this kind of maternalist framework, members of the club carried out charitable work in the slums of Chicago and in the city's jails and police stations. This work, coupled with their preconceived notions of what family life should be like, caused them to believe that families in the poorer sections of the city were on the point of breakdown. Members of the club were horrified to discover that children were left to roam the streets all day because both parents went out to work. From an early age children were sent out to work in factories or to sell newspapers or other wares on the streets. Club members were shocked by this difference in family life in the poorer sections of the city, and some members were not slow to point out the likely consequences for society if this situation was allowed to continue.[16] These fears appeared to be justified by the apparent growth in the rate of juvenile delinquency in Chicago.[17] As members of the club became increasingly involved in projects aimed at preventing children from becoming hardened criminals, it became apparent to them that existing methods of dealing with dependent and delinquent children were not working.[18]

The Chicago Woman's Club was not alone in its concerns about family life in Chicago's slums. It worked closely with another predominantly female organisation – the Hull House community. Hull House was founded by Jane Addams and her friend, Ellen Gates Starr, on 18 September, 1889. They were soon the nucleus of a thriving social settlement in Chicago's Nineteenth Ward. Hull House was not the first settlement house in the United States, but it is arguable that it became the most famous, in large part because of the character of the women who lived there. Like the women of the Chicago Woman's Club most of the residents came from middle-class backgrounds, but, rather unusually, there was a significant minority who came from less privileged backgrounds. It was, however, the college-educated residents who gave the settlement its character, and it was middle-class values that predominated.[19] Like many settlement houses in America, Hull House was dominated by women, although a number of men were associated with it, often as non-residents. It is also significant that many of the women settlement workers were unmarried or, like Florence Kelley and Alzina Stevens, were divorced. Some married couples lived in the settlement, but they were exceptions.[20]

The main purpose of the settlements was that well-educated, middle-class young people should set up residence in slum neighbourhoods and, by living among the poor as neighbours, they should be in a better position to help them. Many of the pioneer settlement workers in America were idealists, who believed that they had a mission to solve the problems of the crowded city and that the best way to do this was to go and live in working-class immigrant neighbourhoods.[21] Their motives, however, were not purely altruistic.

For the first generation of college-educated women in particular the settlement fulfilled a very obvious need. Many of these female graduates experienced difficulty in finding a place for themselves in society, and the settlements provided an outlet for their talents and training which had not previously existed. The knowledge they had acquired at college, joined to the principles of educated motherhood and the growing emphasis on child study, encouraged college graduates to confront the problems posed by industrialisation, urbanisation, and immigration. Settlement work allowed them to apply what they had learned at college to the practical problems of slum life. Their approach to these problems differed markedly from that of traditional female charity workers. They also went beyond purely practical work to investigate the conditions in which their neighbours lived and worked. This change in approach reflected changes in the curriculum taught in female colleges. For while women's colleges continued to be steeped in the traditions of educated motherhood, by the late nineteenth century many women's colleges had begun to introduce a social-science curriculum, which influenced college graduates to use more "scientific" methods in their charity work. [22]

Life in a settlement house supplied further advantages to these women, for it provided an alternative to family life for its residents, at least until they got married and set up homes of their own. Settlement work quickly became an attractive occupation for single middle-class women. To society it appeared as an extension into the slum of the traditional role of women as mother and housekeeper, and settlement workers did little to upset this assumption. [23] Moreover, the community life fostered by the settlements proved an important source of support for the women who lived in them and was also instrumental in their development as reformers. In a period when women still did not have the vote, the settlement gave women reformers the mutual support and ability not just to work with other women's organisations, but also to enter the political realm dominated by men. Thus Hull House gave the network of women reformers centred around it the support and contacts which enabled them to seek legislative redress for some of the problems of their neighbourhood. [24]

The settlement movement allowed women reformers to move fully into civic life, but they still did so as women. For the settlement emphasised women's qualities of compassion, nurture, and sympathy, and also drew upon maternalist ideology with its emphasis upon the role of women as mothers. [25] Their interpretation of this ideology was, however, different from that espoused by the Chicago Woman's Club. For, unlike the "sentimental maternalists" of the Chicago Woman's Club, the majority of the Hull House women were not themselves mothers, and they rejected a sentimental view of motherhood in favour of a more "scientific" approach. These "progressive maternalists", as Molly Ladd-Taylor characterises them, acknowledged the centrality of feminine qualities in their work, but they placed much greater emphasis upon science and professionalism as values equally available to men and women. [26] Thus, while many of them still used the language of "sentimental maternalism" during the 1890s, this was often little more than a strategic posture. In their work the Hull House women placed much greater emphasis upon their professional expertise as social scientists, though the social-science methods and philosophy they advocated remained gendered. [27] Women settlement-house workers used social-science methods to shed new light on social problems and to draw conclusions from their findings – conclusions which were gendered in the sense that they often focused upon the needs of women and children and which demanded reform as an immediate moral necessity.[28]

The earliest efforts of the Hull House residents were directed towards helping the women and children of the neighbourhood. Working with these families, they gained the impression that under the impact of industrialisation, urbanisation, and immigration, the family as they saw it was under threat. It became especially clear to Jane Addams and her colleagues that the children in the slums did not conform to their preconceived ideas of childhood. In this they shared many of the same perceptions as the women of the Chicago Woman's Club, but their experience of living in the Chicago slums and their involvement in compiling social surveys of the area gave them a more realistic understanding of the problems these families faced.[29] A few, like Julia Lathrop, Florence Kelley, and Alzina Stevens, had a very acute understanding of the problems confronting poor families in Chicago as a result of their experience as state officials.[30]

The solutions which the Hull House women sought to the problem of juvenile delinquency and dependency had a different emphasis from those of the Chicago Woman's Club, until the two merged to campaign for legislative change. During the mid-1890s the club's main concern was to ensure the speedy trial of children and their separation from adult criminals wherever possible. The club was able to prevail upon one of the judges to hold separate court sessions just for the trial of boys, but this was accomplished on an informal basis without the sanction of legislation. Attempts to formalise this embryo juvenile court through legislation, in 1895, were abandoned because members of the club were advised that such a law would be unconstitutional.[31] Whereas the Woman's Club was mainly concerned with helping children already involved with the criminal justice system, some of the residents of Hull House were, by the mid-1890s, actively involved in preventing children from ever appearing before the courts; and they were acting as probation officers to those already in trouble with the police. The Hull House probation system seems to have begun simply as an extension of the work of the settlement, a means to help immigrant parents with wayward children who needed help with the police stations and courts.[32] It slowly developed so that Hull House residents began to appear in court when children's cases were being heard; they investigated the home backgrounds of these children and advised the judge how to look after the best interests of the child. Some children were even dismissed into the care of these women.[33]

Although members of the Hull House community and of the Chicago Woman's Club approached the problem of juvenile delinquency from different perspectives, they worked closely together. Several members of the Hull House community were also members of the Chicago Woman's Club, and prominent members of the club were benefactresses of Hull House and were involved in its various activities.[34] At times, indeed, they worked so closely together that it is difficult to distinguish between the initiatives of the two agencies. Although in many respects the two groups of women appeared to be operating from similar motives and in similar ways, substantial differences remained between them. The differences are noteworthy because they show that gender consciousness was not the sole factor in shaping the solutions these women proposed. Nevertheless, from about 1897, the two agencies co-operated increasingly in their efforts for reform.

Their efforts relied upon informal initiatives which had no legal sanction, but the women reformers were increasingly aware that if their initiatives were to have any permanent effect they required the sanction of law. Consequently they campaigned to secure the support of other women's groups to lobby for a change in the law. They stressed it was the duty of women as mothers to ensure that all children, not merely their own, should receive as good a start in life as possible.[35] The Hull House women also used the contacts they had made as state officials to secure the support of influential men. Thus the issue was aired before the Illinois Conference of Charities in 1898, and the Chicago Bar Association was persuaded to draw up the necessary legislation.[36]

Other agencies besides the Chicago Woman's Club and Hull House community were involved in the final agitation for the bill – among them child-saving agencies and other male-dominated organisations. Indeed, co-operation between male and female reformers was important in securing the passage of the Juvenile Court bill. For, although women might legitimately campaign for reforms which were closely related to their interests, a measure too closely associated with women's concerns, and without the endorsement of male reformers, was still unlikely to succeed in the entirely male legislature – especially as women were expected to remain outside the political arena and therefore exercised no political leverage.[37] Male and female reformers needed each other to achieve social welfare legislation. Male political culture as it had come to be defined by the late nineteenth century precluded government interference in many aspects of the social and economic life of the nation. Thus, while men did become involved in reform movements throughout the nineteenth century, they did so as long as these did not extend the boundaries of the state beyond certain limited functions. Women reformers, on the other hand, prompted by their own gender consciousness, began to see the possibilities of using the government to improve conditions for certain sections of society. By the end of the nineteenth century, women had begun to show themselves to be much more willing to use the state to accomplish their reform agenda than were men.[38] Thus, in Chicago, while male reformers seem to have been happy to accept the initiatives of the women reformers and accepted their leadership, the women reformers needed the legal expertise and political clout of male reformers to achieve their aims.

Hull House seems to have played an important part in facilitating this co-operation. It acted as a meeting place for reform-minded people in Chicago, and gave the women reformers involved in the agitation for what became the Juvenile Court Law many contacts and much expertise to draw upon.[39] It also seems to have acted as a centre of operations from which the women reformers lobbied for the passage of the Juvenile Court bill, and tried to influence public opinion to put pressure on legislators at Springfield to pass it.[40] Some features of the bill which had been important to the women reformers were lost as a result of opposition to the bill, but the act that was finally passed clearly acknowledged and reflected the concerns of its originators – the women reformers. Though deficient in some respects, it was hailed by these women as a great step forward in state provision for child care.[41]

The history of the creation of the Chicago Juvenile Court raises some important issues for historians of women's social welfare reform, for the kind of female values that were evident in the Chicago juvenile court movement may also be found in other social welfare reforms in the United States during the Progressive Era and in other parts of the world. Examples in the USA include the provision of mothers' pensions and the foundation of the Federal Children's Bureau. They too may be explained in terms of women reformers' initiatives to preserve the "traditional" American family and to ensure that children were properly nurtured and protected. The juvenile courts were one of the earliest Progressive Era social welfare reforms, and the willingness of women juvenile-court reformers to use the state to achieve their aims foreshadowed later efforts by women reformers to establish the rudiments of a welfare state in the USA.

And, as is shown elsewhere in this book, women were active in the foundation of welfare states in other countries, both in North America and in Europe. Recent comparative work has revealed that many of the concerns of women reformers in the United States were shared by their counterparts in Britain and in other European countries – though little work has as yet been done on Scotland.[42] Other contributors to *Gendering Scottish History* have commented on the fact that historians of gender have only quite recently begun to examine the experience of women in Scotland. In 1986, an eminent Scottish historian could still write:

> The history of the family, and of child upbringing and the place of women within and without the home, is so neglected in Scotland as to verge on becoming a historiographic disgrace.[43]

Though much of the increasing work of the past decade has been largely celebratory, concerned primarily to write women back into Scottish history, more analytical studies drawing upon scholarship on women in other countries are now appearing.[44] This research suggests that middle- and upper-class women in Scotland were involved in similar charitable and reform activities to their counterparts in the rest of Britain.[45] One would therefore expect to find on further investigation that Scottish female reformers were involved, through their voluntary associations, in social welfare activities.[46]

Juvenile courts were established on a formal basis in Scotland by the Children's Act of 1908 which came into operation in Scotland on 1 April 1909.[47] The act consolidated the law for the protection of children from cruelty, danger, exploitation, and neglect, and standardised methods for dealing with juvenile offenders. The act required the establishment of separate courts for children, for as Herbert Samuel who presented the bill in the House of Commons noted:

> the child offender ought to be kept separate from the adult criminal, and should receive at the hands of the law a treatment differentiated to suit his special needs – that the courts should be agencies of rescue as well as the punishment of children.[48]

With the implementation of the Children's Act, two of the key elements of the Chicago Juvenile Court were formally integrated into the Scottish justice system, for probation had been introduced by the Probation of Offenders Act in 1907. Informal methods of dealing with children in trouble with the law had, however, already been developed in some parts of the United Kingdom. For magistrates had been persuaded to hold separate hearings for children's cases and informal systems of probation for children were already well established before 1907.[49]

It is not clear where the initiative for the introduction of new ways of dealing with children in trouble with the law came from in Scotland or the rest of the United Kingdom. A number of women reformers were in communication with American juvenile court reformers; and both formal and informal conferences of social reformers ensured that new ideas spread among the international reform community. Details of how the probation system for children worked in various American states were also reported to parliament.[50] While this might suggest that those concerned with the problem of juvenile delinquency in Britain were merely anxious to emulate the new methods established in the United States, it is clear that demands for changes in the way in which the justice system dealt with wayward children pre-dated the establishment of the Chicago Juvenile Court.[51] The example of the Chicago Juvenile Court suggested to reformers in Britain a solution to these demands. In this sense, the creation of juvenile courts in Scotland may be regarded as a maternalist reform, though until further research is done the precise role and influence of women in this social welfare reform cannot be fully established.

Much of the recent scholarship on the origins of the welfare state in the United States has concentrated on the issue of gender and its role in shaping welfare legislation. While some of this scholarship has been concerned only with writing women back into the history of the welfare state, most recently it has been suggested that women played a pivotal role and often took the initiative in reform. What is also beginning to emerge from this scholarship is that men and women had considerably different visions of welfare, and that this influenced both their perceptions of the problems they faced and their solutions to these problems.[52] As this paper has shown, gender consciousness played an essential role in shaping social-welfare reform. But it has also demonstrated that historians of gender and welfare need to look beyond the differences in welfare vision between women and men and to examine the differences between middle-class women reformers. There were distinct versions of maternalism, and this is clearly illustrated in the women reformers involved in the creation of the Chicago Juvenile Court and in their priorities for reform. Whether similar conclusions may be drawn from a study of the women reformers of Scotland awaits further research.

NOTES

1. Leaflet "To the Women and Women's Clubs of Illinois", dated 15 February 1896 in file on Illinois Federation of Women's Clubs, 1896, reel 41, Jane Addams Papers, microfilm.

2. Herbert H. Lou, *Juvenile Courts in the United States* (Chapel Hill, 1927); Anthony M. Platt, *The Child Savers: the invention of delinquency* (Chicago, 1969); Joseph M. Hawes, *Children in Urban Society: juvenile delinquency in nineteenth-century America* (New York, 1971); Robert M. Mennel, *Thorns and Thistles: juvenile delinquents in the United States, 1825–1940* (Hanover, New Hampshire, 1973); Steven L. Schlossman, *Love and the American Delinquent: the theory and practice of "Progressive" juvenile justice, 1825–1920* (Chicago, 1977); Ellen Ryerson, *The Best Laid Plans: America's juvenile court experiment* (New York, 1978); David J. Rothman, *Conscience and Convenience: the asylum and its alternatives in Progressive America* (Boston, 1980); John R. Sutton, *Stubborn Children: controlling delinquency in the United States, 1640–1981* (Berkeley and Los Angeles, 1988); Eric C. Schneider, *In the Web of Class: delinquents and reformers in Boston, 1810s–1930s* (New York, 1992); Charles Larsen, *The Good Fight: the life and times of Ben B. Lindsey* (Chicago, 1972). Only Platt looks specifically at women reformers.

3. On the concept of maternalism see: Seth Koven and Sonya Michel, "Womanly duties: maternalist politics and the origins of welfare states in France, Germany, Great Britain, and the United States, 1880–1920", *American Historical Review*, vol. 95 (October 1990), pp. 1076–1108; Seth Koven and Sonya Michel, "Introduction: 'Mother Worlds'", in Seth Koven and Sonya Michel (eds), *Mothers of a New World: maternalist politics and the origins of welfare states* (New York, 1993), pp. 1–42; Molly Ladd-Taylor, *Mother-Work: women, child welfare and the state, 1890–1930* (Urbana and Chicago, 1994), pp. 3–7.

4. This definition of maternalism appears in Sonya Michel and Robyn Rosen, "The paradox of maternalism: Elizabeth Lowell Putnam and the American welfare state", *Gender and History*, vol. 4 (autumn 1992), p. 364.

5. On the uses of the language of motherhood see: Molly Ladd-Taylor, "Toward defining maternalism in US history", *Journal of Women's History*, vol. 5 (fall 1993), pp. 110–113. See also, Elizabeth J. Clapp, "Welfare and the role of women: the juvenile court movement", *Journal of American Studies*, vol. 28 (December 1994), pp. 359–383.

6. The Chicago Juvenile Court came into effect on 1 July 1899, as a result of an "Act to Regulate the Treatment and Control of Dependent, Neglected and Delinquent Children", cited in Timothy D. Hurley, *Juvenile Courts and What They Have Accomplished* (Chicago, 1904), pp. 61–66.

7. Henriette Greenbaume Frank and Amalie Hofer Jerome, *Annals of the Chicago Woman's Club for the First Fifty Years of its Organization, 1876–1916* (Chicago, 1916), p. 9.

8. Karen J. Blair, *The Clubwoman as Feminist: true womanhood redefined, 1868–1914* (New York, 1980); Anne Firor Scott, *Natural Allies: women's associations in American history* (Urbana and Chicago, 1993); Theda Skocpol, *Protecting Soldiers and Mothers: the political origins of social policy in the United*

States (Cambridge, MA., 1992), pp. 323–340.

9. Details about the members of the club may be found in Dorothy Edwards Powers, "The Chicago Woman's Club" (MA thesis, University of Chicago, 1939), pp. 55–63.
10. *Annals of the Chicago Woman's Club*, pp. 10–15.
11. Ladd-Taylor, "Toward defining maternalism", pp. 110–113
12. Koven and Michel, "Womanly duties", pp. 1076–1108; Michel and Rosen, "The paradox of maternalism", pp. 364–386.
13. *Annals of the Chicago Woman's Club*, p. 15.
14. On the impact of class on women's reform and philanthropic work, see: Nancy Hewitt, *Women's Activism and Social Change: Rochester, New York, 1822–1872* (Ithaca, 1984); Lori Ginzberg, *Women and the Work of Benevolence: morality, politics and class in the 19th-century United States* (New Haven, 1990). Many of the club's members were also heavily involved in the work of the Charity Organization Society: Kenneth L. Kusmer, "The functions of organized charity in the Progressive era: Chicago as a case study", *Journal of American History*, vol. 60 (December 1973), pp. 657–678. See also note 1 above.
15. Club women were acquainted with the ideas of the child study movement and the kindergarten movement. See for instance, 22 April 1896, box 20, volume 90, Chicago Woman's Club Papers, Manuscript Division, Chicago Historical Society (hereafter CWC Papers).
16. See for instance, Annual Report, 20 May, 1896, box 2, volume 17, CWC Papers.
17. Arrest figures may be found in the *Reports of the Superintendent of Police of the City of Chicago to the City Council* for the relevant years. But see also Lucy L. Flower, "The duty of the state to dependent children", *Proceedings of the Illinois Conference of Charities and Correction*, 1896, pp. 9–16.
18. Flower, "The duty of the state to dependent children", pp. 9–16; *Annals of the Chicago Woman's Club*, for instance, pp. 162–163.
19. Kathryn Kish Sklar, "Hull House in the 1890s: a community of women reformers", *Signs*, vol. 10 (summer 1985), pp. 658–677; Allen F. Davis, *Spearheads for Reform: the social settlements and the Progressive movement, 1890–1914* (New York, 1967). Recent works on the settlement houses which look at the less well-known houses and the middle-class bias of most settlements, include: Ruth Hutchinson Crocker, *Social Work and Social Order: the settlement movement in two industrial cities, 1889–1930* (Urbana and Chicago, 1992); Mina Carson, *Settlement Folk: social thought and the American settlement movement, 1885–1930* (Chicago, 1990); Rivka Shpak Lissak, *Pluralism and Progressives: Hull House and the new immigrants, 1890–1919* (Chicago, 1989).
20. "Hull House: a social settlement", in *Hull House Maps and Papers* (New York, 1895), p. 229; Davis, *Spearheads for Reform*, p. 34; Margaret Gibbons Wilson, *The American Woman in Transition: the urban influence, 1870–1920* (Westport,

Conn., 1979), p. 100.

21. Davis, *Spearheads for Reform*, pp. xi, 38.

22. Sheila M. Rothman, *Woman's Proper Place: a history of changing ideals and practices, 1870 to the present* (New York, 1978), pp. 5–7. *Hull House Maps and Papers* clearly reflects the influence of social-science methods. See also, Kathryn Kish Sklar, "*Hull House Maps and Papers*: social science as women's work in the 1890s", in Martin Bulmer, Kevin Bales and Kathryn Kish Sklar (eds), *The Social Survey in Historical Perspective, 1880–1940* (Cambridge, 1991), pp. 116–129.

23. John P. Rousmaniere, "Cultural hybrid in the slums: the college woman and the settlement house, 1889–1894", *American Quarterly*, vol. 22 (spring 1970), pp. 45–66; Mary M. Kingsbury, "Women in New York Settlements", *Municipal Affairs*, vol. 2 (Sept. 1898), pp. 458–462; Jane Addams, "Woman's work for Chicago", *Municipal Affairs*, vol. 2 (Sept. 1898), pp. 502–508; William Hard, "Chicago's five maiden aunts: the women who boss Chicago very much to its advantage", *The American Magazine*, vol. 62 (1906), pp. 481–489.

24. Sklar, "Hull House in the 1890s", pp. 658–677; Kathryn Kish Sklar, "Who funded Hull House?", in Kathleen D. McCarthy (ed.), *Lady Bountiful Revisited: women, philanthropy and power* (New Brunswick, 1990), pp. 94–115.

25. See for instance the use of "maternalist" rhetoric by Julia Lathrop and Florence Kelley in "To the Women and Women's Clubs of Illinois", dated 15 Feb., 1896.

26. Ladd-Taylor, "Toward defining maternalism", p. 111; Ladd-Taylor, *Mother-Work*, p. 8.

27. Ladd-Taylor, "Toward defining maternalism", pp. 110–113; Barbara Sicherman, "Working it out: gender, profession, and reform in the career of Alice Hamilton", in Noralee Frankel and Nancy S. Dye (eds), *Gender, Class, Race, and Reform in the Progressive Era* (Lexington, KY., 1991), pp. 127–147.

28. Sklar, "*Hull House Maps and Papers*", pp. 116–129; Mary Jo Deegan, *Jane Addams and the Men of the Chicago School, 1892–1918* (New Brunswick and Oxford, 1988), pp. 33–34; *Hull House Maps and Papers*, pp. 3–14. See also, Ellen Fitzpatrick, *Endless Crusade: women social scientists and Progressive reform* (New York and Oxford, 1990).

29. Jane Addams, *Twenty Years at Hull House* (New York, first published 1910, 1961 reprint), pp. 179–181.

30. Julia Lathrop was a member of the Illinois Board of Charities, Florence Kelley and Alzina Stevens were respectively Chief Factory Inspector and Assistant Chief Factory Inspector for the State of Illinois.

31. 27 Feb., 1895, box 20, volume 89, CWC Papers; *Annals of the Chicago Woman's Club*, p. 159; Letter from Mrs Lucy L. Flower, dated May 1917, volume II, Louise deKoven Bowen Papers, Manuscript Division, Chicago Historical Society; Memorandum by Julia C. Lathrop, dated 3 May, 1917, volume II, Bowen Papers; Julia C. Lathrop, "The development of the probation system

in a large city", *Charities*, vol. XIII (7 Jan., 1905), pp. 344–345.

32. Lathrop, "The development of the probation system in a large city", pp. 344–349; *Hull House Bulletin*, October 1896 and from December 1897.

33. Lathrop, "The development of the probation system in a large city", pp. 344–349; Case Studies (Restricted), June 1897–August 1899, supplement 1, folder 7, Juvenile Protective Association Papers, Special Collections, University of Illinois at Chicago; "An interview with Hon. Oliver H. Horton on the juvenile court", *Juvenile Record*, vol. II (January/February 1901), pp. 12–13.

34. For instance Jane Addams, Florence Kelley and Julia Lathrop were all members of the Chicago Woman's Club as well as residents of Hull House. Similarly Lucy Flower and Louise deKoven Bowen were benefactresses of Hull House. On this see, Sklar, "Who funded Hull House?", pp. 94–115.

35. Leaflet, "To the Women and Women's Clubs of Illinois", dated 15 February 1896; unattributed clipping, "To save the child: women's clubs of Chicago tackle an important problem", 10 May 1895, scrapbook 3, Lucy Flower and Coues Family Scrapbooks, Manuscript Division, Chicago Historical Society.

36. *Proceedings of the Illinois Conference of Charities*, 1898; unattributed cutting, "For delinquent children: resolution adopted by the Chicago Bar Association", undated, p. 26, scrapbook 3, Flower Scrapbooks; William M. Lawton, "Father of the Illinois Juvenile Court law", *Juvenile Court Record*, vol. VIII (Dec. 1907), p. 11; Chicago Bar Association Committee on Juvenile Courts, typescript dated 28 October 1899, in possession of Manuscript Division, Chicago Historical Society.

37. Letter from Mrs Lucy Flower, dated May 1917 and Memorandum by Julia Lathrop, dated 3 May 1917, vol. II, Bowen Papers.

38. E. Anthony Rotundo, *American Manhood: transformations in masculinity from the Revolution to the modern era* (New York, 1993), pp. 271–274; Arnaldo Testi, "The gender of reform politics: Theodore Roosevelt and the culture of masculinity", *Journal of American History*, vol. 81 (March 1995), pp. 1509–1533; Skocpol, *Protecting Soldiers and Mothers*; Paula Baker, *The Moral Framework of Public Life: gender politics and the state in rural New York, 1870–1930* (New York, 1991); Maureen A. Flanagan, "Gender and urban political reform: the city club and the Woman's City Club of Chicago in the Progressive era", *American Historical Review*, vol. 95 (October 1990), pp. 1032–1050.

39. This is explored further by Sklar in "Hull House in the 1890s", and in Kathryn Kish Sklar, "The historical foundations of women's power in the creation of the American welfare state, 1830–1930", in Koven and Michel (eds), *Mothers of a New World*, pp. 69–75. See also Jane Addams, "Women's work for Chicago", pp. 502–503.

40. Memorandum by Julia Lathrop, dated 3 May 1917, vol. II, Bowen Papers; Letter from Mrs Lucy Flower, dated May 1917, vol. II, Bowen Papers; Hurley, *Juvenile Courts and What They Have Accomplished*, p. 20; Report of the Chicago Bar Association Committee on Juvenile Courts.

41. An "Act to Regulate the Treatment and Control of Dependent, Neglected and Delinquent Children", as quoted in Timothy D. Hurley, *The Origins of the Illinois Juvenile Court Law*, pp. 26–39; *Hull House Bulletin*, April and May 1899, p. 10.

42. See for instance the essays in Koven and Michel, *Mothers of a New World*; and Gisela Bock and Pat Thane (eds), *Maternity and Gender Policies: women and the rise of European welfare states, 1880s–1950s* (London, 1994).

43. T. C. Smout as quoted in Linda Mahood, *The Magdalenes: prostitution in the nineteenth century* (London and New York, 1990). See also, Jane McDermid, "Placing women in Scottish history", *Journal of Women's History*, vol. 4 (fall 1992), pp. 180–188.

44. McDermid, "Placing women in Scottish history", pp. 180–188; Linda Mahood, *Policing Gender, Class and Family: Britain, 1850–1940* (London, 1995).

45. See for instance, Mahood, *Policing Gender*; Olive Checkland, *Philanthropy in Victorian Scotland: social welfare and the voluntary principle* (Edinburgh, 1980); Pat Thane, "Visions of gender in the making of the British welfare state: the case of women in the British Labour Party and social policy, 1906–1945", in Bock and Thane (eds), *Maternity and Gender Policies*, pp. 93–118.

46. Koven and Michel, "Introduction: 'Mother Worlds'", pp. 1–42; Seth Koven, "Borderlands: women, voluntary action and child welfare in Britain, 1840 to 1914", in Koven and Michel (eds), *Mothers of a New World*, pp. 94–135.

47. Children's Act 1908; Mahood, *Policing Gender*, p. 58.

48. Speech of Herbert Samuel, Under-Secretary of State for the Home Department, 10 February 1908, *Parliamentary Debates (Hansard)*, 8 Edward VII, 4th series, vol. CLXXXIII.

49. "The treatment of youthful offenders", Return to an Address of the Honourable the House of Commons, dated 14 March 1907, *Parliamentary Accounts and Papers: 23 Law & Crime*, 69 [Command 84], 1907; Percy Alden, MP, "Recent social legislation in the British Parliament", *Charities and the Commons*, vol. XXI (3 October 1908), pp. 31–34.

50. Letter from Miss N. Adler of the Committee on Wage Earning Children, London, England, dated 30 July 1905, box 4, folder 3, Ben B. Lindsey Papers, Manuscript Division, Library of Congress, Washington D.C. (hereafter BBL Papers); letter from Homer Folks, dated 12 September 1905, box 93, folder 6, BBL Papers; Samuel J. Barrows (ed.), *Children's Courts in the United States: their origin, development, and results* (The International Prison Commission, Washington DC, 1904); "Memorandum on the Probation System as at present in force in the United States of America", presented to both Houses of Parliament by Command of His Majesty, *Parliamentary Accounts and Papers* [Command 3401], 68 (1907).

51. Howard Association, *Juvenile Offenders: a report based on an inquiry instituted by the committee of the Howard Association, 1898* (London, 1898); "Editorial", *The Law Times*, vol. CXIX (August 12, 1905), p. 332; W. Douglas Morrison, *Ju-*

venile Offenders (London, 1896); William Tallack, *Penological and Preventive Principles, with special reference to Europe and America; and to the dimunition of crime, pauperism and intemperance; to prisons and their substitutes, habitual offenders, sentences, neglected youth, education, police, statistics, etc.* (London, 1889).

52. A review of this literature appears in Clapp, "Welfare and the role of women", pp. 359–383. This subject is explored further in Elizabeth J. Clapp, *Mothers of All Children: women reformers and the rise of the juvenile courts in Progressive Era America* (University Park, PA, 1998).

16

The disbudding of flowers:
the historical construction of female adolescent delinquency

Linda Mahood

Since the Victorian era, definitions of female juvenile delinquency have shifted from a language of "sin", first to one – in the eugenics movement – stressing the influence of "moral deficiency", then to one focusing on the concern of early-twentieth-century psychiatry with impaired "ego formation". Throughout, the recurring theme of social-work rhetoric has been the girl problem. Whether the young female delinquent was cast as a victim of her environment, her genes, or her psychological maladjustment, the "wayward girl" continued to manifest problems for herself and for those who tried to help her. The folk devils of conservative propaganda today – the teen mum and the street girl – would be immediately recognisable to the Victorian and Edwardian child-welfare worker.[1] In this chapter, I explore the construction and regulation of female adolescence between the late nineteenth and early twentieth century, through a historical examination, first, of theories of female delinquency, second, of the child-welfare institutions created to address the problem, and, third, of the gendered disciplinary regimes developed within the institutions for girls and boys. It is argued that notions of working-class feminine respectability were constructed through the interpretation of data; through the elaboration of theory; and also through the child-welfare workers' critique of the poor working-class family culture.

I

For Victorian social reformers, the precursors of the modern social worker, urban problems such as drunkenness, hooliganism, prostitution, and especially crime (which they saw as plaguing Scottish cities and towns) were synonymous with the behaviour of street-corner girls and boys. They did not differentiate between youth who had parents and jobs on the one hand, and the destitute and friendless orphan on the other. They did, however, differentiate the criminal patterns for girls and boys. In the case of street girls, who were by definition working class, early social workers focused on what they interpreted as "sexual promiscuity". It was feared that girls forced to grow up in the overcrowded slums of the large cities were in danger of drifting into prostitution by association with "vice". In 1859 a Scottish physician wrote:

> if the first words a daughter hears are those of cursing and blasphemy; the only example her childhood sees is that of obscenity and vice ... at the age of ten or twelve, she may be both a prostitute and a thief.[2]

In 1864 the editor of Edinburgh's *North Britain* wrote that

> it is a sad sight to see the little daughters of working men fighting with each other for the *honour* of running messages to the prostitute ... [or] to sweep the broken bottles and glasses from the front door of the brothel shebeen.[3]

And, according to a female parish inspector in 1911:

> If the girl lives in a squalid overcrowded slum dwelling ... where the common decencies of life can scarcely be carried out ... where the father of the family bets and drinks, not to mention the mother doing the same, then I say, the girl would hardly be human if she did not fall prey to temptation.[4]

Following World War I, child-welfare workers declared that the slack-

[235]

ening of parental control during wartime, due to the absence of parents on military service, had contributed to a rise in juvenile crime.[5] Most serious was the appearance of a new breed of street-wise girl – the flapper. "Beneath the powder and rouge and despite her laugh and ever ready smiles, the flapper is a very pathetic little figure", an Edinburgh social worker explained in 1918:

> The product of a generation that had largely lost its faith before the war ... she is a thorough-going little pagan.... Her school contemporaries are those boys who provide the problem of the juvenile criminal.[6]

And this social worker's concern was shared by the author of a letter in the *Evening Dispatch* who stated that "all girls with any self-respect would shun being classed as a flapper for the very name breathes vulgarity."[7] In the 1920s tattoo shops were added to the list of factors contributing to female delinquency. A female probation officer indicated that she did not

> think it [was] quite so disastrous for the boys, but with girls it just stamps them as belonging to the street ... no nice girls would work along side a tattooed girl.[8]

Clearly, these observers saw a distinct sex difference in delinquency patterns for girls and boys, where boys fell into thieving and other crimes through hanging about with men at the docks. When girls went "adrift" they went "straight for the streets".[9] Girls at risk were readily identifiable by their defiant and "unfeminine" behaviours – such as using vulgar language, drinking, or smoking cigarettes – and also by their weaknesses for various cheap commercial amusements. Flirting with street-corner boys and keeping late hours with older girls of the promiscuous type provided too great a temptation for girls whose characters were not fortified by strong moral principles. One social worker was careful to point out that

> they certainly don't hang about the streets like old prostitutes, but they run about picture houses and little restaurants and ice-cream shops and these kind of places and everyone clearly knows what they are doing, but they don't actually invite in so many words. They have not the formula that the old prostitutes use.[10]

With regard to paid employment, Victorian social workers stressed that street selling would lead directly to prostitution.[11] They concluded that "the employment of girls in the sale of newspapers and other articles in the street at night, was the cause of much evil."[12] Social workers of the twentieth century noted that hotel and restaurant work, "were the very kind, where [girls] were open prey to the male of 'that kind'". Many would have illegitimate children or very early marriages.[13]

An examination of the reports of various child-protection agencies, such as Scottish branches of the Reformatory and Refuge Union, the National Vigilance Association, the Society for the Prevention of Cruelty to Children, and other child-welfare organisations, suggests that by the early twentieth century the causes of juvenile delinquency were informed by an unstable mixture of environmentalism, eugenics, and Freudian psychology. With few exceptions, early-twentieth-century child-welfare workers saw their clients and the clients' parents as a "race" of moral degenerates, who had to be identified and segregated lest their unrestrained breeding swamp the superior part of the population. The point is made by this description of an Edinburgh slum family:

> To them drunkenness is in no sense disreputable, and sexual immorality no cause for reproach.... They form a distinct *tribe* in the land. Their boys grow up without any manly purity of thought or respect for the honour of women. Their girls are strangers to that maidenly reserve and modesty which are the chief glory and protection of true womanhood and they have no conception either of the holy relationship of marriage or the sacredness of motherhood.[14]

Social workers and therapists of the 1930s continued to argue, as the Victorians had, that girls were harder to reform than boys, but this was no longer simply because they had strayed farther from the path of virtue. According to the psychoanalytic paradigm, female maladjustment was caused by the girl's impaired "ego-formation", brought on by the cruel or neglectful behaviour of a mother who did not return the infant daughter's love and admiration. The first stage in reformatory treatment, which one social worker referred to as "the dis-budding of flowers" was "to help the girl to forget that she was almost grown-up". These social workers believed that the cycle of poverty and deprivation might be broken if proper family values and gender roles could be taught in the reform school.

During the Victorian period social reformers had maintained that the social problems caused by rapid urbanisation could be cured by radical forms of intervention. This mode of thinking inspired a range of social movements including Chartism, temperance, and female suffragism. In the case of poor children, Victorian environmentalism justified moving children deemed "at risk" of falling into criminal and immoral habits from their native slum communities to "better environments" far from friends and family. There was little discussion about such extreme intervention in children's lives. It was believed that delinquency was the result of a variety of environmental, social psychological, and hereditary factors, and that the juvenile penitentiary was a promising place to rehabilitate the delinquent clientele. Consequently, by the end of the nineteenth century, most cities and large towns supported state-licensed, and state-funded, industrial schools and reformatories. These institutions dealt with children sentenced under various sections of the Reformatory and Industrial School Acts (1854). Industrial schools for homeless, vagrant, or convicted children under thirteen years of age and juvenile reformatories for young offenders between twelve and sixteen years of age are just two examples of the range and type of children's homes.[15] In addition to these were various non-statutory girl-only shelters, such as Lochburn Home in Glasgow (previously the Glasgow Magdalene Institution, founded in 1860) for a special class of girl – one rejected by state-funded institutions.

In Scotland, girls and boys over the age of twelve who were convicted of crimes were usually sent to reformatories under section 15 of the Reformatory and Industrial Schools Act (1866). Children charged with status offences such as vagrancy or loitering were charged under section 14; those who were brought to the court by their parents or guardians as uncontrollable were charged under section 16. They were placed in industrial schools or reformatories, depending on their ages and the availability of space. The Reformatory and Industrial Schools Act of 1880 declared that magistrates could send any child under fourteen found in a brothel or residing with reputed prostitutes (including their own mothers) to industrial schools.[16]

Under the Reformatory and Industrial Schools Acts there were two grounds whereby residential school managers could refuse admission to a child sent by the court – "infectious diseases" and "moral considerations".[17] The latter was rarely applied to boys, but girls were frequently rejected when they were suspected prostitutes or had been found living in brothels or had been victims of sexual assault or incest or were suffering from venereal disease.[18] Reformatory and industrial school managers hesitated to take in these "brothel cases", because they feared that regardless of her involvement such a girl would be a "corrupting" influence on the "others in the school".[19] One school board inspector in the 1930s explained that he

> did not like putting a doubtful girl of sixteen or seventeen in the same school as a quite decent girl of twelve or thirteen.... The same argument applies to boys, though I think to a lesser degree.... I think that sexually depraved girls should be kept apart from others.[20]

And a representative of the Scottish Board of Education put it in these terms:

> in the case of the depraved girls, possibly with a strong sex instinct ... I am in complete agreement with the opinion that it would be undesirable to have eight or twelve of that type closely associated together in [a] small [mixed] home.[21]

Throughout the late nineteenth, and well into the twentieth century, girls referred to as "penitentiary cases" were transferred to magdalene homes in Edinburgh and Glasgow. After 1930 they were sent almost exclusively to Lochburn Home[22] – a practice that continued until that institution was closed in 1958, following a riot by inmates alleging ill treatment and physical abuse.[23] Lochburn Home never became certified under any Industrial or Reformatory Schools Act,[24] but this did not stop it from admitting teenage girls who were under a magistrate's warrant. These admissions were authorised under sections of the Reformatory and Industrial Schools Act which stated that children under fourteen found in immoral surroundings could be licensed to the guardianship of private individuals. This process permitted the Juvenile Delinquency Board to place girls in the private custody of the various matrons employed at Lochburn. After the passing of the Probation of Offenders Act in 1907, girls on probation might also be placed in Lochburn if the court considered their homes to be unsatisfactory. In these cases the warrant of probation stated "with place of residence"; and Lochburn was specified as the residence where the girl had to live.[25]

The purpose of the girls reformatory was much more than just training idle, wayward, and "delinquent" teenagers. It was part of a wider programme to make "ideal" proletarian and gendered subjects, who would not only labour in appropriate ways but who would discipline themselves. Learning to behave in sexually appropriate ways was part of this self-discipline. Thus class and gendered subjectivities were constructed through industrial training and sex education. The way the schools functioned; their selection of suitable clients; their power to confine and discipline; their day-to-day management and programme for moral rehabilitation exemplify the value of Michel Foucault's perception that sexuality was not just condemned or repressed "but managed, inserted into systems of utility, [and] regulated".[26]

How, then, was the new self-identity constructed? As with girls, the sexuality of boys was perceived as a dangerous force. Interviews with former inmates and staff confirmed that sexual surveillance was one reason why large dormitories were maintained.[27] Despite the "special care", however, the record books reveal that boys were frequently caned and strapped for sexual misdemeanours – euphemistically described as "extreme perverseness", "gross irregularity", and "filthy habits".[28] While many believed in principle that boys of all ages should be in the same institution, and that senior boys would take on mentorship roles,[29] a former headmaster admitted that while masturbation was regarded as a harmless "part of every young boy's upbringing", occasionally a "bully kind of boy" would sneak into a 'soft' boy's bed, even with a night watchman about".[30] It was recognised that "sexual deviance" in boys was more likely to occur at boarding school than at home. Unlike girls though, boys were not placed in residential schools for precocious sexual activity, although mild forms of punishment might be necessary to contain certain forms of sexual experimentation. Boys' problems of "a certain sort" were not pathologised in a similar way to that which led to the transference of girls to special institutions such as magdalene asylums. For boys, positive solutions were presented in the form of industrial training; merit marks for good behaviour; weekend passes to visit their parents; afternoon trips to town; football matches and organised team sports, and opportunities to participate in youth clubs – like the Boys Brigade and the Boy Scouts – which encouraged training for manliness, sexual hygiene, good citizenship, and self-reliance.[31]

Male reformatories stressed the importance of a boy "keep[ing] in touch with other lads", especially "superior lads to himself".[32] It was almost universally agreed, however, that, owing to their vulnerability, reformatory girls should not have any contact with the community.[33] For girls, it was the world outside the institution that was perceived as the danger rather than the solution. There are statistics which indicate that girls were taken up more quickly than boys[34] and that they were more readily sent to reformatories for a first offence.[35] The majority of industrial school girls were incarcerated for begging; wandering, as homeless or orphaned; being uncontrollable at home; frequenting the company of thieves; or residing with their mothers in brothels. The matron of a girls' industrial school revealed that the majority of her girls had been

found wandering, and having a parent who does not exercise proper guardianship, or is living in circumstances calculated to cause, encourage, or favor the seduction or prostitution of the child.[36]

As Schlossman and Wallach point out in their North American study, "This so-called chivalrous attitude leads to earlier intervention and longer periods of supervision" for girls who are seen as especially "vulnerable to evil and temptations".[37]

Regarding the situation in Scotland, a former residential school head-master observed that the court was more strict with girls

because girls were supposed to have higher standards.... The [court] would have argued that they were going to be made into loose girls ... and so in the sense of being more severe more quickly, they were really trying to protect them. That was their idea of protection.[38]

There is a dark side to the fact that a high proportion of girls was committed for non-criminal offences such as wandering. It illustrates most clearly the contradictions of familial ideology in relation to girls. According to Linda Gordon, the patriarchal authority structure of the nuclear family required girls to be dependent, obedient, and sexually pure, until marriage. They were expected to stay close to home, obey their fathers, and submit to his will and protection – an expectation fully endorsed by child protection agencies.[39] This presented a double bind for girls who could not stay home. The Scottish Society for the Prevention of Cruelty to Children observed that many girls who were afraid to be at home alone with their fathers contracted the habit of wandering.[40] Girls such as these were described in the admission books as syphilitic, shockingly neglected, verminous, and badly knocked about.[41] They re-commended that such girls be sent to industrial schools. The solution to the problem, then, was to catch girls at risk early and to channel them into an appropriate regime of moral rehabilitation in, depending on their age, reformatories or industrial schools.

Gordon has argued that placing the locus of sexual assault outside the immediate kinship group enabled incestuous acts and sexual assault to be reinterpreted through the double process of reconstituting the victim and the assailant. This served to direct scrutiny away from the father-daughter relations to predator strangers and to mother-daughter relations. Thus the "victims" are cast as "delinquents", and the assumptions about the perpetrators shift from male relatives to "men-in-the-street".[42] This logic is observable in Scotland by the first decade of the twentieth century: sensationalistic exposés of casual sex, VD rates among young girls and street-corner boys, and parental neglect tended to focus on the character of working-class girls.[43] Child-protection agencies directed public outrage towards instances of juvenile prostitution – a phenomenon safely outside the home. Moreover, we can see that the social workers' critique of the working-class family was reconfigured as an attack on the girls' mothers. Posing the problem in terms of moral neglect, rather than incest, made it by definition a mother's crime,[44] because it was argued that, whenever girls went wrong, the mother was chiefly to blame. According to a female parish inspector in Glasgow,

> mothers have a mistaken idea that ignorance is innocence and leave the matters at that.... Very often when a mother is spoken to after her girl has gone wrong, the answer one gets is, "but I did not know". I feel I would like to punish every woman who says "I do not know" when she is asked where her girl or boy goes in the evenings.[45]

And, according to one headmistress, it was absolutely necessary to remove such girls from "degrading home environments if they were to become decent citizens and future mothers of the race".[46]

The female matrons, teachers, and other staff played a very important role in the girls' reformatory. It was stressed that the matron be of "a social class superior to [the inmates'] own mothers", as she would mould the inmates in her image. The "wrong done in the home" would thus be corrected.[47] It was hoped that, under the matron's watchful eye and maternal guidance, the girls would learn the domestic skill necessary to become good little maids and mothers. According to the psychoanalytic therapeutic discourse, which is evident by the 1930s, a process called "transference" occurred – whereby the matron, in her dual role as disciplinarian and nurturer, became both the "strict father ... and the loving mother".[48] One therapist described how "in the institution we emphasise the dependence of childhood" in order to develop a retarded ego. The love of their superior, "who symbolises the early childhood mother, will be the reward for suppressing their excessive instinctual wishes." Put simply:

> Girls who become prostitutes ... do not want a man; their desire and longing is unconsciously directed backwards toward the love

of their own mother. That is one reason why a good mother-matron can do them such a lot of good. It is that longing of the girl-child to be protected by her mother, the fear of being alone, which drives her from one man to another. Once in the reformatory the inmates learned that in the reformatory matron they now had a "good mother", one "who would not act as their own mother had done".[49]

While it was hoped that inmates would shake off their "low class" taint by restricted access to their families, it was not intended that girls rise above their station. Unlike boys, who were given a fairly wide range of vocational choices – including carpentry, printing, farming (as preparation for emigration), and nautical training – girls' industrial training was restricted to housewifery, laundry, and sewing. One matron testified that she would not dream of "training [inmates] as clerks or typists.... [And] it would be impossible to make a ... governess out of a reformatory girl."[50] Girls were not apprenticed in the way boys were. They were generally sent to domestic service and lived under the roof of their employer. In 1904 a reformatory school matron stated that it was an "absolute fact" that

> the service girl makes a much better wife than the factory girl.... I can hardly imagine any calling better fitted than domestic service to develop out of the reformatory girl that choicest of God's gift to man – a good wife and mother, the most reliable bulwark a nation can posses.[51]

Girls' reformatories were also confident that respectability was within the grasp of any girl who could learn self-control, discipline, and, above all, chastity. It was also believed to be in the "moral interest" of the senior girls to have little girls in the school to mother; and married former inmates were encouraged to bring their babies to the school. Inviting former inmates back to the schools to show off their tidy clothes and healthy babies was considered "advantageous because [they could] talk to girls, reason with them, and thus they formed ideals".[52] Particular emphasis in a girl's moral rehabilitation was laid on her future role as mother. Sex education was formulated through a language of maternal prospects; and, whereas a precocious interest in sex was held to be improper, an early interest in motherhood and child-care was fully endorsed. According to a matron who followed this new therapeutic approach: "I talk to them of the baby they might have some time in the future. I say: 'One day you will have a baby, and think what it will mean to you.'"[53] Of course they never mentioned the men with whom the girls were to have their sexual experience. The maturity of their female inmates was measured on the basis of the girl's readiness to embrace maternity without showing undue interest in or familiarity with the process by which it would be achieved.

Through their incarceration, infantalisation, and domestic training the inmate would "gradually ... soften from sophisticated young women to teachable school girls again. They begin to feel immature again. They wear school uniforms and have their hair cut short."[54] The regimes of discipline varied greatly from school to school. The use of corporal punishment had decreased by the mid-nineteenth century. Ventilated isolation rooms replaced Dickensian cells, and new approaches to rational punishment evolved. A former inmate of the early 1950s remembers being subjected to the "holding therapies" that were popular at that time. She recalled that during her early teens she would get extremely angry – as many teenagers do. Her matron handled her by enlisting older girls to pin her against the floor until the tantrum passed. She remembered "laying on the floor when one or two of them was on me, and I was in a temper" and "screaming at the matron: 'when I get out of here I'm going to marry a Teddy Boy and I don't care what you say, I'm going to marry a Teddy Boy!'"[55] Regarding the inmates' desire to return to their families upon release – which was regarded as a failure by the child-saving agencies – interviews with former students, and an examination of the punishment books, reveal that acts of resistance to the institution's efforts on their behalf ranged from innocuous gestures like swearing at, or disobeying, teachers, and smoking to absconding, and overt acts of aggression.[56] The records also reveal a number of riots.[57]

While some female child-welfare workers often identified male brutality, desertion, and drunkenness as the special problems of the women and children (who had to put up with their consequences), the majority remained bound by ideologies of gender, class, and family and by various beliefs about what constituted appropriate work for women and ideal family relations. The "conception of passive womanhood",[58] espoused in these institutions, was totally alien to lower-class inmates. Yet domestic service continued to be looked upon as the best means of protecting girls, even though the records revealed a growing refusal by these girls to enter, or to remain in, this occupation. It was the opinion of the director of the YWCA's St Katherine's Girls Clubs that the "only safeguard that a girl is going to have" against going astray is "if she has a strong instinct for homemaking.... We cannot over-develop the womanly side.... We don't even mind if a girl powders and paints."[59]

In spite of the growing demand for skilled and unskilled female labour in the factories and the new light industries, especially after World War I, domestic service continued to be looked upon as the best means of rescuing girls. But it was not a realistic option for all girls, and many were "terribly opposed" even to the mention of it.[60] A female health inspector from Aberdeen testified that there were inmates who were unfit for service: they "drift to the mills, or become what is known in Aberdeen as fish girls".[61] She also reported that many of the sixteen-year-old girls one industrial school placed in service were "rather knocked about by their employers, resulting in a considerable amount of immorality."[62] A former industrial-day-school girl recalled that, when she left school in 1916, she could not go into service because her mother wanted her to earn higher wages, so she took a job in a carpet factory.[63] Other girls simply refused to go into service, preferring to go to "work and have their evenings free".[64] A former inmate of the Lochburn magdalene home recalled that the girls there taught themselves to faint in order to get themselves out of the laundry work.[65]

Female protection agencies like the National Vigilance Association and the YWCA recognised that the system did not enable all inmates to escape the cycle of poverty; and, as the decades passed, the reformatories and industrial schools dealt with a significant number of children whose parents had been through the system.[66] The best the institutions could offer these girls was to set up homes for unwed mothers in the 1920s. The SSPCC established social schemes, mothers' meetings, and girls' clubs to assist poor young women "to struggle on".[67] They held baby competitions, with prizes for well-kept babies and organised home employment schemes for mothers.[68] After World War I, the St Katherine's Girls' Club in Aberdeen recruited its members from among the factory girls, and fish-workers, between fourteen and sixteen years of age. According to the club's director:

> We have arranged our membership so that all the girls come from the poorest parts of the city. It would be easy to fill the club with middle class girls. Our girls are chosen for low physical condition, bad homes, or difficult working conditions.

And she divided the club members into seven categories: young offenders, headstrong girls, girls of bad parentage, girls without homes, vicious girls, subnormal girls, and girls on probation. The club's goal was to teach every girl housewifery and homemaking skills and to develop in her a sense of "responsibility as good Christian citizens". [69]

By the end of World War II, it was admitted that, while girls and young women continued to be taken out of the community for their own protection, this method of protection really did not work. According to a former headmaster, the experience of being in a reformatory, possibly for years, affected girls in ways "that did not affect boys". One reason was that, while both boys and girls were being trained to reject their families – to stand on "their own two feet" – there were, he admitted, special problems for girls. The inadequate education and training the girls received in the schools did not prevent them from falling into "loose living, early marriage and lots of children". So the schools "were trying to be kind, but in actual fact in many ways there were creating the climate" in which the problem grew. [70]

Meda Chesney-Lind and Randall Sheldon have recently argued that girls' experience of, and treatment within, child protection agencies are best understood if they are placed within the history of this unique set of institutions. [71] This chapter has suggested that, in the period studied, the language of gender and sexuality remained an integral part of the child-welfare movement. The late-nineteenth- and early-twentieth-century child-welfare movement was part of a massive intervention into private life, the strategies, institutions, and consequences of which are still being debated by historians and social scientists. Then, as they are now, children were frequently the targets of theories and practices aimed at the wider regulation of family life. [72] Certainly, since the late nineteenth century, public interest in children has been the lever used to force the family open. [73] It has been argued, both in popular and in expert discourses, that sexual practices – whether real or imaginary – were the key marker of the "delinquent" status of girls and young women; in the same way that criminal activities, like theft or vandalism, established a criminal identity for boys. A girl's sexuality was seen in almost totally negative terms. Once a girl had fallen, there was little to be done other than to contain the danger. For a special class of girl, on the run from male abuse and violence, the juvenile reformatory provided a refuge and a way out. But institutionalisation – as case after case in the latter years of the twentieth century has confirmed – is no guarantee against physical or sexual abuse. Certainly the way that the juvenile justice system has dealt with girls has had a direct impact on the lives of clientele. The current public outrage over issues such as domestic violence and child abuse, juvenile crime, homelessness, and well-publicised cases of the apparent "failure" of child-protection agencies, has its roots in the late-nineteenth-and early-twentieth-century child-welfare ideologies and institutional regimes.

NOTES

1. L. Mahood and B. Littlewood, "The 'vicious' girls and the 'street-corner' boy: sexuality and the gendered delinquent in the Scottish child-saving movement, 1850–1940", *The Journal of the History of Sexuality*, vol. 4 (1994).
2. J. Miller, *Prostitution Considered in Relation to its Causes and Cure* (Edinburgh, 1859), p. 6.
3. J. Bertram, *Glimpses of the Social Evil in Edinburgh and Elsewhere* (Edinburgh, 1864), p. 13.
4. Parish of Glasgow, *Memorandum on the Social Evil in Glasgow and the State of the Law for Dealing with Certain Forms of Immorality*, (Glasgow, 1911), p. 58.
5. Report of the Glasgow Special Committee on Probation of Offenders, *Seeking and Saving* (May 1919), p. 138.
6. *Evening Dispatch*, 23 March 1918.
7. *Evening Dispatch*, 25 March 1918.
8. D. Maitland (Female Probation Officer), Report of the Departmental Committee on Reformatory and Industrial Schools in Scotland, Minutes of Evidence taken before the Youth Offenders Committee, 1925 (cited hereafter as PP.YOC, 1925–26), Q: 4869.
9. PP.YOC, 1925–26, Q: 4846.
10. PP.YOC, 1925–26, Q: 4868.
11. Report of the Departmental Committee on Reformatory and Industrial Schools in Scotland, Appendix VIII, PP 1896–97 xv (cited hereafter as PP.SC, 1896–97), p. 231.
12. Edinburgh Magdalene Asylum, *Annual Report*, 1887, p. 6.
13. Ibid.
14. *Emphasis added*. Rutherford Hill (Edinburgh Band of Hope), "Some helps and hindrances in rescue and preventive work among women and girls", *Reformatory and Refuge Union: National Conference*, (Edinburgh, 1911), pp. 55–56.
15. The Youthful Offenders Bill was passed in 1854 for the regulation of reformatories; and Dunlop's Act (17 & 18 Vict.c.74) in 1854 dealt with industrial schools. The Reformatory and Industrial Schools Act (1866) consolidated industrial schools and reformatories in Scotland and England under the Home Office of the Secretary of State. See chapter 3 of my *Policing Gender Class and Family*, (London, 1995).
16. PP.SC, 1897, p. 91.
17. PP.SC, 1897, p. 224.
18. Ibid.

19. Ibid.
20. Scottish Education Department, *Approved schools: methods for dealing with difficult girls and boys: special status for Glasgow Magdalene Institution*: extract from Mr Pleck's minutes to HMI Mr Forbes, 17 February 1932 [ED15.136]).
21. Scottish Education Department, *Approved schools, department minute*, 1 March 1934: letter to Mr Brewer (Glasgow Magdalene Institution).
22. "It seems to be generally agreed among people with experience of [*sic*] the management of delinquent girls is often much more difficult problem than in the case of boys. The reasons are obscure: it may be because the offences for which girls tend to be put under custody or supervision are of a special nature; it may be because girls respond less well to supervision or institutional custody. Another possibility is that a high percentage of girls committed to institutions are in need of psychological or psychiatric treatment.... In post-war years we have had public trouble at Lochburn Home for Girls (now closed as a result)." Margaret Geddes, *Some notes on remand homes and approved schools*, paper no. 6, Scottish Advisory Council on the treatment and rehabilitation of offenders (November 1964). In the 1950s these girls were described in Home Office schools inspectors reports as "in need of psychiatric treatment", "unstable", "potential suicides", "depressives", "neurotic-schizoid". According to one psychiatrist: "One would expect some unstable girls to express instability or promiscuous sex behaviour." See Scottish Education Department, "Proposed working party on management of approved schools for girls: methods for dealing with difficult girls", 3 March 1952, Scottish Records Office, ED/1/5/274.
23. A study of Scottish Magdalene institutions is found in L. Mahood, *The Magdalenes: prostitution in the nineteenth century* (London, 1990).
24. Glasgow Magdalene Institution, *Homes committee minute book*, 1920–1935, 10 April 1934.
25. For example: "The Secretary for Scotland had consented to the girls Robina Stewart being licenced to the care of Miss Paterson, matron, for three years." See Glasgow Magdalene Institution, *Homes committee minute book*, 10 March 1914. And, from the same source, on 14 November 1916: "... a girl of fifteen was sent on license to Miss Paterson, by the Juvenile Delinquency Board.... [S]he will not be admitted as an inmate until she is 16."
26. Michel Foucault, *The History of Sexuality, volume I: an introduction* (New York, 1980), p. 24.
27. Interview with former industrial school headmaster (retired in 1980), Glasgow, September 28, 1989.
28. Mossbank Industrial School, *Register of Offences and Punishments*, 1893–1924; Empress Training Ship, *Punishment Returns*, 6 July 1923.
29. W. Smith (Superintendent, Oakbank School), Report of the Select Committee on Reformatory and Industrial Schools in Scotland, Minutes of Evidence, PP., 1896–97, Q: 23,220; E. McGee (Superintendent, St Joseph's Industrial

School, Tranent), ibid., Q: 23,988.

30. Interview as in footnote 27.
31. F. Mort, *Dangerous Sexualities: medico-moral politics in England Since 1830* (London, 1987), p. 194.
32. J. Campbell (Superintendent of Dundee Industrial School), PP.SC., 1897, Q: 24,728–24,730.
33. Dow, PP.YOC, 1925, Q: 1452.
34. Mahood, *Policing Gender*, p. 79.
35. S. Schlossman and S. Wallach, "The crime of precocious sexuality: female juvenile delinquency in the Progressive era", *Harvard Educational Review*, vol. 48 (1978), p. 66.
36. C. Dow (Superintendent of Maryhill Industrial School for Girls), PP.YOC, 1925, 19 November, Q: 1303.
37. Schlossman and Wallach, "The crime of precocious sexuality"', p. 66.
38. Interview with former industrial school headmaster (retired 1980), Paisley, September 28, 1989.
39. L. Gordon, *Heroes of Their Own Lives: the politics of the history of family violence* (London, 1989), p. 205.
40. Francis Hepburn (Secretary, Edinburgh Division, Scottish Association for the Prevention of Cruelty to Children), Report of the Departmental Committee on Reformatories and Industrial Schools in Scotland, Minutes of Evidence, PP. 1915, Q: 7919. (cited hereafter as PP.DC, 1915).
41. Maryhill Industrial School, *Admissions Book*, 1914–16; 1920–1925 (Strathclyde Regional Archives, Glasgow).
42. Gordon, *Heroes*, pp. 219, 223–226.
43. Glasgow Parish Council, *Immorality and Venereal Disease* (Glasgow, 1911), pp. 4, 60; A. H. Gray, *Exempted Shops. Report II: Ice-cream Shops* (Glasgow 1911), p. 7.
44. L. Gordon, *Heroes*, p. 226.
45. Parish Council of Glasgow, *Immoral houses and venereal diseases*, (Glasgow, Glasgow Parish Council, 1911), p. 60.
46. M. Maclauchlan (Superintendent, Guthrie's Girls' School), PP.YOC, 1925–26 (1 February 1926), p. 2.
47. PP.SC, 1896–97 p. 31.
48. E. Rosenfield, "Re-education of delinquent children", *The Approved Schools Gazette*, January 1946, pp. 186–199.
49. Ibid.
50. Catherine Hunter-Craster, Report of the Departmental Committee on Reformatory and Industrial Schools in Scotland, Minutes of Evidence PP.DC, 1915, Q: 3461, 3583. Catherine Hunter was matron of Chapelton Girls' Reformatory in Glasgow between 1893 and 1904. She married John Crastor, the superintendent of Wellington Farm Industrial School for Boys in 1904 and became matron of that institution. She testifed before the Departmental

Committee in 1897.

51. *Seeking and Saving* (September 1904), p. 442.
52. Mrs Cameron (Superintendent, Maryhill Industrial School for Girls), PP.SC, 1896–97, Q: 75,82. The practice was still followed in 1915: see Hunter-Crastor, PP.DC, 1915, Q: 3480
53. Rosenfield, 1937, p. 190.
54. "Wayward girls", *Approved Schools Gazette* (January 1946), pp. 303–304.
55. Interview with former industrial day school girls (1945–55), Perth, 25 May 1993.
56. *Daily Telegraph*, 6 June 1876; *Reformatory and Refuge Union Journal* (November 1876), p. 134, (July 1878), p. 410; (January-March 1882) p. 27; *Glasgow Herald*, 19 February 1889.
57. *Reformatory and Refuge Union Journal* (November 1876), p. 134, (July 1878), p. 410; Interview with Jim Henderson (former *Daily Express* reporter) in *Washing Away the Stain*, BBC Documentary, 1992.
58. N. Williamson, "Factory to reformatory: the founding and the failure of industrial and reform schools for girls in 19th-century New South Wales", *Australia and New Zealand History of Education Society*, vol. 9 (1980), p. 39.
59. Walker, Q: 10, 351.
60. B. Walker (Leader of St Katherine's Club, Scottish Division, YWCA), PP.YOC, 1925–26, Q: 10,457.
61. Dr Anne Watson (Medical Officer, Aberdeen Girls' Industrial School), PP.DC, 1915, Q: 6526.
62. Watson, PP.DC, 1915, Q: 6556–6557.
63. Interview with former industrial day school girl (1907–16), Glasgow, August 1989.
64. Hepburn, PP.DC, 1915, Q: 7996.
65. *Washing Away the Stain* (BBC Documentary, research notes, December 1992).
66. Hepburn, PP DC, 1915, Q: 7984–7985.
67. Scottish National Society for the Prevention of Cruelty to Children (Edinburgh District) *Annual Report* (1912), p. 22.
68. Scottish National Society for the Prevention of Cruelty to Children (Edinburgh District)), p. 23.
69. Bella Walker (leader, St Katherine's Club and Division Secretary, Scottish Division, YWCA) PP.YOC, 1925 (26 January 1926), Q: 10,502–10,503.
70. Interview as in footnote 27.
71. Meda Chesney-Lind and Randall Sheldon, *Girls: delinquency and juvenile justice* (California, 1992), p. 101.
72. C. Steedman, C. Irwin and V. Walkerdine (eds), *Language, Gender and Childhood* (London, 1985), p. 8.
73. B. Bellingham, "The history of childhood since the 'invention of childhood': some issues in the eighties", *Journal of Family History*, vol. 13 (1988), p. 354.

PART THREE

W*omen's history, Scottish history, historical theory*[1]

Terry Brotherstone

W*hatever his political sins*, the English humorist P. G. Wodehouse, often had a word for it. "It is never difficult," he observed in his story "The Custody of the Pumpkin", "to distinguish between a Scotsman with a grievance and a ray of sunshine."[2] The phrase has, just occasionally, forced itself uninvited into my mind when my thoughts were supposed to be focused on enjoying a book on modern Scottish social history or political analysis. Recently, however, I heard it quoted with guiltless approval by a fellow-Scot, a female "cultural commentator" who said she thought most Scottish women would know exactly what Wodehouse meant.[3] Whether the remark was originally intended to be gender-specific I am not sure. But if it is indeed the role of Scotswomen to bring the "pursuit of happiness", into Scottish life, it is to be hoped that they will soon be doing so even more uninhibitedly than at present in the sphere of Scottish history.

The time is ripe. Since the conference from which this book derives, the Scottish Women's History Network (SWHN) has been reinvigorated and has held several lively meetings. The latest (in October 1999) took place a few months after the opening of Scotland's first modern parliament and at a time when there was an unusually public discussion taking place about how to promote a serious understanding of the country's history. In a session at the SWHN conference about the state of affairs today, the election of a relatively high percentage of female Members to the Scottish Parliament (MSPs) was properly celebrated, though there was a cautious, "we must wait – actively vigilant – and see" attitude towards the future.[4] Were the Scottish parliamentary elections a stepping stone to gender parity, or might the gains made be clawed back? And would the social agenda of the new, more female parliament necessarily be more progressive? The effect of having an improved (albeit still small) cohort of women in, and supporting, Tony Blair's post-1997 New Labour government at Westminster suggested that this was very far from a foregone conclusion.[5] While these matters were alluded to rather than discussed, the session reinforced the impression that the new political situation in Scotland is likely to give a much higher profile – and, it is be hoped, greater depth of analysis – to the debate about such issues.

But is the profile in Scotland of female historians, women's history and gender analysis, commensurate even with the modestly dramatic gains being made in the political sphere? The perception at the SWHN conference, it seemed to me, was that it is not; or at least that the situation is highly contradictory. Contributors could talk without undue self-congratulation of "the rejuvenation of Scottish women's history" over the past few years; but also enunciate their distress that "Scottish history is being rewritten ... and women aren't in there." This perception was also evidenced by a Glasgow reader of the newspaper *Scotland on Sunday's* apparently rather hastily assembled, six-part series "The Story of a Nation". Its early instalments were "devoid of any mention of women, other than some cursory references to the great and the good," s/he wrote; and the editorial apologia that most Scots women have left no records would not wash. The series' authors were simply marginalising all the "painstaking research and interpretation" that has been published in order to perpetuate "the story of the white Scottish male". [6]

Some contributors to the new histories of Scotland scheduled to coincide with the first year of the parliament, will complain that it is unfair to accuse them of leaving women out. But the debate about the importance of women's history generated when some of its results are included, can be almost as jejune as mere ignorance. Tom Devine, whose *The Scottish Nation 1700–2000* may well be seen as a standard synthesis for some time to come, is not responsible for the fellow historians who review his work. One of them, however, observed that the significance of Devine's inclusion of chapters on women and ethnic minorities was that it meant the book would appeal even to the "politically correct".[7] It is apparently still possible in such circles to conceive of a satisfactory, non-PC, general history of Scotland, which pays no attention to women whatsoever.

Gendering Scottish History will be read, I hope, as one contribution to a historical discourse which is beginning to treat women's history and gendered analysis not as necessary gestures, but as vitally interwoven into the process by which we usefully and accurately understand our social past. In a very practical way, therefore, it is also a contribution to another activity which tends to be underrated in historical discussions in Scotland – debate about historical theory. If history is to be more than just interesting, if it is meaningfully to inform decisions women and men take about what to do now, there has to be some contextualising conception of why we study it, what approaches we are adopting, and how we theorise the relationship between past and present. Otherwise the most excitingly presented facts and interpretations may ultimately rely for their general acceptance on nothing more than a particular historian's claim to have read more archival material than somebody else; and/or on his/her established reputation.

This book is about women and about Scotland; but it is also about approaches to history more generally and about internationalism. Its particular chapters may be differently adjudged to represent "women's history", "feminist history" and "gender history"; and many will sit easily in more than one category, or at an intersection of all three. As an outsider to the discipline (or disciplines), it is certainly not my part to attempt to provide a summary (an impossible task), to propound some essential thesis, or to make programmatic pronouncements about where research should go from here. But I was an insider at the fifth Mackie conference from which *Gendering Scottish History* derives; and this chapter is the result of personal reflections prompted by it.

*   *   *

The discipline of women's history has had, and continues to have, a vital function in uncovering and telling the story of fifty per cent or more of the human race. But it has also served (and been served by) the cause of feminism. The relationship between history and political ideas has always posed problems for historians trained in the empirical tradition;

and feminists have been prominent amongst those who have shown that the practice of historical scholarship and involvement in political discourse are compatible, even essentially interconnected, activities. For an outsider to the discipline in Scotland, the scholarly stimulation generated in the SWHN by academic and non-academic researchers alike – as they probe a past that is absent from, or under-represented in, the official histories – is striking. But more exciting still is the sense of the relevance of this work, even when the particular subject is the quite remote past, for now. Women's history has, by providing part of the indispensable scholarly groundwork for the "gendering" of history helped to raise afresh questions of historical theory; certainly if one means by that, not so much the more abstruse areas of postmodernist discourse, as the simple – but necessarily contested – issues which arise when we ask why it is important to study history at all.

Historical work in the 1960s and 1970s (when modern women's history began) was deeply influenced, whether in a relationship of attraction, association or antagonism, by Marxism. For many, there was at least an implication that to do history was, in however mediated a way, to contribute to a class consciousness which could help to change the world and make society truly human. What has been called "British Marxist" history, moreover, saw serious and original research on the past as crucial to the re-humanising of a theory conservative thinkers would have liked to dismiss as fatally poisoned by Stalinism. The achievements of the "British Marxist historians" have been well celebrated, and a strong case could be made that anglophone historiography would have been in a sorry state without them.[8] Yet the way in which the writings of this school were founded so determinedly on rigorous empirical work – necessary though this was in the light of the perception that abstract theory had been used to rationalise the political lies on which the actually existing soviet system was based – had the downside that little attention was paid to the reworking of Marxism's theoretical basis. As a consequence "Marxist history" never explicitly or fully (despite some honourable efforts) settled accounts with the mechanical misconceptions of which Stalinism represented the most ghastly form.

This must be an important factor in explaining why the Marxist approach to social history, which appeared to offer so much in the 1960s, seemed moribund in the 1980s, and – despite the continued official celebrity of historians like Eric Hobsbawm – dead after the events of 1989–91.[9] What is conventionally called "the collapse of communism", moreover, was preceded by a growing scepticism about any sort of historical theory which seeks to explain the past in terms relevant to present-day political problems. But the study of history has always derived much of its fascination for the general public from the idea that what we know about the past will assist us to understand the possibilities of our own times. And feminist history has been prominent – notwithstanding recent divisions in the feminist camp – amongst the intellectual trends which never abandoned such a theoretical purpose. [10]

If, then, it is the case that – whatever may have been its other achievements – feminism in Scotland has had difficulty (notwithstanding some fine work) in establishing a strong, visible tradition of historical writing, it follows that Scottish historiography has been doubly disadvantaged. It lacks not only full acceptance of the importance of the history of women, but also the benefits a feminist discourse can bring to the historian's theoretical agenda. From this point of view it is worth adding to remarks made elsewhere in this book one further instance illustrating the perception that a predominantly male Scottish historical establishment has tended to marginalise women's history. In 1996, Scottish historians gathered to discuss how Scotland's history has been written from the earliest times to the present. Pointing out a number of omissions – as "flags" rather than "criticisms" – T. C. Smout (whose *History of the Scottish People* in the late 1960s was seminal in the development of a modern Scottish historiography) reported that no mention was made of "the intellectual history of ethnic and gender consciousness" nor of "women's history", despite the fact that "these are fields that excite younger scholars".[11] It is important, of course, that the Historiographer Royal for Scotland chose to highlight the fact that women's history deserves proper recognition. But the comment neatly evades the need for analysis of why such recognition has been so slow in coming, or reference to the significance of the involvement in the discipline of scholars of all ages. Arguments over women's history are not merely about generational shifts in intellectual taste: they are also theoretical and political.

This is not to suggest that there is no such thing as a generational shift, and the mention of Smout and his major role in the modernising of Scottish historical scholarship allows for an interesting aside on this question. In a recent videotaped interview Smout talks to his former colleague, Rosalind Mitchison, who was the doyenne of female scholars involved in the revival of modern Scottish social history in the 1960s and 1970s: her *History of Scotland* both complemented and vied with Smout's *History of the Scottish People*.[12] Mitchison speaks of being conscious of prejudice against her in the Scottish academic world of the 1960s "not as a woman", but "as a married woman." The previous generation of women had established the right of women "to do all sorts of jobs, but not to link it up with marriage." She acknowledges that theory is her "weak point". Feminist theory particularly "frightens" her because she thinks it is "too doctrinal" for her generation: it makes her worry about saying the wrong thing. But she admires the good work done in women's history in Scotland: since "slightly more than half the human race are women" it is "important to establish their point of view". Women's history also serves, she thinks, as a critique of the "slightly disreputable" side of labour history: "labour historians, and people in the labour movement have been extremely hostile to the independence of their women-folk." Suspicious of feminism, in favour of women's history, is how her position is summarised.

* * *

This seems a world away from the story of the feminist historian Catharine Hall, a representative of a younger generation, and working in English universities. Hall's autobiography provides one illustration of the way in which arguments about women's history raise theoretical and political questions. She has written about how she engaged with "feminism and history" in the 1970s and 1980s. Committed to the empirical values of historical scholarship, she argues, however, that history must always be premised "on a relation between past and present". It is "about investigating the past through the concerns of the present". And Hall insists that feminism has contributed in important ways to how "the meaning of being an historian" and "of trying to do certain kinds of historical work" changed significantly during the 1970s and 1980s. [13]

At school and university, Hall was influenced by the work of Christopher Hill, Rodney Hilton and those other "British Marxist historians" who set out "to challenge British historiography" and to "construct a new body of Marxist history that would both connect with popular politics and engage with the academic establishment". But her early research on the medieval period in episcopal archives proved disillusioning, and marriage imposed its own constraints. Then came 1968, which signified not only the "student activism, the demands for a new curriculum [and] the insistence that the history syllabus should include discussion of theory and historiography", but also "the familiar discomfort, not yet recognized for what it was, of being a woman active in left politic ." Pregnancy hampered her sense of being a revolutionary by making it impossible for her to sleep on the floor of the occupied Great Hall at Birmingham

University. But she was inspired by the first women's movement conference in England in 1970, and by reading Juliet Mitchell and Sheila Rowbotham. A second child made trips to the Public Record Office even more difficult, and an article by an American feminist on Victorian womanhood was "an eye-opener". It was this combination of personal experience and participation in a new discourse that, as child-care problems became more manageable, guided Hall into her successful career.

There are several reasons for referring to this story in the context of a discussion of women's history in twenty-first-century Scotland. First, it reminds us that English historiography in the late 1960s was at a different stage of development from that of Scotland. Establishment political history had been subject to the practical revisions of a new school of social history. And this body of work, it can be seen in retrospect, helped to make possible – and invited – a feminist critique. In Scotland, the creation of a basic body of work to modern empirical standards was the perceived priority; and the pre-feminist (but already substantially post-Marxist), English social-history paradigm provided the basis for a methodology. There is considerable evidence of an aspiration for a more specifically Scottish interpretative discourse and theoretical critique, but it is more to be found in relatively marginal magazines than in mainstream historical work.[14]

Second, commitment to feminist history, for Hall, arose from a combination of personal, political, and academic factors; and it may be that a similar convergence is possible in a Scotland which, at the turn of a new century, is self-consciously at an "historical moment". Much historical work necessarily takes the form of scholars "revising" previous orthodoxies in a manner internal to the profession. For a more fundamental critique, new questions have to asked, often inspired by considerations coming from outside an exclusively professional discussion. Hall's story is specific to its times, but it shows how the conservatism of the academy can be challenged by those whose intellectual rationale is not conditioned exclusively by academic concerns.

Third is the insight Hall provides into the role of 1968 and after, and her evident conviction that a generation of historians who did not experience that period will benefit from knowing what it meant to do so. There is a danger in Scotland that the "new politics" and the new situation associated with the Scottish parliament are seen as coming into being on a kind of post-Thatcherite *tabula rasa* rather than arising, at one remove, in response to the historical, socio-economic crisis which first appeared in the late 1960s. Historical strategy, pronounced one Scottish history professor in the mid-1990s, should be "shaped not by the false revolutionary dawn of 1968, but by the cataclysmic collapse of communist regimes since 1989". Had he been female, she might, at the very least, have expressed the point more dialectically.[15]

Fourth, Hall is an English feminist historian who, along with others – notably Clare Midgeley – has shown in practice how women's history, important in itself, can also be a stepping-stone to a much more general critique of the established historical agenda.[16] Hall, Midgeley and others have demonstrated this with regard to imperial history in particular, a subject of especial relevance in Scotland, where the Empire served for two hundred years to cement the Union with England, and where its collapse in the third quarter of the twentieth century underlies the politics of devolution and Scottish nationalism.

* * *

A book cannot reproduce the spirit of a living event, so it should be recorded that the fifth Mackie conference was particularly stimulating, co-operative and devoid of academic point-scoring.[17] In terms of the diversity of topics addressed, places visited and periods covered, it violated the classical unities. But there was a more important unity – a sense of common purpose. The conference developed a logic of its own, constantly prompting reflections going beyond the immediate interest of particular papers. Indeed, the claim to originality I would make for *Gendering Scottish History* as a whole (the specific qualities of the particular chapters speak for themselves) lies not in its insistence that women's and gender history need to be taken more seriously in Scotland. That case has already been well made by the work referred to above by Elizabeth Ewan and Jane McDermid. It lies rather in its attempt, in line with the conference, to show that an explicitly international approach can cast Scottish women's history into a sharper light.

More even than other international meetings on women's history, said one participant in the concluding discussion, the Mackie conference had created at the same time a "shock of recognition" at common problems being encountered in particular national situations, and a "shock of difference". The ensuing discussion ranged widely but focused on this problem. On the one hand there were differing emphases on what were the most pressing tasks and the most effective strategies. On the other, there was a sense of the need, not so much for a common agenda as for the further development of an integrated international discourse – with

Scotland included. The conference, some thought, had shown that there was a surprisingly large amount of work published on the history of women in Scotland, which requires more confident promotion. And regret that the Scottish male historical establishment was largely absent was tempered by the fact that the men who had come, as one overseas contributor commented, had stayed, listened, and refrained from making "the usual patronising comments".

Not everyone agreed that male historians were generally indifferent to the rise of women's history. Integration had to be the way forward, not the acceptance of a kind of successful "ghettoisation" which, some thought, was a danger facing women's history in North America. To revise national histories for a new generation, while at the same time putting into practice the results of a paradigmatic shift making women crucial in the story, is difficult. But the very fact that there is a growing consciousness of this problem, it can be argued, shows that the paradigm which excluded women has indeed been shifted. However, modern social history had been the new approach of the 1960s, and its implementation took a long time. To synthesise different emphases in the discussion, it might be said that working with male historians was recognised as important, but that it should not be forgotten that they had had a long time to do something on their own initiative and, by and large, had signally failed.

Plain speaking about men and career structures led to the argument that women's history could be seen as threatening. It might be accepted, but only on condition that it did not disturb the established ways too much in practice. The triad in recent historical work of race, class and sex ("blacks have race, the workers have class, and women have ... gender") assumes that white, middle-class males don't need any particular category. They deal with "History", and they still determine the dominant discourses in university history departments. Male fears that serious archive-based work on women's history may pose a competitive threat, some stressed, should not be underestimated.

The idea that women's historians have been in some measure the victims of their own success was developed in an exchange on publishing. There is now a self-created market for women's history, and for gender history (which wrongly tends to be taken simply as code for the same thing). A book written for the mainstream, with gender in the subtitle, will appear in the "gender studies" section of a catalogue rather than under the subject – the national history or whatever – it is about. That reflects the fact that women's history is one of the few areas in which the student and general book-buying public converge around the same bookstore shelves. This "commodity fetishism" can actually militate against the fuller integration of the subject, and can draw attention away from the idea of "gender history" as a new analytical approach to history as a whole.

Some of the most optimistic comments were based on Spanish experience, a matter of particular interest in Scotland. In Spain the emergence of women's history was tied up with political change, not only in the sense that feminism and the development of women's history were everywhere interconnected, but also more generally. There may be no direct comparison between the electoral resistance of the Scots to Thatcherism in the 1980s and Spain's reaction to the end of the Franco years,[18] but the juxtaposition of the two experiences can be instructive. The Spanish and Scottish cases have a point of contact in the much-discussed role of the nation-region in European politics; but the intellectual association being suggested here is more specific than that. The coming of women's history in Spain in the 1970s occurred when the country as a whole was debating the post-Franco agenda. Its emergence in Scotland in the 1980s took place amidst a growing consciousness of the need to develop new political institutions – not least because of the perception that a Scottish parliament would have been a chamber of resistance to Thatcherism.

Serious historical work was politically difficult in Spain for more than a generation after the Civil War. When the Franco regime was sinking to its deathbed, everything about how to approach Spanish history was potentially challengeable. Feminist historians were able to take an initiative, insisting – and showing through translations of important texts – that women's history was in the forefront of historical work internationally. It had to be a major element, and to be so recognised by publishers and male academics, in the more general enterprise of restoring Spain to the community of world scholarship. Even if Scotland's new parliament and Spain's emergence from fascism are not directly comparable historical moments, it seems not too far-fetched to suggest that one of the tests of the enterprise of writing histories useful for the citizens of Scotland's twenty-first-century democracy will be the degree to which historians follow this particular Spanish practice in "gendering" Scottish history.

This point occurred to me again more recently on reading *Women and Socialism / Socialism and Women*, edited by Helmut Gruber and Pamela Graves. This is an impressive volume of collective scholarship examining what Geoff Eley describes as "women and the socialist question" in interwar Western Europe. Throughout the book, writes Louise Tilly in a concluding reflection, is the search for an answer to the question, "Why did the ballot fail to endow women with full citizenship, not to speak of gender equality?".[19] Informing this major exercise in women's historical scholarship, in other words, is a discourse directly relevant to all who understand at the end of the twentieth century – as many who thought themselves progressive in the 1960s did not – that gender equality is not a postponable option in the struggle for real democracy. The particular question, moreover, is of especial interest in Scotland where one of the main justifications of the claim that the new parliament will herald a "new" and more democratic politics rests on the moves it has made in the direction of gender parity. Yet there are no references to Scotland in *Socialism and Women* … .

In one sense this is not surprising since the book is organised around studies of the major European nation states. But if Scotland is not a nation state, neither is Catalonia, and the Spanish contribution to the Gruber-Graves book comes from Barcelona rather than Madrid.[20] In Spain, on this evidence at least, the overcoming in historical work of the "peripheralisation" of the "nation-region", and that of "women", is apparently being accomplished in tandem. In Scotland, by contrast, the reassertion since the 1960s of the importance of a national past requiring the attention of professional historians apparently relegated women's history to a marginal position; and this has been made all the more noticeable by the advances the discipline in general has made. Can the conjuncture at which the Scottish parliament has created a sense of political change and Scottish women's history is being rejuvenated provide the opportunity for qualitatively changing this relationship?

* * *

The idea that a gendered scholarship is of special relevance to Scotland at this historical moment may also be addressed by a side-glance at literary studies. Feminists have played a major role in the revival of creative writing in Scotland in the 1980s and 1990s; and, in 1995 Christopher Whyte edited a volume with a title cognate with that of this book, *Gendering the Nation: studies in modern Scottish literature*. "Nationalism," he writes, "is always bad news for women"; but this is not his own view. It is the reported remark of someone he calls an "English-identified" participant in a seminar, at which, it seems, everyone could be either "English-" or "Scottish-identified". Whyte, first, thinks that, if sustained, this view "would mean that cultures where nationalism [is] an acknowledged issue" are by definition "less tolerant of women" and, he adds, "therefore of other marginal groups, be they black, lesbian or gay". And, second, he explains the statement as "part of a larger polemic" to discredit nationalism "by appearing to champion women." Whyte is concerned with the gendering of national cultures because "thanks to the collapse of the Soviet Union, the crucial issue in Europe" (including the former "Eastern Europe") is now, he thinks, nationalism, or rather "nationalisms".[21]

The civilising of national cultures rather than the pursuit of humanist goals more directly on the international stage, it seems to follow, is the context within which, Whyte thinks, scholarship must now operate. And he goes on to deal with the need to gender the study of Scottish literature with practical goals in mind. It is particularly important to do so, he argues, in what has previously been seen as a masculine, even macho, literary culture. Like Margery Palmer McCulloch above (pp. 98–111) – coming from the rather different angle of a literary scholar concerned with using literature as evidence for social history – he cites Hugh MacDiarmid, Neil Gunn and William McIlvanney particularly. But he is also concerned with the need, when discussing the formation of nation-based identities, to foreground other so-called "minorities", whether black, gay or lesbian. In this context he quotes Jackie Kay, "a black, lesbian, Scottish-identified poet", who, when asked aggressively by a white Scottish woman about her origins, replied to the effect that Scotland is "where she comes from".

Looking at how to hear women's stories and to promote gender analysis within the male-dominated literary culture of a small nation, Whyte has to argue about what he thinks that nation is, and has to become, in human terms. His nation will encompass a society which will not simply permit white, straight women full equality with white, straight men on the basis of a common "Scottish-identification". It will also ensure real equality for Jackie Kay. (It will also, one presumes, hesitate to be too complacent if its parliament moves towards gender parity while failing – as was the case with the Scottish parliament after the 1999 election – to have a single non-white MSP.) Whyte postulates a nationalism that is "good news" for both genders, all races and people of different sexual orientations; and relevant to how this is achieved is a gendered critique of literature.

* * *

Is such a nationalism possible? Can the capitalist nation state be reinvented as a humane form of social organisation, free of the internally repressive and externally aggressive associations of the ideologies which have sustained it in the past? Or is this mere wishful thinking, ignoring historical insight and born of a desperation arising from the disastrous collapse of the grand experiments which claimed to be socialist? Can real gender equality be achieved within the context of the social organisation which sustains the hegemony of capital? Or must the struggle for it march together, in some way or other, with the project of transforming social relations as a whole? I do not of course propose to answer these questions here, nor to suggest that this book provides the basis for doing so. But I do want to conclude by arguing briefly that these are questions historians, with their own particular types of expertise, can – with advantage both to themselves and to the common good – involve themselves in discussing.

In a recent article, Theodore Koditschek reviews new work on the gendering of the history of the working class – a process inspired by Joan Scott's post-structuralist critique of E. P. Thompson. Much of this work may be the product of thinking which eschews "grand theory". Yet it can be read as pointing towards an approach which aims afresh at the ambitious goals of the 1960s in a theoretically more sophisticated way. For Koditschek, himself the author of a major study of nineteenth-century Bradford written in a post-Thompson tradition, it now becomes possible to debate the effect of the "monopoly in the grand narratives of working-class formation" of "the largely male club" of Marxists and labour historians. The picture they produced was of "valiant, emancipatory struggles against capitalism whose final consummation had unaccountably become derailed or at least delayed."

The new gendered histories, Koditschek argues, suggest "why this derailment was probably inevitable from the start." The movement was always "to a considerable extent (though never entirely) a movement of masculinist privilege." Too often "it advanced the interests of working men (frequently only white, European or skilled working men) by excluding women or minorities from its benefits and ranks." And despite "its periodic movements" of revolutionary militancy, it has "proven all too willing" to make

> strategic alliances with its structural antagonist, capital, so as to stabilise the new system of capitalist patriarchy at the expense of those working people whose experience, interests and identities

[263]

were never seriously meant to be encompassed within its emancipatory project.[22]

Whatever may be the merits of, or problems with, this argument, it opens
one particular door on a new, mutually critical (and self-critical), relationship between what remains lively and forward-looking in the labour
history of the 1960s, and the developments in feminist history which have
taken place since the early 1970s. Scotland – where labour history has
been a major strand in historical writing, but is now itself in danger of
marginalisation in the historical canon – could provide productive
ground for the development of such a discourse.[23]

To place the discussion in a yet wider frame – again proposing no more
than *one possible* way in which the theoretical implications of the gendering of history might be developed – reference may be made to the work
of István Mészáros, the philosopher and political thinker.[24] In an article
on the "rise and fall of historical temporality", Mészáros argues that the
ideological crisis of the late-twentieth century is tied up with the attack
on "historical temporality" – the understanding of the specificity of historical periods, including the present. Today's ruling élites, he suggests,
are furnished with a crucial ideological weapon by the failure of leading
theoretical figures (Mészáros makes a detailed critique of Hannah Arendt
in particular) to grasp the historical temporality of the contemporary
world. As a result such thinkers, whatever their intention, rationalise a
political discourse within which the programmes of the élites are judged
by appearance rather than in terms of the real limits of the existing social
system. While Mészáros comes to the question from a different angle, his
ideas must have their place within the agenda Tilly points towards, in her
reflections on *Socialism and Women* ..., in which she stresses the need for
"a theoretical approach for evaluating the dimensions of inequality".[25]

For Mészáros, the subordination of women, historically analysed, is not
simply a function of personal relations but necessary to "the established
conditions of hierarchy and domination" of what he calls the capital system – historically a much older formation than capitalist society itself.
The "historic cause of women's emancipation", the demand for
"substantive equality", he insists, can only be realised in direct conflict
with capital itself since "substantive equality within the family" cannot
be achieved without structural reverberations "across the whole of the
existing social 'macrocosm'".[26] On the other hand, however, the particular effect of this historical constraint on women means that their
"irrepressible demand for meaningful equality" is "a crucially important

constituent" in the broader struggle to transcend the ever more restrictive limits today's actually existing social organisation (which includes the nation state) places on any movement towards a society based on the achievement of real human equality.

Divisions in the feminist movement are, for Mészáros, one piece of evidence of a qualitative change in the crisis of the social system as a whole. The earlier (1960s and 1970s) unity was founded on the expectation of improvement in the conditions of women within the established order. As the system's room for manoeuvre has shrunk, exemplified by the Thatcherite/Reaganite programme of degrading the social-meliorative provisions of the post-World War II "consensus", this became more clearly unrealisable, and the "divisiveness within the feminist movement ... more pronounced". The "shrinking of the margins" places more pressure on those advocating "strategies ... to secure advancement in women's emancipation" to be ready "to question the structural limits set by the parameters of the capital system as such...."

It is not necessary to accept such an analysis to agree that the questions it raises should have their place in historical discourse. Professional historians can, of course, ply their trade well without feeling obliged to debate why history matters and what it means for now: methodologically, indeed, much of their research depends on creating sufficient space and detachment to be able to examine evidence on its own terms and, as far as possible, without anachronistic sensibilities. But the results of their work will ultimately be read by people whose life struggles require all the consciousness they can acquire of where to locate themselves in the wider crisis of human society. If the historical work called forth by the sense that the turn of the twenty-first century represents a new moment in Scottish history is to play its full part in arming women and men to make rational decisions about the future, it must surely at least address itself to such questions.

* * *

In its empirical explorations, internationalist contextualisation and demonstration of the importance of historiographical approaches lie *Gendering Scottish History*'s main interest and significance. But, along with other recent work, the book perhaps shows too that women's history in Scotland could be on the verge of what, to adapt Siân Reynolds' remark above (p. 2), should be "one of the biggest and noisiest conversations" of our times. This conversation must surely contribute crucially to whatever new Scottish histories emerge to serve Scotland's much-vaunted "new politics". My own view is that the humane direction such a conversation (and the research work on which it is necessarily based) must logically take, will increasingly clash with the ideological and resource-related constraints within which those who participate in it are forced to converse. This should ensure that the discussion will not only be noisy: it will also challenge some conservative assumptions about the proper limits of historical discourse, and about what, in terms of the real improvement of human society, it can help to accomplish. This may not be exactly what Reynolds meant when she observed that women's history "remains potentially disruptive to accepted frameworks of historiography"; but, for me at least, putting this gloss on her comment brings an exciting intellectual prospect into view.[27]

NOTES

1. Duncan Forbes, Hilary Horrocks, Liz Leicester, Debbi Simonton and Oonagh Walsh all read earlier drafts and made different criticisms. My thanks to them all for helping me rescue some hostages to fortune: those that remain are given by myself alone. If apology is needed for the addition of this chapter it rests on the fact that making women's history the theme of the fifth Mackie conference was my idea. The remit for the Mackie symposia (as the conferences were originally called) is the study of Scottish history in an international context. Initially that was taken to mean aspects of Scottish history which involved overseas connections, and three volumes were produced, all edited by Grant G. Simpson. These make up the Mackie Monograph series, and are: *Scotland and Scandinavia 800–1800* (Edinburgh, 1990); *The Scottish Soldier Abroad, 1247–1967* (Edinburgh, 1992); and *Scotland and the Low Countries, 1124–1994* (East Linton, 1996). The fourth conference dealt with the influence of Scottish education abroad. For the fifth, the remit was extended to include Scotland's relations with the rest of the world considered in more methodological or historiographical terms. Accordingly this book is published under the separate series title of Mackie Occasional Colloquia. Future publications based on Mackie conferences – unless they seem more appropriately described as colloquia – will be referred to as the Mackie Symposia. The first symposium to be published will be Allan I. Macinnes, Thomas Riis and Frederik Pedersen (eds), *Ships, Guns and Bibles in the North-East and the Baltic States* (East Linton, forthcoming). It is also proposed to launch, with the support of the Mackie Trust, a series of Aberdeen Monographs, which will normally be single-authored books on particular topics in Scottish history.

2. See P. G. Wodehouse, *Blandings Castle and Elsewhere* (London, 1935).

3. I think it was the ubiquitous writer and moralist Joyce Macmillan on the BBC radio programme "Quote ... Unquote", broadcast on 4 and 10 October 1999.

4. Just under 40% of MSPs in the 1999 parliament were women.

5. Harriet Harman, Blair's first Social Security Secretary, achieved notoriety when – in the name of financial rectitude – she piloted through the Westminster parliament the government's proposals to cut benefits to single mothers, an enterprise in which she was supported by most of the New Labour majority, men and women alike.

6. *Scotland on Sunday*, 3 October 1999; "The Story of a Nation" was published as a supplement to the paper from 5 September to 10 October, 1999.

7. T. M. Devine, *The Scottish Nation 1700–2000* (London, 1999); Michael Fry, *The Herald* (Glasgow), 30 September 1999.

8. The starting-point for this argument is still probably Harvey J. Kaye, *The British Marxist Historians: an introductory analysis* (2nd edn, London, 1995).

9. Hobsbawm became a Companion of Honour, an élite award in the gift of HM the Queen in the mid-1990s.

10. For major interventions in recent debates on historical theory by female historians, see for example Joyce Appleby, Lynn Hunt and Margaret Jacob, *Telling the Truth About History* (New York and London, 1994); and Ellen Meiksins Wood and John Bellamy Foster (eds), *In Defense of History: Marxism and the postmodern agenda* (New York, 1998).

11. T. C. Smout, "Writing Scotland's history: preface", *Scottish Historical Review*, vol. lxxvi (April 1997), p. 3; and see his *A History of the Scottish People 1560–1830* (Glasgow, 1969; London, 1985; many reprints).

12. Rosalind Mitchison, *History of Scotland* (London, 1970, 1982; many reprints). The videotape is available from the Institute of Historical Research in London in its "Interviews with Historians" series.

13. Catharine Hall, "Feminism and feminist theory", in her *White, Male and Middle Class: explorations in feminism and history* (Cambridge, 1992), pp. 1–40, esp. pp. 1–5.

14. See, for example, *Crann-tàra* (quarterly, Aberdeen, 1977–81), later as *Radical Scotland* (monthly, Edinburgh, 1982–91); *Scottish International* (monthly, Edinburgh, 1968–74); *New Edinburgh Review* (quarterly, Edinburgh, 1969–84), since 1984 as *Edinburgh Review*; *Cencrastus* (irregular, Edinburgh, since 1979); *Scotlands* (semi-annual, Edinburgh, since 1994). Hamish Henderson's "The women of the glen: some thoughts on Highland history", in his *Alias MacAlias: writings on songs, folk and literature* (Edinburgh, 1992), for example, appeared originally in *Cencrastus* under the title, "Give me the daggers".

15. Allan I. Macinnes, "A strategy for history", *Aberdeen University Review*, vol. LV(4) (1994), pp. 350–51. Coincidentally this issue of the *Review* was the "Women's Centenary Number": on which, too, see Mary R. Masson and Deborah Simonton (eds), *Women and Higher Education: past, present and future:*

proceedings of a conference held to mark the centenary of the admission of women to degree study at the University of Aberdeen (Aberdeen, 1996).

16. See esp., Clare Midgeley (ed.), Gender and Imperialism (Manchester, 1998).

17. The short account of the concluding discussion at the fifth Mackie conference which follows is a personal one based on my notes and on tape recordings in my possession. It has not been checked by the participants, and, at the risk of impersonality, it seemed better not to identify individuals. I have tried to convey the collective "feel" of the discussion rather than to dwell on particular opinions.

18. Though Baroness Thatcher's enthusiastic support for General Pinochet, when he was detained in Britain during 1999 awaiting possible extradition to Spain to answer for crimes against humanity in Chile, makes one wonder: see for example press reports of the Conservative Party conference in the last week of October 1999.

19. Helmut Gruber and Pamela Graves (eds), Women and Socialism / Socialism and Women (Providence, RI, and Oxford, 1998): Gruber and Graves, "Introduction", p. 8; Louise Tilly, "Women, citizenship and power", at pp. 507–15, esp. p. 507; and Geoff Eley, "From welfare politics to welfare states: women and the socialist question" at pp. 516–46.

20. Mary Nash. "'Ideals of Redemption': socialism and women on the left in Spain", in Gruber and Graves, Socialism and Women, pp. 348–80. On Catalonia, see esp. pp. 362, 368, 373, 535.

21. Christopher Whyte, Gendering the Nation: studies in modern Scottish literature (Edinburgh, 1995), pp. ix–xiv.

22. Theodore Koditschek, "The gendering of the British working class", Gender and History, vol. 9 (1997), pp. 333–63, esp. pp. 356–57. The main books reviewed by Koditschek are Deborah Valenze, The First Industrial Woman (New York and Oxford, 1995); Anna Clark, The Struggle for the Breeches: gender and the making of the British working class (Berkeley, Cal. and London, 1995); Sonye Rose, Limited Livelihoods: gender and class in nineteenth-century England (Berkeley, Cal. and London, 1992); and Ellen Ross, Love and Toil: motherhood in outcast London (New York and Oxford, 1993). See too Koditschek's "Marxism and the historiography of modern Britain: from Engels to Thompson to deconstruction and beyond", in Terry Brotherstone and Geoff Pilling (eds), History, Economic History and the Future of Marxism: essays in memory of Tom Kemp (1921–1993) (London, 1996), pp. 103–48.

23. For the link between labour history and women's and/or feminist history, see, inter alia, Eleanor Gordon, Women and the Labour Movement in Scotland (Oxford, 1991); Elspeth King, The Hidden History of Glasgow's Women: the Thenew factor (Edinburgh, 1993); and Joseph Melling, Rent Strikes: peoples' struggle for housing in west Scotland 1890–1916 (Edinburgh, 1983). This last, it could be argued, was one of the pioneering works of Scottish women's history, arising out of an evidence-based critique of the male bias of previous

historians of "Red Clydeside": see Helen Corr's interesting introduction at pp. v–xi.

24. István Mészáros, "The rise and fall of historical temporality", in Brotherstone and Pilling (eds), *History, Economic History and the Future of Marxism*, pp. 251–92.
25. Tilly in Gruber and Graves, *Socialism and Women*, p. 507. See too Joan Wallach Scott, "Introduction", to her edited volume *Feminism and History* (Oxford, 1996).
26. István Mészáros, *Beyond Capital* (London, 1995), pp. 190–94.
27. For a randomly selected example of the sense of excitement which can be generated when such frameworks are challenged, see Leila J. Rupp writing about feminism and internationalism in *Gender and History*, vol. 10 (November, 1998), pp. 535–38, where she envisages the development of "truly global feminisms that can ... change the world". There may be scholarly as well as politically conservative reasons for the unlikelihood of such a statement appearing in the more respectable Scottish history journals; but the possibility of an occasional utopian speculation might bring a new readership to the appreciation of the real and important virtues of those publications.